Literature and the Marketplace addresses one of the great ironies of nineteenth-century British and American literature: the fact that authors of that era, in voicing their alienation from middle-class readers, paradoxically gave expression to feelings of alienation felt by those same readers. As William G. Rowland Jr. points out, romantic writers "thought of the market as conspiring against 'imagination' (Blake) or 'telling the truth' (Melville)" and consequently felt frustrated with literary institutions. Yet their "frustrations," writes Rowland, "helped to energize romantic work and explain its subsequent and continuing appeal."

The book opens with a survey of reading publics in Great Britain and the United States in the early years of the nineteenth century. Rowland then presents individual writers—including Wordsworth, Shelley, Hawthorne, Poe, and Emerson—and their relations to their readers. Finally, Rowland shows how the idea of genius was developed by writers as different as Coleridge, Blake, Whitman, and Dickinson and how that idea evolved as an antidote to the commercial literary marketplace of the nineteenth century.

A wide-ranging and provocative book, *Literature and the Marketplace* describes the relations between important British and American authors and the audiences and publishing industries of their era—relations that were troubled, uncertain, and remarkably productive of literature.

William G. Rowland Jr. is the Director of Studies at Hereford Residential College, University of Virginia. This is his first book.

WILLIAM G. ROWLAND JR.

Literature

and the

Marketplace

Romantic Writers
and Their Audiences
in Great Britain and
the United States

UNIVERSITY OF NEBRASKA PRESS
LINCOLN AND LONDON

© 1996 by
the University of Nebraska Press
All rights reserved
Manufactured in the United States of
America

♾ The paper in this book meets
the minimum
requirements of American National
Standard for
Information Sciences—Permanence
of Paper
for Printed Library Materials,
ANSI Z39.48-1984.

Library of Congress Cataloging-
in-Publication Data
Rowland, William G.
Literature and the marketplace : romantic
writers and their audiences
in Great Britain and the United States /
William G. Rowland, Jr.
p.   cm.
Includes bibliographical references and index.
ISBN 0-8032-3918-1 (alk. paper)
1. English poetry—19th century—
History and criticism.
2. Authors and readers—Great Britain—
History—19th century.
3. Authors and readers—United States—
History—19th century.
4. American literature—19th century—
History and criticism.
5. Authors and publishers—
History—19th century.
6. Books and reading—
History—19th century.
7. Authorship—History—19th
century.   8. Reader-response criticism.
9. Romanticism.
I. Title.
PS590.R68   1997
821'.709145—dc20   96–33836
CIP

Dedicated to the memory of
Helen Strasburg,
1900–1992.

"In quietness and in confidence
shall be your strength."

Contents

Preface:
Current Interest
in Audience

Since the mid-1980s, literary scholars have shown a growing interest in "the reader," "the audience," or "the reading public" and this entity's role in shaping the form and influencing the content of works of literature, both canonical works and newly discovered or revalued ones. Studies of readers often proceed by studying reviewers, publishers, and book buyers or borrowers who, in the British romantic and antebellum American periods, are often called "the literary marketplace," "the institution of letters," or "the profession of letters." These studies infer from contemporary reviews (which may or may not have been puffs), publishers' comments in letters and advertisements, authors' letters to publishers, sales figures, library records, and so on, what the climate of reception for romantic works might have been or possibly was, at least in those circles of readers whose responses have been preserved. But clearly these studies, which have been both celebrated and dismissed as sociological, are more easily focused on living readers, whose responses can be queried and surveyed, rather than dead ones.[1] We simply do not know and cannot find out what most readers of the past thought about a particular book. Sales figures and library circulation records can tell us what people were buying or borrowing, but can they tell us whether the buyers or borrowers read the book more than once, or read it carefully from cover to cover, or even read it all the way through, or at all?

Take, for example, a simple but rarely asked question: How many readers reread a given book? That is the practice of academics and students, but is it a characteristic practice of many or most readers, or an unusual one? We know that adolescents in the late twentieth century go to see popular movies repeatedly. Did the feminine readers of ante-bellum America read *The Lamplighter* and *The Wide, Wide World* more than once? Did the readers of Hawthorne and Melville give them a second, more informed reading or only one perhaps uncomprehending perusal?

Current studies of the reader, the audience, the profession of letters, and the literary marketplace owe much to Richard Altick and William Charvat.[2] Their research is still valuable and worth consulting, but it was not built upon in any systematic way as long as the focus of literary studies was the text rather than the reader, partly because the New Criticism and its deconstructionist heirs fostered such a dominant interest in the text, and partly because information about readers and their responses to books is not easy to come by. With the rise of the New Historicism in the early 1980s, a renewed effort began to place readings of literary texts in a social and historical context using Marxist theory, Foucault's investigations of institutional power, and neglected contemporary documents that shed light on the cultural assumptions authors shared with their readers (or, in the case of the studies of Renaissance drama associated with Stephen Greenblatt, playwrights with their audiences).[3] In romantic studies the leading New Historicist practitioners were Marilyn Butler and Jerome McGann and, in American nineteenth-century studies, Sacvan Bercovitch, Eric Sundquist, and others. Partly as a result of the new interest in cultural studies, including politics, history, sociology, and anthropology, scholars began to take a new, or renewed, interest in the ground that Altick and Charvat had earlier explored.

My study of literature and audience uses readings of traditionally major romantic authors from Wordsworth to Melville, and other authors (primarily in the United States) who questioned romantic formulations, to find the dynamic between writer and reader inscribed within romantic literary works. Like Stephen Railton in his *Authorship and Audience*, I study the reader assumed by the writer and then subject those assumptions to criticism and analysis. I begin in chapter 1 by setting romantic writers within their working context—publishers, reviewers, other published writers—that was changing sometimes for the better and sometimes for the worse in the nineteenth century. My sense of how this working context helped writers, in spite of their protests, and hindered them, in spite of their successes, will appear in the following chapters.

Chapters 2 through 7 are given over to careful, sociohistorically informed readings of several major authors. I am assuming what Ian Jack assumed when he selected this quote from Graham Greene as the epigraph to his study of poets and audience: "I doubt if the best work has ever been produced in complete independence of a public . . . . The awareness of an audience is an essential discipline for the artist" (vi). Romantic writers sometimes denied this assumption and sometimes, either grudgingly or enthusiastically, agreed with it. But, as I think my study shows, this awareness of audience shaped romantic works and can reveal, when isolated and analyzed, interesting interpretations of the works, facts and myths about the reading public that we are only just beginning to separate, and clues that romantic writers were in a peculiarly good position to give us about the private and public histories of people in their times.

The British romantic and American Renaissance writers lived at a juncture in history that was exciting and difficult and, to students of the period, rather familiar: the industrial revolution; the French revolution and the reaction to it in England; the Napoleonic wars; the rise of modern political nationalism, whose links to romanticism have been frequently noticed and studied; the first hints of commercial society and mass culture in the nineteenth-century United States; rising secularism, punctuated by religious revivals and other efforts to combat declining religiosity in everyday life with new private, literary, artistic, and social myths; and, primarily for the British writers but also for those in the United States, a time when past, preindustrial arrangements were available in living memory and the consequences of industrialism such as pollution, social fragmentation, and both rural and urban poverty were just becoming evident. From the prefaces and reviews written to define and engage an audience to the most esoteric and difficult of romantic works, romantic writing gives us today a peculiarly good insight into the lived experience of the times in which they were written. I believe that the dynamic between author and reader found in romantic works is unusually revealing, perhaps uniquely so.

My study uses, and is in fact dependent on, New Historicist insights into the romantic writers and their period, as well as more properly sociological studies of actual readers, insofar as we can find out about them. But, as Mark Edmundson points out in his review of some New Historicist studies of Wordsworth, something is lost as well as gained by the New Historicist insistence on privileging things that the romantic writers could not have known, and by using the critical vantage point of a particular late-twentieth-century sociohistorical perspective that romantic writers could not have had. What is lost is roughly the sense of the generations of romanticists that the New Historicists sought to supersede, the sense that literary works have something to teach us and contain insights that we can admire and even apply to our lives.[4]

I agree with the New Historicists that older generations of romanticists tended as a group to regard romantic works as a source of truth, even quasi-religious, ultimate truth, and that these approaches need to be viewed skeptically and modified. For example, Hubert Zapf writes in his paper on English and American romantics that "trancendentalism in its initial stages was not primarily a literary but a fundamentalist project. For this purpose, it used the model of English Romanticism, responding not to its artistic achievement but to its parareligious self-rationalizations" (95). This insight is also noted and repeated in several places by Butler and McGann, although their primary concern is with the religious language of twentieth-century literary critics. As McGann puts it in *The Romantic Ideology*, "literary criticism too often likes to transform the critical illusions of poetry into the worshipped truths of culture" (135). I would like to study romantic works both by contextualizing them in the literary institutions that produced them (like a New Historicist; see chapters 1 and 8) *and* by reading the writers closely for truths we cannot possibly discover about the texture and feel of their times, except by close readings aided by the sociohistorical information in front of us that has been discovered by past and more recent scholars. As Edmundson writes, "a more accurate way to understand Romantic writing, I think, is to recognize it as being itself historicist, always striving to render experience in such a way that it cannot be assimilated to existing normative principles, or to those that are likely to arise in the future." "[N]o stabilizing analysis," he goes on to say, "will do Romantic work justice" (130). A close analysis of the romantic writers in Britain and the United States as they were most actively engaged in the struggle to define themselves in relation to their audience helps us to understand the same struggle to define themselves being undertaken by many individuals in industrial and commercial society.

Acknowledgments

On the acknowledgment pages of many scholarly books, authors list more intellectual allies and creditors than I have living relatives or friends. My list is brief and includes some of those relatives and friends.

For reading early versions of the manuscript, I would like to thank Paul Cantor, Jerome McGann, Dorothy Ross, and Andrea Rowland.

For bibliographical and methodological advice from first to semifinal drafts, I would like to thank Stephen Railton.

For reading a late draft of the manuscript, I would like to thank Melvin Cherno, Dawn Fisher, E. D. Hirsch Jr., and, once again, Andrea Rowland.

For advice about navigating the rough waters of contemporary criticism and academic publishing, I would like to thank Mark Edmundson and Michael Levenson.

And for intellectual, moral, and departmental support from the inception of this project to its completion, I would like to thank Raymond Nelson.

LITERATURE AND THE MARKETPLACE

Introduction:
The Romantic Response
to Mass Society

Writing literary works is a social activity as well as a solitary one. Writers, no matter how esoteric or committed to their vision, imagine some audience for their work.[1] Ian Jack, in his 1984 study *The Poet and His Audience*, caught Byron in an unguarded moment when writing to his friend James Hamilton Browne: "I shall adapt my own poesy, please God! to the fashion of the time, and, in as far as I possess the power, to the taste of my readers of the present generation" (88). It is the romantic writer's highly charged, highly conflicted, and highly ambivalent response to "the taste of . . . readers of the present generation" that I intend to study here. This book is about what romantic writers on both sides of the Atlantic thought about their audience, their "reading public," as it came to be called in the early nineteenth century. Because major writers tend to be acute, intelligent, and sensitive people, their thoughts on audience are sometimes good clues to what the actual reading public was like. But "the reading public" was also an abstraction imagined in response to the romantic writers' professional frustrations with the literary institutions of the nineteenth century: publishers, reviewers, magazine editors, other published writers, and the ideas of the reading public half perceived and half created by the authors themselves.

Romantic attacks on the literary institution and romantic hostility toward the first signs of a "mass" audience often were the result of finding existing groups of readers hard to reach or even identify. However, these frustrations also helped to energize romantic literary work and explain its subsequent and continuing appeal, for those frustrations were analogous to the difficulties experienced by middle-class and working-class people in a rapidly evolving industrial society.

British romantic works seem heroic to us today, partly because they are products of the last group of writers who could even think of trying to hold together the disparate audiences coming into being in the nineteenth century. As Jon Klancher has written,

> What made [the romantic period] a particularly poignant moment of cultural transformation was that, perhaps for the last time, it was still possible to conceive the writer's relationship to an audience in terms of a personal compact. The small, deliberative, strategic world of early-nineteenth-century reading and writing still allowed for Wordsworth to imagine the reading of a poem as a personal exchange of "power" between writer and reader. . . . Political and periodical writers shifted between this world of cultural strategy and that cultural epoch emerging everywhere around them, the one that Byron and Scott awakened to, a massive audience for which they would perform, but a public they had never attempted to make. (14)

Even by the time of the American Renaissance, the ideal of a communion of writer and reader seemed to be a nostalgic dream. Hawthorne felt that he had seen the death of the "gentle reader" in the course of his own working lifetime,[2] and Melville's often fierce distaste for actual readers dramatizes for us both the death of a dream and the cost in pain and thwarted energy of letting such a dream die.

Nineteenth-century discussions of literature's social irrelevance, such as Thomas Love Peacock's *Four Ages of Poetry*, coincide historically with the initiation of romantic efforts to define literature as a special and privileged kind of writing (see chap. 2 below). In the very process of defining a realm of literature, romantic theorists imagined it as under attack, as in Shelley's response to Peacock, *A Defence of Poetry*. In a way, the romantics marginalized literature in the very act of bringing it into being. In part this is an ironic repetition of the division of labor going on throughout the socioeconomic and cultural realms: some human functions were elevated and others inevitably devalued. The romantics tried to escape this specializing tendency by defining literature as an activity that encompassed all other human functions; Wordsworth's prefaces to the *Lyrical Ballads* discussed in chapter 2 are key documents in this effort.[3] But while this strategy gave literature a supreme cultural value, it seemed to remove literature and culture from the social realm of most other human functions. The realm of culture was becoming the realm of "Culture," an important and powerful sphere that was paradoxically above or detached from, and therefore not essential to, the "real work" of society. In antebellum America, both the attacks on and the defenses of literature took as their starting point literature's perceived uselessness, even though publishing was a major industry and a "high-culture" publishing sector was just beginning to define itself.[4]

The major romantic authors are still interesting because their response to their audiences was acute and yet anxious. Nineteenth-century writers on both sides of the Atlantic were active polemicists for their works in prefaces, critical articles about other writers, theory, and manifestos. They also created works such as Blake's *Jerusalem* or Melville's *Pierre* in which the author's relationship to his or her audience is a major source of dramatic tension. At the historical moment of English romanticism, the middle classes began to develop the sense of themselves as individuals who were in but not of industrial society. The English romantics worked at a time when the individual was increasingly thought of as an autonomous and discrete entity limited only by will and talent, while society was often viewed as an indifferent, faceless, and hostile arena. Marx expressed this view in the *Grundrisse*:

> Only in the eighteenth century, in "civil [bourgeois] society," do the various forms of social connectedness confront the individual as a mere means towards his private purposes, as external necessity. But the epoch which produces this standpoint, that of the isolated individual, is also precisely that of the hitherto most developed social (from this standpoint, general) relations. The human being is in the most literal sense a political animal, not merely a gregarious animal, but an animal which can individuate itself only in the midst of society. Production by an isolated individual outside society . . . is as much of an absurdity as is the development of

language without individuals living *together* and talking to each other. (223)

The new social relations that directly affected writers included larger, more diverse, and more contentious groups of readers; a more powerful and sophisticated publishing industry; and more writers competing for success in a market system that promised lucrative rewards to winners such as Scott, Byron, or Moore, but often less than subsistence to losers. As Klancher puts it in *The Making of English Reading Audiences*, "the intense cultural politics of the Romantic period obliged writers not only to distinguish among conflicting audiences, but to do so by elaborating new relations *between* the individual reader and the collective audience. For a reader is just as surely constituted among audiences when he is apparently abstracted from *all* audience-belonging as when he is firmly embedded within it" (II).

Wordsworth, Blake, and Shelley are prominent in this study while Byron is not, because Byron's success with the reading public obviated the need to question his art's relationship to that public. He did not need to define his art for an audience that was accepting his work more readily than they were accepting Shelley's and (though he was more successful even early on than he would admit) Wordsworth's.[5] On the American side, I study Emerson, Hawthorne, Poe, and Melville rather than Thoreau because he was ultimately, I believe, a profoundly private individual who gave up the struggle to bring his art before the public.[6] What I find representative in the writers I have chosen to study is the drama of engagement with an audience—and by extension with a society—that was growing and becoming more diverse, at first slowly in late-eighteenth- and early-nineteenth-century England, then rapidly from the 1830s on in the United States.

Despite the instability of the romantic canon at the present time, no one to my knowledge has suggested that Wordsworth, Blake, and Shelley are less interesting poets than the most popular English poet of the period, Hemans, or that Emerson, Hawthorne, Poe, or Melville were poorer writers, and less worth reading today, than best-selling antebellum authors such as Warner or Cummins.[7] In spite of attacks on, revisions to, and protests about the canon, these writers continue to be read, taught, and written about, and are still referred to by most literary critics and historians as major writers or great authors who remain interesting, though perhaps for different reasons than we in the literary-critical profession formerly thought.[8]

The main theme of this study is that, while romantic writers often presented their works as timeless, transcendent, and removed from social and historical dislocations, they managed to produce great literature, often in spite of their theories, because their activity as writers forced them to confront a general feeling of their epoch, sometimes called alienation and sometimes called modern selfhood. One of the most powerful historical responses to alienation was the creation, in literary works, of the private, transcendent self, a process that was also going on in society in the romantic historical moment and has been frequently studied, not only under such rubrics as "the rise of modern selfhood," but also "individualism" and "individuality."[9]

As Hubert Zapf put it in a 1992 conference on romanticism, in the course of comparing the English romantics with the American transcendentalists, "the reaction of English Romanticism to this change [the industrial revolution and the machine age] was quite ambiguous, because in the central role [romanticism gave to] the self-determined individual subject it was itself an expression of a distinctly 'modern' state of consciousness. . . . This means that the aspect of *alienation* is central to English Romanticism, which is in an important sense and probably for the first time in literary history a response to that experience of alienation and to the 'disenchantment of the world' [Max Weber] caused by the rise of science and technology" (95). Richard Poirier also notices alienation in a most optimistic American writer, one who seems fully engaged with his society and the opportunities with which it presented the individual:

Emerson's might be called an American form of alienation in which, as George Kateb puts it in his study of Hannah Arendt, 'the moral unit . . . is the individual, not humanity or the masses of people heaped together traumatically. The individual is the democratic individual, not some unconditioned and unsituated ghost.' Thus imagined, the self is 'loose fitting,' indifferent to social identification, and capable of the 'doubleness' which makes it possible to be inside and outside society all at once, inside and outside the self. The self becomes a form of the Other. (77)

In Britain, the romantic response to alienation was to write internalized epics or conversation poems addressed to a single intimate friend and to write polemics and prefaces that were in part manifestos reflecting their authors' dissatisfaction with the nascent mass audience and, by extension, with the nascent mass society.

Romantic writers had difficulty formulating their relationship to audiences and to the new social order because their work was to observe, record, and respond to the very changes in social and economic life that were creating new conditions for their work. The self-reflexivity so often noted in romantic writing was both paralyzing and energizing, and romantic writers frequently wrote polemical prefaces and other theoretical statements because, like other members of a rapidly evolving social order, they had to find and justify a place for themselves within it.

In many British literary works and manifestos, the poet replaced the actual readers of the time who were buying books or borrowing them from the new circulating libraries with auditors built into the poems themselves, because actual readers were assumed to be unaware of the great writer, unsympathetic to great literature, and unable to comprehend the writer's deepest feelings. American Renaissance writers borrowed British romantic formulations about the writer in part because they explained the professional frustrations that shaped every major American writer's career. Hawthorne spent his writing life insisting that he addressed only a small circle of friends. Emerson, though he spent much of his long career addressing people directly from lecture platforms, created a persona of the sage who had access to another world from his hearers, even as he still spoke to them and for them. Perhaps more than any other figure of the period, Emerson was aware of and shaped by his sense of the paradoxical nature of writing as both solitary and social. Take for example a passage in *Nature*:

> The poet, in utter solitude remembering his spontaneous thoughts and recording them, is found to have recorded that which men in crowded cities find true for them also. The orator

distrusts at first the fitness of his frank confessions, his want of knowledge of the persons he addresses, until he finds that he is the complement of his hearers;—that they drink his words because he fulfills for them their own nature; the deeper he dives into his privatest, secretest presentiment, to his wonder he finds this is the most acceptable, most public, and universally true. (74)

Melville embraced the professional ethos more fully than Hawthorne or Emerson and was a professed democrat in the world of letters as well as in politics, but he alternately accepted and abused the audience he was both choosing and forced to address. *Moby-Dick* and *Leaves of Grass* are among the greatest works of the American Renaissance period, not because Melville and Whitman refused to compromise with the audience but because they made a profound effort to engage the existing reading publics with what they were most moved to say, even while the romantic conception of authorship isolated the writer from his audience and from the marketplace and its demands and peculiarities.

The idea of the romantic poet held by Victorian and antebellum middle-class readers included among its prominent features the romantic idea that the poet is tragically misunderstood. The writers we now consider major shared and enacted the belief that the great writer is above worldly entanglements but destroyed by them. This idea of the writer was already a part of the romantic myth in 1830s America and in part explains the popularity of the Philadelphia publisher J. Griggs's edition of *The Poetical Works of Coleridge, Shelley, and Keats* (1832) when commentators among the intelligentsia could see no reason for grouping the three. The political and artistic differences among the writers faded before the public sense of Coleridge as a thwarted genius and Keats and Shelley as angels called home from this world. The same sense of rediscovering neglected geniuses would energize later readers of Blake, Whitman, and Melville.

By the mid–nineteenth century, romantic writers were becoming paradigmatic, especially the poets.[10] Wordsworth was poet laureate; Keats, Shelley, and Byron provided the image of the poet's eccentric and tragic career; and Blake was about to be discovered as a visionary genius. Later in the century, Whitman would become for a growing number of disciples the good gray poet, while the success of Emily Dickinson's posthumously published work would startle her editors, friends, and family. Romantic work is interesting not because of its consciously adversarial posture, but for the assumptions it shares with the middle-class public that eventually did adopt it. Like the members of the middle class, romantic writers had to come to grips with a widely shared vision of society as a hostile arena in which the individual struggles to realize himself or herself outside the realm of social class.

The self in middle-class culture and romantic writing is very often a unique individual who is paradoxically engaged in the same struggle as a faceless mass of other autonomous selves. Like John Stuart Mill, middle-class readers sought in romantic work consolations grounded in the opposition between Nature (and the self that loves her) and the world of social, economic, and political struggle that was creating the middle-class way of life. Poets and readers alike used romantic work to suppress and at the same time subconsciously acknowledge this contradiction.

In romantic work and myth (Byron's writings and career would be the prime examples) the writer is often a sacrificial figure destroyed for the sins of his society. Middle-class readers could condemn the figure's antisocial urges and yet secretly identify with his autonomy, freedom, and transcendence of worldly complications—the very view of the self that bourgeois society encourages and yet must control if it is to function. Writers like Wordsworth and Emerson who lived and worked long enough to see themselves transformed from radicals to sages exemplified the appropriateness of much of the romantic project to middle-class needs.[11] As this study shows, one historical force at work during the period was romantic writing itself and its reception. I will argue that the romantic project was most interesting and most heroic when it sought to perform a healing function for a divided society—that is, when the major writers worked strenuously to unite groups of readers that were divided among themselves and from each other.

The existence of a large, inevitably diverse, and sometimes inscrutable mass reading public put the same pressure to succeed on individual writers that the open market put on individual businessmen, especially in the United States. Antebellum writers worked in a boom market, but competition for the audience was intense. As Stephen Railton puts it in his description of the antebellum American literary institution, "the audience presides over the space in which literature happens" (20). Railton elaborates:

> the American faith in the theology of majority rule meant that writers could not look to the structures of a literary establishment to mediate between their work and the larger reading public. In essence, each writer was alone on the stage of literary performance. Writers did not necessarily have to tremble, but it was directly before the public that they had to perform. For almost any validation of his or her identity *as* an American artist, the writer was directly dependent on their response. (20)

Emerson's claim that "poetry was all written before time was" ("The Poet," 5) and Hawthorne's remark that "America is now wholly given over to a d——d mob of scribbling women" who produced "trash" (qtd. in Ticknor, *Hawthorne and His Publisher* 151) were both responses to professional crisis—and very similar responses, despite the difference in tone. Both men were trying to differentiate the great writer from the hack, and both were trying to define a place for their work in a competitive and rapidly changing situation.

As Henry Nash Smith has said, Hawthorne "may have been partially correct" that he was competing with women authors, "but the sales of the new women writers were so much larger than those of any earlier American novelist that new groups of readers must have been involved" (8). Everyone agrees that the antebellum American reading public was larger, better educated, and better provided with books, newspapers, and magazines than contemporary publics in England and Europe. The English publisher Charles Knight wrote in the 1850s that "the American people are much more universally readers than the English people. They are better educated. They have a Government that considers it a duty to educate the young without distinction, and to afford the adult every means of intellectual improvement. The American Government has created a reading nation" (273). Americans were quick to point out this aspect of American cultural superiority. In July 1856, a *Putnam's* writer admitted, "There are more writers in France, and better writing in England, no doubt, than among ourselves," but he could still argue that "these nations cannot compare with us in the number of intelligent readers" (qtd. in Madison 45). Historians such as Russel Nye and Lawrence Cremin accept these observations and note that the American audience was not only larger but less fragmented than its European counterparts. "Reading in the United States was not restricted to the well educated, the wealthy, or even the upper classes," writes Nye, who puts the literacy rate of the white American public at over 90 percent (*Unembarrassed Muse* 23). Cremin suggests that the actual percentage of literate white adults may have been slightly lower, particularly among women, but he offers these figures by contrast: the only European rate approaching that of the United States was Scotland's, with 80 percent literacy in 1830 and 85 percent by 1878; for the same years, England recorded 56 and 77 percent, France 36 and 70 percent (491).

Alexis de Tocqueville was among the first to note the connection between democratic ideology and the spread of education:

> when every man derives his strength from himself alone, it becomes evident that the chief cause of disparity between the fortunes of men is the mind. Whatever tends to invigorate, to extend, or to adorn the mind rises instantaneously to high value. The utility of knowledge becomes singularly conspicuous even to the eyes of the multitude; those who have no taste for its charms set store upon its results and make some efforts to acquire it.
>
> People do not read with the same notions or in the same manner as they do in aristocratic communities, but the circle of readers is unceasingly expanded, till it includes all the people. (2: 9, 40–41)

William Ellery Channing made the same point more succinctly in his popular lecture of 1838, *Self-Culture*: "Books are the true levellers" (42). Like Bryant before him, Channing emphasized the progressive possibilities of the new mass market, and rebutted Tocqueville's charge that widespread education is necessarily narrow and utilitarian. Channing felt that mass education subverted the tyranny of the majority rather than reinforcing it: "men are now learning to study and reflect alone, to follow out subjects continuously, to determine for themselves what shall engage their minds, and to call to their aid the knowledge, original views, and reasonings of all countries and ages; and the results must be, a deliberateness and independence of judgment, and a thoroughness and extent of information, unknown in former times" (42). The Sunday school movement, the national library movement—which "made more and better books far more generally available" (Antczak 57)—and the rapid increase in the number of schools at all levels after 1830 were all responses to the demand for education, specifically in literacy, fostered by democratic ideology.

A literate audience is not necessarily an audience that reads literature, but as Nina Baym has established in *Novels, Readers, and Reviewers*, there was a significant audience for fiction throughout the American romantic period, and, according to Nye, "the position of the poet in early nineteenth-century America was more elevated and secure than at any other period in American history" (*Unembarrassed Muse* 100). The structure of American society, often seen as hostile to literature, in fact established its necessary preconditions, an audience with leisure and money. In 1836, novelist William Gilmore Simms wrote that "the finish of art can only be claimed by a people with whom art is a leading object. No other people are well able to pay for it—no other people are *willing* to pay for it" (qtd. in Bank 213). Two years later, Orestes Brownson claimed that the often criticized materialism of the country was already creating a "nation of readers." In response to Emerson's "literary ethics," Brownson wrote, "Now this very business world, against which we war, is the most active in teaching all to read, in providing the means of universal education. And how, without this general and absorbing devotion to money-getting, is the general wealth of the country to be sufficiently augmented to allow the leisure we have determined to be necessary?" (13). Brownson attacked Emerson's romantic definition of the literary life as solitary, above the mob, and opposed to "low and utilitarian concerns" ("Literary Ethics," *Nature* 113) by arguing that the first duty of the scholar was to cultivate the audience being formed by capitalist expansion: "Now in this country the whole people must constitute the audience, the public. The scholar here must speak not to a clique, a coterie, but to the entire nation. The first thing to be done, then, is to make the whole nation a 'fit audience.' To talk of a 'fit audience though few,' betrays an entire ignorance of the age and the country" (13). Brownson was not simply reciting the democratic responsibilities of the writer but was arguing that the public was "an indispensable condition of [the writer's] existence" (13), a fact that every American writer admitted at some point but that each responded to differently.

These opportunities were inseparable from the problems facing the young man or woman who would choose writing as a career. Writers faced an extreme form of the professional dilemma described by Donald Scott:

> an intellectual or professional career almost of necessity was at least partly oriented toward an indeterminate, diffuse, and miscellaneous audience. In mid-nineteenth-century language, the problem was how "to come before the public" and "make a mark," how to secure support or clients from an immediate audience as well as gain the attention of a broader, unknown public beyond. (796)

The problem for writers in antebellum America, as for all professional groups, was to find an audience to support them within a fluid society that had few formal networks or institutions to promote group coherence. But members of the would-be audience found themselves in the same state of flux and confusion. The professional struggles of the major American writers were thus representative, even (perhaps especially) when the writers perceived themselves as isolated amidst an uncomprehending or hostile mass public.

The careers of major American writers were marked by the constant threat of exhaustion and futility. After writing *Mardi*, Melville wrote to Evert Duyckinck, " Would that a man could do something & then say—It is finished.—not that one thing only, but all others—that he has reached his uttermost, & can never exceed it. But live & push—tho' we put one leg forward ten miles—its no reason the other must lag behind—no, *that* must again distance the other—& so we go till we get the cramp & die" (*Letters* 83). It was a feeling that pursued Melville throughout his career. Even at the height of his powers, when he was composing *Moby-Dick*, he wrote to Hawthorne, "I feel that I am now come to the inmost leaf of the bulb, and that shortly the flower must fall to the mold" (*Letters* 130). Hawthorne could sympathize with Melville's feeling. In his 1844 sketch, "The Intelligence Office," he has a character say, " I want my place!—my own place!—my true place in the world!—my proper sphere! my thing to do, which nature intended me to perform when she fashioned me thus awry, and which I have vainly sought, all my lifetime!" (*Tales and Sketches* 874). The cry reflects Hawthorne's personal situation as a struggling writer with a family to support. But "finding a place" was a problem facing nearly everyone. Hawthorne's Intelligencer turns down the desperate man with the reply, "were I to [offer you a place], I should have the whole population of the city upon my shoulders; since far the greater proportion of them are, more or less, in your predicament" (874).

Historians and social scientists have confirmed the Intelligencer's description of antebellum professional life. In his discussion of the nineteenth-century public lecture circuit, Scott has shown that the major problem facing professional men was to find a place by reaching the democratic audience:

> Getting a hold on a career can be construed, in part, as a problem of audience and public. The dimensions of the problem varied according to particular circumstances, but those seeking professional and intellectual careers nonetheless had a common need to secure or even create the audience necessary to sustain them. The problem has several dimensions. First, in the 1830s and 1840s, there appears to have been a glut of young men trying to forge such careers. . . . Overcrowding was a lament common to lawyers, physicians, and ministers; and those in the demiworld of urban intellectual and literary life inhabited an intensely competitive jungle. (796)

As observers since Tocqueville have noted, the openness of American society was at once opportunity and problem. In Scott's words,

> Those who sought professional or intellectual careers in mid-nineteenth-century America faced a chaotic, confusing, and frequently unpredictable occupational life. Few whose adulthoods spanned these decades had careers that followed a course that they could have either planned or predicted. They frequently made their way by moving into or through a series of institutions, places, and activities that had not even existed when they started out and that

they themselves often had to invent. . . . Their problem was not that of selecting and gaining access to a position or profession that would give them a predictable purchase on mobility, prosperity, and status. It was how to create or improvise a career. (795)

The problem of self-definition was not restricted to writers, and the self-reflexivity of much nineteenth-century writing was but one example of the self-consciousness characteristic of young professionals.

The problems of antebellum professional men are reflected in literature in the romantic theme of self-creation. Self-creation was not merely a literary trope or the exclusive activity of great writers, but a cultural task imposed on all would-be professionals. As Scott puts it, life appeared to many antebellum Americans "less a matter of settling into an established niche than a process of continuing self-construction" (801). In his 1832 article on Sidney's "Defence of Poesie," Longfellow wrote that in America, "every man is taught to rely upon his own exertions for a livelihood, and is the artificer of his own fortune and estate" (qtd. in Ruland 243). Frank Sanborn, a midcentury precursor of the American social-science movement, took his cue from Emerson's claim that "all men of power and originality nowadays make their own profession" and wrote that the minister must create his audience by first creating himself: "wherever a clergyman maintains his authority, it is not so much by virtue of his office as by his personal weight of character" (qtd. in Haskell 59). Marvin Meyers, a historian of Jacksonian America, also sees self-creation as a general cultural activity: "The American who was involved in the continuous re-creation of his social world, the continuous relocation of his place within it, became the anxious witness of his own audacity. . . . In this situation the American is more than self-made according to the usual meaning; he is self-created, out of an image of common sense which all the elements of his past and present suggest to him" (56, 66). Perry Miller has described the "youthful soul-searchings" and the "highly developed self-consciousness" of young antebellum literary reviewers as they tried to "formulate the role they intended to play in the nation" (77). And R. Jackson Wilson has linked professional crisis and the appeal of certain American romantic ideas this way: "The steady decline of the ministry and the increasingly obvious failure of politics as a career resulted in a vocational vacuum. . . . most of the intellectuals of the period simply lacked clearly understood roles. Within such a context, the ideal of transcendence made perfect sense and answered real needs" (19). Like ministers and lawyers, writers had to improvise their careers, find and hold an audience, and create an identity for themselves.

But the essential similarity between the writer's and other middle-class careers was obscured by cultural forces that were shaping "literature" at the same time that they were shaping the self-perception of individuals. In *The School of Hawthorne*, Richard Brodhead describes how publishers such as James Fields of Ticknor and Fields were creating "a differentiated realm of literary writing" and associating this realm with "a previously unimaginable level of cultural prestige" (56). Fields linked the category of "literature" with the names of well-known writers such as Hawthorne and Longfellow. He did not simply market literature, but established "'literature' as a market category": "At a time when the paying audience for imaginative writing was expanding . . . , Fields found a way to identify a certain portion of that writing as distinguished—as of elevated quality, as of premium cultural value; then to build a market for that writing on the basis of that distinction" (55). In creating a nineteenth-century canon, Fields was using romantic conceptions of literary work.

Hawthorne conceived of Fields as a mediator between himself and a mysterious and threatening public. Fields conceived of Hawthorne as a "nervous man of genius" and a "gentle dreamer," removed from the day-to-day affairs of the world, yet with a mysterious power over them. "I have known rude people," wrote Fields, "who were jostling him in a crowd, give way at the sound of his low and almost irresolute voice, so potent was the gentle spell of command that seemed born of his genius" (54, 69, 87). Fields thought of Hawthorne the author as a man "shut up in his tower, [where] he could escape from the tumult of life, and be alone with only the birds and the bees in concert outside his casement" (95).[12] Caroline Ticknor, daughter of Fields's partner, also remembered Hawthorne as a dreamer in the shadows behind the green curtain of Fields's Old Corner Bookstore, "not actively engaged in any occupation, but passively gazing out on the world surrounding him, from a half shadowy hiding place," customarily sitting "in a secluded niche where he could see and yet be out of sight" (*Hawthorne and His Publisher* 10). This was the self-image that Hawthorne preferred and one that Fields helped him to foster. It was also a self-definition significantly aligned with the definition of self held by members of the middle-class culture.[13]

Because of this feeling of being cut off from others, romantic writers often found existing groups of readers hard to reach or even identify, even though (in a central irony of the period) this feeling of isolation was just what they shared with their readers. This helps to account for the democratic, even republican, sympathies of Blake, Shelley, and Melville, among other romantic democrats, which at first seems contradicted by the sometimes obscure and difficult forms of their works. In an earlier draft of this book I asked the question, How can a poem be in any genuine sense political if it can only be understood by a few readers? This question, while it is not as easy to answer as I once rhetorically supposed, should at least trouble more teachers, critics, and scholars than it seems to. I have in mind poems like Shelley's *Prometheus Unbound* as opposed to his *The Mask of Anarchy* or "England in 1819"; or Blake's *Jerusalem* as opposed to his *Songs of Innocence*, meant to be a book that "all may read."

The major romantic writers experienced the general feeling of being cut off from "developed social relations" alternately as freedom and as despair. They felt free to explore the growth of their own minds (*The Prelude*) or to create inner apocalypses (*Prometheus Unbound, Jerusalem, The Confidence-Man*), but they sometimes despaired of communicating their insights to the public. Romantic literature, which both reflected and perpetuated the idea of the individual as isolated, thus penetrated deeply into the lived experiences of the members of industrial society, particularly the middle class. The romantics produced a great literature because their activity as writers forced them to confront a general experience of their historical period: the feeling of being cut off from other people and from the social and historical processes that determine one's life.

CHAPTER ONE

The Anglo-American Literary Profession in the Nineteenth Century

The term *reading public* was first used in the early nineteenth century to describe several emerging social developments: an increasing number of readers and new forms such as reviews and newpapers to serve them; rapid increases in the annual output of new books; and new methods of distributing reprinted works and remaindered new books (Jack, *English Literature* 43). This term was echoed by publishers and critics who thought that the market conditions that made more books available to more readers at less cost were progressive phenomena, and by the romantics themselves, who, unlike publishers and readers, often thought of the market as conspiring against "imagination" (Blake) or "telling the truth" (Melville). Some publishers saw that the reading public presented an opportunity that the "great" publishers and the romantic writers they represented often failed to grasp. Archibald Constable, Walter Scott's publisher, recognized this opportunity in the 1820s. He wrote to Scott, "there has been, and there exists at present, a desire of knowledge and a demand for books in the middle ranks and manufacturing classes of society altogether unprecedented, to supply which will occasion a demand to fully ten times the amount of any hitherto existing" (qtd. in Collins 199). He also saw where the real problem in serving that demand lay: "the sale of cheap books in this country is at present carried on to an extent altogether astonishing, but almost entirely in the hands of the most inferior class of traders" (199). That is, the new audience was being exploited by the publishers of the cheap novels and pirated editions that Wordsworth fulminated against in the 1800 preface to the *Lyrical Ballads*: he attacked "frantic novels, sickly and stupid German tragedies, and deluges of idle and extravagant stories in verse" (*Prose* 1:128).

The publishers of the works now considered major at first stood aloof from this new market. Charles Knight, one of the originators of the cheap-literature movement in the 1820s and an astute observer of turn-of-the-century publishing practices, noted:

> there are still many evidences that the commerce of books at that period, and subsequently, did not contemplate the existence of a large class of buyers, beyond those who were at ease in their fortunes. . . . Nor had the booksellers discovered that there were essentially two, if not more, classes of customers for books—those who would have the dearest and the newest, and those who were content to wait till the gloss of novelty has passed off, and good works became accessible to them, either in cheaper reprints, or "remainders" reduced in price. (224–26)

The great, well-established publishers of expensive books, Knight observed, "hated cheap books" and combined against innovative publishers such as John Bell, who brought out a series of English poets in 1777, and James Lackington, who protested against the regular practice of destroying unsold books to keep prices high (246). Publishers still equated high price with literary excellence and refused to enter the market that Bell, Lackington, and John Cooke, another publisher of reprinted classics, had discovered. Continued high prices were, in Knight's words, "to be ascribed to the determination of the great publishers not sufficiently to open their eyes to the extension of the number of readers," a determination that resulted in "a system of extravagantly high prices" (238).

The English romantic writers were among the earliest to experience the reading public as a social fact and to conceive of it as a problem that would later be called the mass reading public. From the beginning, the romantics were ambivalent about the new reading audiences, and particularly about signs of the developing mass audience. Coleridge expressed his contempt for readers in a passage that has been quoted or echoed so often that it is received as a description of his sociohistorical moment rather than as an expression of his own personal frustration:

For as to the devotees of the circulating libraries, I dare not com-
pliment their *pass-time*, or rather *kill-time*, with the name of *reading*. Call it rather a sort of beggarly day-dreaming, during which
the mind of the dreamer furnishes for itself nothing but laziness,
and a little mawkish sensibility. . . . We should therefore transfer
this species of *amusement* (if indeed those can be said to retire *a
musis*, who were never in their company, or relaxation be attribu-
table to those, whose bows are never bent) from the genus, *reading*, to that comprehensive class characterized by the power of rec-
onciling the two contrary yet co-existing propensities of human
nature, namely, indulgence of sloth, and hatred of vacancy.
(*Biographia*, ch. 3, 48)

At this point the familiar battle lines are in place between the serious artist and the reading public.

Publishers such as James Lackington were aware of the social as well
as the economic pressures on new readers of the period—the pressures
of ignorance and of unfamiliarity with a pursuit formerly restricted to
small, sophisticated, and wealthy groups. Lackington himself attested
to the difficulties facing the new reading audiences. In 1794 he wrote,

I made the most of my little stock of literature, and strongly recommended the purchasing of Books to [a friend]. But so ignorant
were we on the subject, that neither of us knew what books were
fit for our perusal, nor what to enquire for, as we had scarce ever
heard or seen even any *title pages*. . . . And here I cannot help
thinking that had Fortune thrown proper books in our way, we
should have imbibed a just taste for literature, and soon made
some tolerable progress; but such was our obscurity, that it was
next to impossible for us ever to emerge from it.

As we could not tell what to enquire for, we were ashamed to go
into the bookseller's shops; and I assure you, my friend, that there
are thousands now in England in the very same situation; many,
very many, have come to my shop, who have discovered an en-
quiring mind, but were totally at a loss what to ask for and who
had no friend to direct them. (88–89)

Robert Chambers, who started a secondhand bookshop in 1818, corroborated Lackington's observation: "Hundreds, I found, as Lackington had done before me, would buy books from a stall, who would not purchase them equally cheap in a shop" (qtd. in Collins 188).

When many critics of the romantic poets do mention the socioeconomics of publishing, it is to cite how little this or that poet was paid for a book, not how much the reader was charged for it. But Bell, Cooke, and Lackington made significant cultural contributions during this period. Augustine Birrell wrote of John Cooke, "He believed both in genius and his country. He gave people cheap books, and they bought them gladly" (qtd. in Altick 54). Lackington made a fortune by cultivating this new audience using new methods to distribute books: remaindering newly published but unsold books that were usually destroyed or sold for waste paper; selling secondhand books; and selling books on a cash-only basis in order to maintain his current inventory at high levels. He could justly claim that his innovative business practices made an important cultural contribution.

In his memoirs, Lackington wrote,

> Thousands . . . have been effectually prevented from purchasing (though anxious to do so) whose circumstances in life would not permit them to pay the full price, and thus were totally excluded from the advantage of improving their understandings; and enjoying a rational entertainment. And you may be assured, that it affords me the most pleasing satisfaction . . . when I reflect what prodigious numbers in inferior or *reduced* situations of life, have been essentially benefitted, in consequence of being thus enabled to indulge their natural propensity for the acquisition of knowledge, on easy terms: nay, I could almost be vain enough to assert, that I have thereby been highly instrumental in diffusing that general desire for READING, now so prevalent among the inferior orders of society. (218)

Lackington exaggerates the number of lower-class readers in what is of course a piece of self-puffery, but the consensus among students of the British reading public is that by the early nineteenth century there were indeed more readers from more classes than ever before.

What compelled them to read was, in the words of a contemporary, "'the irrepressible passion for discussion which succeeded the fall of old systems on the French Revolution,'" and, as John Gross points out, "the stirring up of fundamental social questions by the steady advance of industrialism" (2). The increase in the number of readers meant an increase in the number of kinds of readers and many different reasons for reading. The entrepreneurial middle class had more time for reading and more money to spend on books, which connoted luxury and status. As Richard Altick notes, "in the middle class, even to some extent in its lower reaches, growing prosperity and the cheapness of labor enabled men and women to hire others for tasks they had hitherto done for themselves. . . . Hence to scores of thousands of families touched by the prosperity of the new age, relief from household duties provided a degree of leisure undreamed of in earlier generations" (85–86). These were the patrons of the circulating libraries at whom Coleridge sneered but whose reading habits and tastes were similar to those of earlier eighteenth-century upper- and middle-class readers. They read the new journals and magazines as well as novels, histories, poetry, and the classics.

Other sorts of readers for whom circulating libraries were still too expensive were appearing and demanding to be addressed. These men and women were drawn to print largely by the political and social controversies of the age. Working-class readers, whom Blake tried to address in some of his poems, were the largest part of the audience for radical pamphlets and newspapers, which achieved such wide circulation that taxes and censorship were instituted to suppress them. Such readers had little leisure, yet were compelled to read by what Wordsworth called in the 1800 preface "the great national events which are daily taking place" (*Prose* 1:128). R. K. Webb concludes in *The British Working Class Reader*, "The rapidly expanding output of political pamphlets and handbills played an important part in the widening political interests of the eighteenth century. But in the nineties one finds a persistent overtone of novelty. The strangeness lay not so much in the variety and extent of publication as in a new complexity in the audience. For the first time the working class reader had specifically to be reckoned with" (36). So the period was marked by more readers but not quite yet by a "mass" of readers. Distinct groups were arising with distinct needs.

The new reading publics would require new forms of publication and distribution to meet new demands. Publishers and writers recognized this in a vague way but were slow to respond creatively. Early efforts to reach the new reading publics, particularly the working-class public, were flawed by palpable ulterior motives and condescension. The free tracts distributed by groups such as the Christian Knowledge Society were intended to persuade workers to resign themselves to their place in the new industrial order and were treated by the workers with contempt. Until Byron and Scott became best-selling poets, the major publishers serving the middle and upper classes continued to issue new works in small and expensive editions. Scott and Byron ushered in an age of large and, in spite of economies of scale, expensive editions. Other romantic writers who complained of public neglect and the precedence of "cheap literature" offered no solutions. They produced a nominally democratic literature but continued to distribute it through publishing arrangements aimed at a well-to-do middle-class audience that represented only a small part of the existing reading public.

Like any new and dynamic situation, this one was difficult for the participants to interpret. Some members of the "reading public" had the money and leisure for new books, many more were willing to buy cheap reprints and pirated editions, while others were able to read but had little access to published books of any sort. Ironically, Wordsworth himself wrote from Grasmere to a friend in 1801, "We live quite out of the way of new books; I have not seen a single one since I came here, now 13 months ago" (*Letters* 1:318). When the established houses failed to serve the obscurer publics, other publishers stepped forward to exploit them. Among these were the Minerva Press, which published the "frantic novels" of which Wordsworth complained, and the firm of Thomas Tegg, which specialized in carelessly produced reprints of the classics. Though Wordsworth announced in 1815 that every author "has had the task of *creating* the taste by which he is to be enjoyed" (*Prose* 3:80), romantic writers and their publishers at first did little with regard to existing taste except to caricature and bemoan it.

Other writers of the period with political and social views similar to those of the romantics were reaching tens of thousands of readers with every cheap pamphlet and newspaper they printed. In 1816 William Cobbett responded to the declining circulation of his *Political Register* by producing a cheap version sold for two pence. Circulation rose to between 40,000 and 50,000 copies a week (Jack, *English Literature* 313). Cobbett was demonstrating, in Jon Klancher's words, "how effectively an older and now discredited publishing practice [self-publishing] could be taken over and reworked for a new audience" (48). By 1820 Cobbett was able to write this of his audience:

> I always say that I have derived from the people . . . ten times the light that I have communicated to them. A writer engaged in the instruction of such a people, is constantly upheld, not only by the applause that he receives from them, and by perceiving that his labours are attended with effect; but also by the aid which he is continually deriving from those new thoughts which his thoughts produce in their minds. It is the flint and the steel meeting that brings forth the fire. (qtd. in Thompson, *English Working Class* 758)

An audience existed for works of social and political relevance and high quality. But the works had to be affordable and available. The *Lyrical Ballads*, though they used a folk genre and plain language and touched on radical themes, remained in the booksellers' shops frequented by the upper and middle classes.

The cost of books was not the only issue to be considered in cultivating the new reading publics. As Charles Knight said, "those who have to deal with 'Literature for the People' must bear in mind that time as well as money has to be economised by those who of necessity must labour hard either by hand or head" (247). The refusal to consider simple facts about the material circumstances of different groups of readers, such as how much time they had to read, how much energy they could spare from work to devote to books, how much privacy their homes afforded, is perhaps the most galling aspect of attacks, then and now, on the "reading public." One could argue, for example, that many potential readers were benighted far more effectively by want of candles, windows, and daytime leisure than by any lack of intellectual light. The availability of gas lighting in the early nineteenth century is as important as the rise of the novel in any discussion of the new reading publics (Webb 23).

The first-generation romantics—Blake, Wordsworth, and Coleridge—all began their careers as radical democrats and so felt obliged to address "the People." But when faced with the difficulty of addressing the new reading publics, romantic theory transformed "the People" into an increasingly abstract concept. Shelley, the most politically radical of the romantics, finally developed a poetic theory that separated literature completely from the response of its immediate audience. He wrote in *A Defence of Poetry,*

> And let us not circumscribe the effects of the bucolic and erotic poetry within the limits of the sensibility of those to whom it was addressed. They may have perceived the beauty of those immortal compositions, simply as fragments and isolated portions: those who are more finely organised, or born in a happier age, may recognize them as episodes to that great poem, which all poets, like the cooperating thoughts of one great mind, have built up since the beginning of the world. (qtd. in Brett-Smith 40–41)

In reaction to his own unhappy age, Shelley developed a theory in which poets no longer address their contemporaries but participate instead in an inhuman abstraction, the "great poem" which is eternal and addressed to the ideal audience that actual readers cannot ever be.

The romantics faced a time not just of political but also of professional crisis and frustration. Book prices were high, great public issues demanded the attention of readers, and the industrial revolution was radically transforming social arrangements. As historian Fernand Braudel puts it, "the composition of every society undergoing long-term growth is inevitably affected by the division of labour. . . . An example would be the way a cultural sector (from education to the theater, newspapers, publishing houses and learned societies) was gradually emerging as an increasingly independent world. . . . By the end of the eighteenth century all the professions were expanding steadily and tending to change their structures and traditional forms of organization" (598–99).

Some writers and publishers quickly grasped the effect of these changes on their activity. Thomas De Quincey wrote that "literature must decay unless we have a class *wholly* dedicated to that service, not pursuing it as an amusement only with wearied and pre-occupied minds" (qtd. in Chilcott 200). Leigh Hunt said that Wordsworth was at the head of the profession of letters in his age. But the major romantic writers, even successful ones such as Byron and Longfellow, began to define their activity as being above the confusing and arbitrary world of trade.

In his standard history *Publishing and Bookselling*, F. A. Mumby explains that, in the eighteenth century, successful authors had dominated the literary institution, but by 1800 authors had to collaborate with the great publishers and the reviews they controlled. He cites this letter from John Murray as representative of the changed status of nineteenth-century authors: "I am in the habit of seeing persons of the highest rank in literature and talent, such as . . . Southey, Campbell, Walter Scott, Madame de Stael, . . . Lord Byron, and others; thus leading the most delightful life, with means of prosecuting my business in the highest honour and emolument." Mumby then comments, "Murray's words illustrate the changed relations which he had so largely helped to bring about between authors and publishers. Instead of the eighteenth-century custom of, say, Dr. Johnson's lifetime, when the literary lion of the day would be surrounded by an association of publishing-booksellers, the publishers' drawing-room was now the centre of an appreciative crowd of authors" (191).

Clearly the literary marketplace had as much power over authors' lives as the capitalistic social and economic arrangements had over those of other individuals in bourgeois society. In an 1825 letter to Samuel Rogers, Wordsworth revealed his nostalgia for the eighteenth-century situation, which he characterized as more manageable and more favorable to authors:

> I am obliged by your kindness in taking so much trouble about my Poems, and more especially so by the tone in which you met Mr Murray when he was disposed to put on the airs of a patron. I do not look for much advantage either to Mr M. or to any other Bookseller with whom I may treat; and for still less to myself, but I

assure you that I would a thousand times rather that not a verse of mine should ever enter the Press again, than to allow any of them to say that I was to the amount of the strength of a hair dependant upon their countenance, consideration, Patronage, or by whatever term they may dignify their ostentation and selfish vanity. You recollect Dr Johnson's short method of settling precedence at Dilly's, "No, Sir, authors above booksellers." (*Letters* 4:327)

In contrast, Bernard Barton's 1822 letter to Robert Southey gives a more accurate account of the prevailing relationship between writers and publishers: "The Notice of [Murray's] *Quarterly Review* is an understood passport to an extensive Circle whose attention I certainly could wish to obtain" (qtd. in Barcus xiii). That circle included the new middle-class reading public.

Wordsworth and Coleridge attacked reviewers in order to reassert the writer's authority within the literary institution. Wordsworth directly linked critics with the reading publics, the passive consumers of literature: critics, to his mind, were "men of palsied imaginations and indurated hearts; in whose minds all healthy action is languid, who therefore feed as the many direct them, or, with the many, are greedy after vicious provocatives;—judges, whose censure is auspicious, and whose praise ominous!" (*Prose* 3:66). In the *Biographia Literaria*, Coleridge accused the critics of fostering the public's indifference to romantic work: "But alas! as in other despotisms, [the public] but echoes the decisions of its invisible ministers, whose intellectual claims to the guardianship of the muses seem, for the greater part, analogous to the physical qualifications which adapt their oriental brethren for the superintendence of the Harem" (ch. 3, 59). The snide and accusatory tone that often characterizes professional struggles reveals Coleridge's need to mount some sort of self-defense against a literary institution that, like society, appeared to the individual as a hostile, impersonal arena.

Coleridge saw the literary institution being dominated by publishers, reviewers, and other more popular writers, and, like Wordsworth, attacked them as part of the market system that in his view vulgarized literature:

But alas! the multitude of books and the general diffusion of literature, have produced other and more lamentable effects in the
world of letters. . . . now, partly by the labours of successive poets,
and in part by the more artificial state of society and social intercourse, language, mechanized as it were into a barrel-organ, supplies at once both instrument and tune. Thus even the deaf may
play, so as to delight the many. . . . Hence of all trades, literature at
present demands the least talent or information; and, of all modes
of literature, the manufacturing of poems. . . . hence individuals
below mediocrity not less in natural power than in acquired
knowledge; nay, bunglers that had failed in the lowest mechanic
crafts . . . have been able to derive a successful trade in the employment of booksellers, nay, have raised themselves into temporary
name and reputation with the public at large. (ch. 2, 38–41)

Coleridge objects to being forced to compete with other writers in a
boom market that encouraged all, and at the same time he asserts his
own priority within the existing competitive system. The vocabulary
of imagination used by romantic poets reflects a common fear and a
common need to assert oneself and one's selfhood; this assertion was
one example of the belief in the power of the private self to overcome a
hostile social and historical environment, and the fear that it could not.

By the second decade of the nineteenth century, the great publishers
were being forced by market pressures to cultivate the new reading
publics. In his account of John Murray's Family Library, Scott Bennett
writes, " it was the 'discovery' of the common reader that excited publishers most during the period and stimulated their most innovative
practices. The discovery might be a fearful or a hopeful one, depending
on the publisher's attitude toward the established order, but all were
alike eagerly involved in both responding to and creating the conditions for the democratization of the printed word" (140). When the
publishers finally moved into these new markets, the writers they published were forced to redefine their role, and to undertake the task,
sometimes a confusing and threatening one, of inventing new relationships with the existing reading publics.

In his 1815 "Essay, Supplementary to the Preface," Wordsworth distinguished between the public, "that small though loud portion of the community, ever governed by factitious influence" (that is, critics), and the people, "philosophically characterized," to which "his devout respect, his reverence, is due" (*Prose* 3:84). The identical distinction along with its contempt for actual readers can be found in Keats: "I never expect to get any thing by my Books: and moreover I wish to avoid publishing—I admire Human Nature but I do not like *Men*.—I should like to compose things honourable to Man—but not fingerable over by *Men*" (qtd. in Chilcott 203). Many other authors would come to equate publishing with contamination and disgusting physical contact, while financially independent authors like Byron continued to treat writing as a gentleman's avocation rather than as a profession or trade, often refusing to accept payment for their work.

In the *Biographia* Coleridge depicted the relationship between writers and readers as steadily degenerating over time:

> In times of old, books were as religious oracles; as literature advanced, they next became venerable preceptors; they then descended to the rank of instructive friends; and, as their numbers increased, they sunk still lower to that of entertaining companions; and at present they seem degraded into culprits to hold up their hands at the bar of every self-elected, yet not the less peremptory, judge, who chuses to write from humour or interest, from enmity or arrogance, and to abide the decision (in the words of Jeremy Taylor) "of him that reads in malice, or him that reads after dinner." (ch. 3, 57)

In the second decade of the nineteenth century, neither Wordsworth nor Coleridge could see the progressive and, as Bennett points out, democratic aspects of the literary marketplace: that it could serve larger and more diverse groups of readers and that it could free writers from patronage and the isolation of the coterie. Instead, they characterized the new situation as the rule of an impersonal mob whose tastes and standards were not immediately accessible to the writer, as in the supposedly more personal patronage relationship. Coleridge reacted to the new situation with undisguised contempt for the reading public:

The same gradual retrograde movement may be traced, in the relation which the authors themselves have assumed towards their
readers. . . . Poets and Philosophers, rendered diffident by their
very number, addressed themselves to *"learned* readers;" then,
aimed to conciliate the graces of "the *candid* reader;" till, the critic
still rising as the author sunk, the amateurs of literature collec-
tively were erected into a municipality of judges, and addressed as
THE TOWN! And now, finally, all men being supposed able to read,
and all readers able to judge, the multitudinous PUBLIC, shaped
into a personal unity by the magic of abstraction, sits nominal despot on the throne of criticism. (ch. 3, 58–59)

Coleridge describes the new social formations perceptively—indeed,
he and the publisher Lackington describe closely related stages of the
same process, though each values it differently. In fact, Coleridge
chronicled actual social formations when he portrayed the evolving urban culture as a faceless and unknowable rabble rather than as a potential audience (Klancher 96). Coleridge parodies the inevitable conces-
sions writers had to make to the new audiences—readers who were at
first learned or merely well intentioned began to form themselves into
an impertinent "TOWN" and finally disappear into a faceless and hostile crowd. Like Wordsworth, Coleridge felt that proper relations between writers and readers had been reversed; the writer should be the
despot, not his readers.

Coleridge's "Kubla Khan" is a direct response to the situation of authorship that frustrated him. He published the poem, he says, "at the
request of a poet of great and deserved celebrity," Lord Byron, who
represented for every early-nineteenth-century writer the new and
mystifying conditions of mass success. The prose headnote then re-
counts a tale of visionary power thwarted by the concerns of the everyday world, represented by the man from Porlock. The poem itself then
seeks and finds compensation for this creative frustration in a vision of
the artist as a fascinating yet dangerous seer who can be approached
only with "holy dread." Coleridge's ideal reader is a seeker of religious
truth, not someone who wants to be entertained, informed, or roused
to action. As Marilyn Butler and others have noticed, much romantic

criticism, including later academic criticism of romantic writers, envisions reading as a fundamentally religious activity in which readers declare themselves sheep or goats by their willingness to enter the authorial "world" or "universe," metaphors that traditionally equate the author with God.[1] American Renaissance writers then borrowed English romantic formulations of the writer's role in society and literature's value as a guide toward ultimate, quasi-religious truth.

However, Byron was a best-selling author, one of the first, along with Scott, in part because he captured the experience of the alienated self in his poems that many actual readers were also experiencing. Wordsworth too was more well known than he would admit, and looked down on the activity of publishing, even while claiming to be "a man speaking to men." Coleridge transformed himself from a vatic bard to a working journalist; Blake and Shelley wrote accessible works at some points in their careers, but they grew increasingly obscure as their difficulties in reaching the reading public became more and more pronounced. Keats reenacted in his career the common experience facing most members of his society: whether to escape into the realm of the transcendent imagination, the romantic version of private selfhood, or to be "up and doing" in the social arena, in Keats's case as a practicing physician. Keats experimented with public forms like the drama, though with the lyric ode he found the perfect vehicle to express modern selfhood, as subsequent generations of readers would attest.

Wordsworth tried to replace the contending, sometimes mutually hostile audiences he faced with a universal human audience—men— and to universalize the writer's work as the vocation that addressed fundamental human concerns, not that which constructed the specialized, class-based discourses that Klancher anatomizes as the actual products of early-nineteenth-century writers (4). However, in early-nineteenth-century England the pressure from the mass audience was more sensed than felt. Wordsworth and Blake in particular struggled with a nascent mass audience in a way that would anticipate American struggles in a demographically different situation, where the mass audience was a more palpable reality. Indeed the British romantic writers were "prophetic," but in a more practical sense than has traditionally been seen, for they anticipated the phenomenon of the mass reading public that would perturb but also energize later generations of writers in the United States. The success accorded Byron and Scott provided only a hint of the rewards successful writers could gain, rewards that were countered by the pressures to enact oneself and one's work on an exhilarating, baffling, and impersonal stage. In mid-nineteenth-century America, however, the mass audience was becoming a quantifiable reality—the sales figures for works by Stowe, Cummins, and Warner were well known to the American Renaissance writers (Railton 74). We know from studies like Ronald Zboray's *A Fictive People* and Ezra Greenspan's *Walt Whitman and the American Reader* that the literary profession in the United States was inaugurated by Irving and Cooper, grew as the modes of publishing technology and distribution became more sophisticated and rapid, and culminated in the self-congratulatory Crystal Palace dinner in New York, in 1855, when authors and publishers gathered to celebrate the growth of a new culture founded on both democracy and technology.

Was there no place for the American romantics on the bookshelves of the readers who were supporting this new culture? Thoreau did not think so; Whitman did. Melville thought in rapid oscillation that the reading public would accept his greatest work and was too stupid to accept his greatest work. However, even at his gloomiest point, in *The Confidence-Man*, Melville was fully engaged with American literary culture, as that book's parodies of Emerson and Thoreau reveal. But even before the rise of the best-selling American novelist, American writers were adapting British romantic formulations of the writer's work to their own situation and using them to explain and to compensate for their professional frustrations.

The effect of the mass market on American letters was not to debase taste but to make taste unpredictable. As Zboray notes, "the reading public conformed to no monolithic model, but instead reflected in its diversity the chaotic course of antebellum economic growth" (xx). The recurrent word in Zboray's sociocultural analysis of the antebellum reading public is *chaos*—economic chaos that forced Americans notable for their diversity to seek an order amidst that chaos in a national print culture that was as diverse as the reading public: "Here, in the common plight of families and friends scattered by the winds of economic circumstance, and not in any deliberate attempts at cultural unification, can be found the seeds of a national way of life. For a subtle transfer of self-construction took place . . . until eventually the symbolic community of the printed word replaced or compromised much direct personal contact" (xx). *The Scarlet Letter* was a moderate success, *Moby-Dick* a relative failure; Poe was a journalist whose work was notorious and fairly familiar, while Whitman was a journalist whose poetry was notorious and (at first) unread.

But the growing feeling among American writers (canonical, forgotten, and newly rediscovered) was that the audience was a mass whose tastes were mysterious and could be penetrated only by fortunate hacks who struck the right chords. The English romantics had the tradition of "the English poet" to sustain them in their frustrating struggles with the new audiences, but major American careers were often marked by abrupt breakdowns or silences and a feeling of alienation, often exaggerated, from contemporary audiences. Hawthorne and Melville are key examples, but so is Dickinson's conflicted refusal to enter "the Auction / Of the Mind of Man."

Though it was not possible in the United States for a significant number of authors to be self-supporting until the 1860s, the inevitability of professional arrangements was evident much earlier. Literary work became professionalized in America much more rapidly than in England because commercial expansion and democratic ideology made it difficult to continue thinking of literature as a gentleman's activity. In the late eighteenth and early nineteenth century, nearly every regional population center from Hartford to Richmond supported a publisher-bookseller who served a small regional market. In the 1820s, books were still distributed by cart or boat; in winter, poor roads and frozen rivers suspended deliveries for months (hence the traditional spring publishing season). With the coming of canals and railroads, a national market that included the Midwest became a possibility. New York's access to these distribution channels (particularly the Erie Canal) accounts for its continuing dominance as a publishing center. During the 1840s it surpassed Philadelphia and Boston by aggressively exploiting the huge midwestern market, a fact which led Hawthorne to remark of Emerson in the mid-1840s, "I wish he might be induced to publish this volume in New York. His reputation is still, I think, provincial, and almost local, partly owing to the defects of the New England system of publication" (qtd. in Mellow 258).

The best account of these changes and their effect on major American writers remains William Charvat's *The Profession of Authorship in America, 1800–1870*. He notes that "during the twenties and thirties writers like Irving, Cooper, and Emerson, who began as patrician amateurs, were transformed into hard-working professionals" even though they "never ceased resenting the forces that brought about that change" (293). After the panic of 1837 temporarily curtailed the book trade, publishers rebuilt their market by lowering prices for books and inventing cheaper newspaper formats for novels. According to Frank Luther Mott, magazines and reviews began paying their contributors more or less adequately after 1840 and thus became a major source of income for writers. Rewards for the highest-paid writers were substantial, as they had been for Byron and Scott, and they established the economic situation within which writers such as Melville, Thoreau, and Whitman had to define themselves.

Like their British counterparts, the American romantics found themselves working in a competitive market dominated by highly visible popular writers, many of whom could not automatically be dismissed as inferior scribblers. Cooper resented being called the American Scott, and Longfellow resembled Byron only in his immense popular appeal and financial success. But Cooper and Longfellow were to American writers what Byron and Scott were to British ones: a paradigm of authorship which combined greatness, fame, and financial success. By 1860, as Charvat notes, "many American writers were deriving an adequate income from the home market, which had not been possible during the first half of the century. . . . During this period writing ceased to be a part-time avocation and became a profession capable of supporting authors in middle-class respectability" (*Profession* 313).

The dominant American publishers, such as Harper's and Putnam's, were serving and accessing the mass market through more efficient distribution and advertising. In the 1850s the book trade emerged from the period of cutthroat competition; prices increased, gentleman's agreements among publishers at home and abroad were struck, and the book trade, in James Barnes's view, "enjoyed its image of prosperity and respectability" (29). Russel Nye concludes that "conditions were more favorable to the American writer during the middle decades of the nineteenth century than ever before" (*Society and Culture* 75). However, individual writers in antebellum America faced a grating professional truth: a Cooper or an Irving could achieve fame, a Longfellow, fortune, a Stowe or a Cummins, huge sales, but the standards for success were neither agreed upon nor automatic, and talented writers could prosper, subsist, or fail, and sometimes all three at different stages of their careers.

In his 1828 *Notions of the Americans*, James Fenimore Cooper observed, "Writers are already getting to be numerous, for literature is beginning to be profitable. Those authors who are successful, receive prices for their labors, which exceed those paid to the authors of any country, England alone excepted" (Ruland 228). Cooper noted that American writers and publishers made less money than the English but could reach a wider audience because "the same work which is sold in England for six dollars, is sold in the United States for two" (Ruland 228). Despite unfair competition from publishers who paid no royalties to foreign authors, by the 1840s American works were dominating the American market, in sales if not in cultural prestige (Cremin 302). In 1845, Evert Duyckinck was echoing De Quincey's demand that the profession of authorship "be rescued from mere amateurs and quacks, and restored to its legitimate followers, the modest sincere men, who are now driven into silence or poverty" (qtd. in P. Miller 125).

American writers also dealt with the marketplace and the increased literary professionalism of the mid–nineteenth century by attacking critics and the reading public, complaining about successful but inferior competitors, idealizing literature as beyond the realm of trade, and by using other British romantic formulations. Like the British romantic period, the antebellum American period was an age of polemical prefaces, theoretical essays on writing and on national literature, and works in which the artist is a central character.

For example, Longfellow's autobiographical *Hyperion*, published just before his rise to public prominence, includes several discussions of "the private sufferings of authors by profession." "Next to the New-gate Calendar, the Biography of Authors is the most sickening chapter in the history of man" (68), he wrote. Longfellow has one of his characters suggest that the "calamities of authors . . . spring from false and ex-aggerated ideas of poetry and the poetic character" (70)—that is, romantic definitions of the poet as a visionary or a legislator. In response, Longfellow invokes the concept of the literary genius as a redeemer: "It would seem, indeed, as if all their sufferings had but sanctified them; as if the death-angel, in passing, had touched them with the hem of his garment, and made them holy; as if the hand of disease had been stretched out over them only to make the sign of the cross upon their souls!" (75). In *Hyperion* Longfellow transmuted professional struggles into spiritual triumphs. Even after his great success in the literary market, Longfellow continued to recite the conventional complaints. In his 1849 *Kavanaugh* he tweaked critics as "sentinels in the grand army of letters, stationed at the corners of newspapers and reviews, to challenge every new author" (64). He satirized his popular competitors as uninspired hacks writing only for money: "To many [authors] the trumpet of fame is nothing but a tin horn to call them home, like la-borers from the field, at dinner-time; and they think themselves lucky to get the dinner" (64). Despite his great commercial success, Long-fellow could still disparage any attempt to associate literature and trade.

Though he single-handedly proved that a poet in America could gain a wide audience while winning the respect of his peers, Long-fellow asserted in his last work, *Michael Angelo*, that

> an artist
> Who does not wholly give himself to art,
> Who has about him nothing marked or strange,
> But tries to suit himself to all the world,
> Will ne'er attain to greatness. (382)

In this work, Longfellow uses the figure of Michelangelo to atone for his own popular success. The audience that revered Longfellow was composed of

many people
Who see no difference between what is best
And what is only good, or not even good;
So that poor artists stand in their esteem
On the same level with the best, or higher.
(166)

The great artist demands "sequestration from the world around us" and "consecration of the world within us" (381), and repudiates the audience and the mediocre work it prefers. The public, of course, turns on such artists, "Calls them strange people and fantastical, / Morose, discourteous" (381), but their disapproval is the seal of the artist's greatness. Longfellow never finished this work, but it leaves one with the eerie sense that he went to his grave after a long and successful career wishing that he had more actively courted failure.

The century-long debate about creating a national literature was another attempt to find a place for literary work in a rapidly expanding capitalist society and to resolve the professional confusion facing nineteenth-century American writers. There was much talk about creating a democratic as opposed to an aristocratic literature and using American subjects rather than European ones, but James Russell Lowell revealed the central issue when he wrote in his 1855 "The Function of the Poet" that "gradually, however, the poet as the 'seer' became secondary to the 'maker.' His office became that of entertainer rather than teacher" (5). Lowell formulated the decline in the writer's status using the same terms that Coleridge used in the *Biographia Literaria* and that Emerson echoed in *Representative Men*. Lowell's essay is another romantic literary "history" whose subtext is the contemporary writer's plight in a commercial society, forced to meet the demands of an audience of consumers rather than dictating inspired wisdom to a passive group of believers.

Lowell echoes Coleridge's ideologically motivated nostalgia when he claims that "the poet and the priest were united originally in the same person" (4), and he echoes Wordsworth's (and Emerson's) attempts to elevate poetry over more practical reading matter and over other professions by claiming that "formerly science was poetry" (13).

By claiming a vatic function for the poet, Lowell tried to create for him a noncommercial role:

> Till America has learned to love art, not as an amusement . . . but for its humanizing and ennobling energy, for its power of making men better by arousing in them a perception of their own instincts for what is beautiful, and therefore sacred and religious, and an eternal rebuke of the base and worldly, she will not have succeeded in that high sense which alone makes a nation out of a people, and raises it from a dead name to a living power. (19)

Like Shelley in his *Defence of Poetry*, Lowell argued that the poet, not the businessman or the politician, shapes contemporary reality: "It is not by any amount of material splendor or prosperity, but only by moral greatness, by ideas, by works of imagination, that a race can conquer the future" (19). Lowell did concede that the poet must write about the present ("steam and iron and telegraph wires" [18]), and address the contemporary audience, but, as in most romantic polemics, he is not so much arguing for a "function" for the poet (which implies well-defined service to a society of equals) as trying to return him to some imagined past where he was an acknowledged cultural arbiter and dispenser of wisdom. The poet is not part of "the dusty path of our daily life" but "an interpreter between man and his own nature" (8). The debt to Wordsworth's prefaces to the *Lyrical Ballads* is clear.

Like Melville's 1850 "Hawthorne and His Mosses" or Whitman's 1855 preface to *Leaves of Grass*, Lowell's essay is an attempt to define an audience suitable for the romantic artist and to will that audience into being. Lowell feared that the American poet already had a function—to divert the reading public. The rather embarrassing length of the search for a great American writer, and the inability of the reviewers to settle on a host of plausible candidates, indicates that the literary nationalists were in fact reluctant to replace vague, "absolute" standards of literary greatness with the obvious standard of marketplace success, which would have been both democratic and concrete.

The new publishing media, a literate public, and democratic ideology made it seem more and more possible to establish direct contact with the people, and many writers such as Stowe and Longfellow were doing so. As Leslie Fiedler has written, "with the invention of printing, the growth of literacy and, especially, the appearance of a 'free market' for the exchange of cultural commodities, literature seemed on the verge of total emancipation" (57). Yet questions about whether a distinctive American literature could exist, whether the modern world offered poetic subjects, whether literature was inherently aristocratic and above the crass and material concerns of the age, continued to be obsessively repeated. Writers were most uneasy about creating American literature at the very historical and cultural moment when that literature was being created.

CHAPTER TWO

Wordsworth
and the Difficulty of
"Speaking to Men"

In the 1802 preface to the *Lyrical Ballads*, Wordsworth defined the poet as "a man speaking to men," thus substituting an idealized relationship between the poet and his audience for the complex relationship to diverse publics that characterized the early nineteenth century (*Prose* 1:120). Wordsworth's sense of the audience for the *Lyrical Ballads* was understandably uncertain. The advertisement to the 1798 edition seems confidently addressed to leisured upper- and middle-class readers. There Wordsworth defines his reader as one who is "conversant with our elder writers, and with those in modern times who have been the most successful in painting manners and passions," and also one capable of "severe thought, and a long continued intercourse with the best models of composition" (*Prose* 1:116). But he will not exclude "the most inexperienced reader from judging for himself," an egalitarian sentiment that reveals Wordsworth's awareness of other audiences than the traditional one for poetry (*Prose* 1:116–17).

As Leslie Chard notes, Wordsworth clearly was "striving to reach a larger audience than that of most contemporary poetry" (255). The ballad form itself had egalitarian and radical implications. The 1797 edition of the *Encyclopaedia Brittanica* defined *ballad* as "a kind of song, adapted to the capacity of the lower class of people; who, being mightily taken with this species of poetry, are thereby not a little influenced in the conduct of their lives. Hence we find, that seditious and designing men never fail to spread ballads among the people, with a view to gain them over to their side" (qtd. in Ryskamp 358). Yet the *Lyrical Ballads* looked very much like the magazine verse familiar to polite readers, and were accepted as such. The 1798 volume cost five shillings, expensive for a small, anonymous collection. The circumstances of publication suggest a narrower intended audience than "men," "the most inexperienced reader," or "the vast empire of human society" mentioned by Wordsworth in the 1802 preface (*Prose* 1:141). Wordsworth's decision to enter the existing market for polite literature seemed to contradict, or at least complicate, his democratic hopes for his work.

Wordsworth's conception of his intended audience is both abstract—"the vast mass of human existence"—and an accurate response to nascent social conditions. Wordsworth seems to have tried to imagine a direct relationship to all mankind in place of his actual relationship to the existing audiences, perhaps because the actual relationship to diverse groups of readers caused him creative uncertainty. This tension between the poet's willed and his actual relationship to his audience is at the heart of many of the contradictions in the 1802 preface.

The impression Wordsworth gives in the 1802 preface is that the poet, like other people, is not equipped to deal with the new social order on its own terms. His rejection of industrial society's tendency to divide and specialize human functions is clear: "the Poet writes under one restriction only, namely, the necessity of giving immediate pleasure to a human Being possessed of that information which may be expected from him, not as a lawyer, a physician, a mariner, an astronomer, or a natural philosopher, but as a Man" (*Prose* 1:139). In order to combat the social fragmentation resulting from industrialization and class conflict, Wordsworth conceived of Man in terms of a general human nature rather than in terms of particular social roles. In a letter to Charles Fox accompanying his presentation copy of the *Lyrical Ballads*, Wordsworth discussed the relationship of his work to current social upheavals:

> It appears to me that the most calamitous effect, which has followed the measures which have lately been pursued in this country, is a rapid decay of the domestic affections among the lower orders of society . . . recently by the spreading of manufactures through every part of the country, . . . by workhouses, Houses of

Industry, and the invention of Soup-shops &c. &c. superadded to the encreasing disproportion between the price of labour and that of the necessaries of life, the bonds of domestic feeling among the poor, as far as the influence of these things has extended, have been weakened, and in innumerable instances entirely destroyed. (*Letters* 1:313)

In *Michael* and *The Brothers*, Wordsworth hoped to combat social fragmentation by calling attention to the domestic affections being lost and by making his polite readers aware of growing class distinctions. His success depended on his demonstration that there was a pure human nature beneath material circumstances, affected by them and even threatened by them, but fundamentally separate from them. He told Fox, "The two poems which I have mentioned were written with a view to shew that men who do not wear fine cloaths can feel deeply" (*Letters* 1:315). By addressing a pure human nature instead of actual people in society, Wordsworth attempted to resist new and destructive material relations by replacing them with bonds forged in the poet's consciousness: "the Poet binds together by passion and knowledge the vast empire of human society, as it is spread out over the whole earth, and over all time" (*Prose* 1:141). The poet's function is to heal a divided society and divided selves within that society—just what John Stuart Mill looked for and found in Wordsworth.

"Tintern Abbey," first published in the 1798 *Lyrical Ballads* and the poem in that volume most praised by contemporary reviewers, is for the most part about transcending social reality. Wordsworth admits to being puzzled by "the heavy and weary weight / Of all this unintelligible world" (lines 39–40), a burden that can be lightened only by achieving a contemplative perspective:

> with an eye made quiet by the power
> Of harmony, and the deep power of joy,
> We see into the life of things.
> (lines 47–49)

In "Tintern Abbey" Wordsworth presents the poet's function exactly as he defined it in the 1802 preface: the poet penetrates to the essential and discovers a pure human nature. To make this function plausible, Wordsworth must subordinate social reality to an act of individual perception. In the poem the rural poor are mentioned briefly and tentatively: "With some uncertain notice, as might seem / Of vagrant dwellers in the houseless woods" (lines 19–20). As Jerome McGann and Marjorie Levinson point out, the ruined abbey was known during the 1790s as a haunt of beggars and vagrants, the socially displaced whom Wordsworth mentioned in his letter to Fox (McGann, *Romantic Ideology* 86; Levinson chap. 1). But the movement of the poem is to subsume these particular concerns in a more general and "universal" meditation and finally to enfold them into

> The still, sad music of humanity,
> Nor harsh nor grating, though of ample power
> To chasten and subdue. (lines 91–93)

Wordsworth achieves this magnificent effect of universality by transforming a general feeling of his historical period—that the individual is a discrete soul apart from and opposed to society—into an affirmation of the individual's power to harmonize social turmoil by an act of individual consciousness.

"Tintern Abbey" expresses the prevalent sense of its cultural moment that social life is an unpleasant business that takes place "out there" but need not influence private life. Men and women can achieve inner serenity when they feel a sense of connection with the real "image of things." Thus nature is invoked as that which

>   can so inform
> The mind that is within us, so impress
> With quietness and beauty, and so feed
> With lofty thoughts, that neither evil tongues,
> Rash judgments, nor the sneers of selfish men,
> Nor greetings where no kindness is, nor all
> The dreary intercourse of daily life,
> Shall e'er prevail against us, or disturb
> Our cheerful faith, that all which we behold
> Is full of blessings. (lines 125–34)

The Nature that "never did betray / The heart that loved her" (lines 122–23) is a projection of the private life of the discrete individual, which Wordsworth opposed to the unkindness of men in society and the dreary actuality of daily life (lines 130–31). By 1798, Wordsworth felt that contemporary political and social trends had indeed betrayed him. The affirmation in "Tintern Abbey" was made against the climate of political reaction that isolated Wordsworth and his friends at Alfoxden and finally drove them to Germany, and against the social upheaval caused by industrialism that Wordsworth decried in his letter to Fox.[1]

Wordsworth clearly perceived the changes being effected by industrialization and their consequences for men and women:

> For a multitude of causes, unknown to former times, are now acting with a combined force to blunt the discriminating powers of the mind, and, unfitting it for all voluntary exertion, to reduce it to a state of almost savage torpor. The most effective of these causes are the great national events which are daily taking place, and the increasing accumulation of men in cities, where the uniformity of their occupations produces a craving for extraordinary incident, which the rapid communication of intelligence hourly gratifies. (*Prose* 1:128)

Wordsworth's description of the problem is of a piece with his proposed solution; he does not focus on the consequences of industrialism for people's health or economic well-being or on the alteration of the structure of their daily lives, but on how these changes affected their minds. This formulation of the problem allows the poet to use his particular talents for social welfare. "For the human mind," writes Wordsworth, "is capable of being excited without the application of gross and violent stimulants; and he must have a very faint perception of its beauty and dignity who does not know this" (*Prose* 1:128). Wordsworth believed that by addressing the higher capacities of the human mind, the poet could keep those capacities alive and defend them from the attack mounted against them by modern society.

To defend this solution, however, Wordsworth had to separate "certain inherent and indestructible qualities of the human mind" (*Prose* 1:130) from the minds he saw being destroyed, thus distinguishing the

Human Mind that transcends material circumstances from the minds of men and women who are dominated by them.

In the 1800 and 1802 prefaces it is often not clear whom Wordsworth felt he was addressing: an idealized Human Mind that is indestructible or actual men and women who were sunk into savage torpor. Wordsworth separated an eternal Mind from a confusing and arbitrary social reality because he saw the existing social organization as too complex to be described, let alone combatted. In *The Prelude*, Wordsworth pictured the city as a human invention apparently no longer under human control:

> there, see
> A work completed to our hands, that lays,
> If any spectacle on earth can do,
> The whole creative powers of man asleep!
> (7, lines 678–81)

Urban society presented problems that Wordsworth felt had already gone far beyond diagnosis. In some ways in the 1800 preface he was already throwing up his hands: "When I think upon this degrading thirst for outrageous stimulation, I am almost ashamed to have spoken of the feeble endeavor made in these volumes to counteract it" (*Prose* 1: 128, 130). He had begun to confuse the symptoms of social turmoil ("this degrading thirst for outrageous stimulation") with the causes, of which he had spoken so eloquently in his letter to Fox. Though he reasserted his faith in the "inherent and indestructible qualities of the human mind," a split was already evident between his conception of man as a victim of social forces and the tendency to blame individuals for their inability to withstand those forces that would be reflected in his later conservatism.

This is a characteristic split in the poetry as well:

> Earth has not any thing to show more fair:
> Dull would he be of soul who could pass by
> A sight so touching in its majesty.
> ("Composed Upon Westminster Bridge," lines 1–3)

Two sorts of reader are implied here. One is the ideal reader often invoked by Wordsworth: the kindred spirit like Dorothy in "Tintern Abbey," Coleridge in *The Prelude*, or the lover in "Strange Fits of Passion" who empathizes with the poet and can be addressed intimately, without constraint or fear of misunderstanding. The other is the dull reader thirsting for "outrageous stimulation" whose sensibilities are too blunted to appreciate the scene that moves the poet. Wordsworth could at times see how the economic and material compulsion at work in modern life conspired against the faculties of men, diminishing their ability to respond to beautiful scenes or to poetry by unfitting their minds "for all voluntary exertion" (*Prose* 1:128).

But in "Composed Upon Westminster Bridge" the possible connection between the average man's dullness and the savage torpor caused by industrialization and urbanization seems forgotten. In this sonnet, as in "Tintern Abbey," Wordsworth separates pure human nature from particular aspects of social life in a vision of urban life that anticipates that of his later Victorian readers. The reproach to the dull reader occurs in a description of a city with no people evident—"the very houses seem asleep" (line 13)—and the calm of an idealized city replaces the sordid confusion of real social life represented by Bartholomew Fair in *The Prelude* (7, lines 722–28). "Composed Upon Westminster Bridge" is addressed to an idealized reader who, like Wordsworth, has transcended the crowded business of daily life and can meditate upon a sight that is touching primarily because of its solitary calm.

Despite his republican sympathies, Wordsworth soon began describing men and women living in industrial society as a mass against which the authentic individual had to define himself. In *The Prelude* we find the characteristic separation of the isolated individual from an impersonal society:

That huge fermenting mass of human-kind
Serves as a solemn back-ground, or relief,
To single forms and objects.
(7, lines 621–23)

In 1812 he wrote to Catherine Clarkson, "For upwards of thirty years, the lower orders have been accumulating in pestilential masses of ignorant population" (*Letters* 3:21). Wordsworth's instinctive revulsion from mass society made it difficult to address readers because it eliminated any sense of common purpose with them; but his revulsion is typical: Wordsworth expresses the common sense of the time, that the self is private and other selves are fundamentally unknowable:

> How oft, amid those overflowing streets,
> Have I gone forward with the crowd and said
> Unto myself, "The face of every one
> That passes by me is a mystery!"
> (7, lines 626–29)

By defining the existing members of his audience in advance as unknowable, Wordsworth had difficulty maintaining the sense of contact with readers that is vital to literary art.[2]

In the remainder of the additions to the 1802 preface, Wordsworth emphasizes the distinction rather than the similarity between the poet and other men. For example, the poet has "a disposition to be affected more than other men by absent things as if they were present; an ability of conjuring up in himself passions, which are indeed far from being the same as those produced by real events, yet . . . do more nearly resemble the passions produced by real events, than anything which, from the motions of their own minds merely, other men are accustomed to feel in themselves" (*Prose* 1:138). As in "Tintern Abbey," what makes the poet like some men and separate from others is his ability to assume a detached perspective on the material events that affect others trapped by mass society. Like Shelley in *A Defence of Poetry*, Wordsworth defines the poet's concerns as the soul and the universe rather than the public affairs of men. Because the poet expresses "those thoughts and feelings which, by his own choice, or from the structure of his own mind, arise in him without immediate external excitement" (*Prose* 1:138), he can substitute an imagined realm of freedom for the turmoil, insecurity, and uncertainty of urban industrial society, a society he can neither choose nor control.

The power of Wordsworth's *The Ruined Cottage*, written around 1797–98, depends on the imaginative structure that surrounds the narrated events. If these events are not perceived as part of a poem, if they cannot be subsumed by an imaginative structure, they are literally meaningless, part of "the dreary intercourse of daily life." Contrast this to one of Wordsworth's contemporaries and rivals, George Crabbe, whose tales are intended to achieve what Jerome McGann calls an "effect of reality" rather than transcendence (*Beauty of Inflections* 302). The tales depend on a context of shared social perceptions and values rather than on an imaginative structure created by the poet. Often such consolations are presented in Crabbe's poems only to be crushed by social or material realities, as in the "Dream of the Condemned High-wayman" with which he ends "Prisons," in which the experiences of imprisonment and impending execution are powerfully rendered by contrasting them to the prisoner's dream of being free to walk with a lover.

Wordsworth occasionally praised Crabbe because of the dream of freedom and the concern for social injustice that they shared, but he also accused him of writing only in response to "the spur of applause he received from the periodical publications of the day" (Pollard 293) as if Crabbe's professional success discredited him. He objected to Crabbe's habit of concentrating on "matter *which it does not soothe the mind to dwell upon*" (Pollard 291), matter that Wordsworth himself addressed (in *The Ruined Cottage*, for example), but for which he sought a more soothing perspective. The most revealing charge was that Crabbe was "unpoetical," the most damning of romantic criticisms (Pollard 290). For in one crucial way, Crabbe's theory of poetry resembles Wordsworth's: both endeavored, in Wordsworth's phrase, to look steadily at their subjects (*Prose* 1:132). This apparently straightforward statement of method conceals an ideological position, as Wordsworth's most familiar complaint against Crabbe reveals: "After all, if the Picture were true to nature, what claim would it have to be called Poetry? At the best, it is the meanest kind of satire, except the purely personal. The sum of all is, that nineteen out of twenty of Crabbe's Pictures are mere matters of fact; with which the Muses have as much to do as they have with a Collection of medical reports, or of Law Cases" (Pollard 290). Wordsworth dismissed Crabbe because he made poetry out of facts, which were the province of the historian and the biographer and the ordinary professional man, not the poet.

The contrast between Wordsworth's transcendence and Crabbe's "realism" is evident in Wordsworth's confrontation with the blind beggar in *The Prelude*:

> Thus have I looked, nor ceased to look, oppressed
> By thoughts of what and whither, when and how,
> Until the shapes before my eyes became
> A second-sight procession, . . .
>
>   Amid the moving pageant, I was smitten
> Abruptly, with the view (a sight not rare)
> Of a blind Beggar, who, with upright face,
> Stood, propped against a wall, upon his chest
> Wearing a written paper, to explain
> His story, . . .
>   an apt type
> This label seemed of the utmost we can know,
> Both of ourselves and of the universe;
> And, on the shape of that moving man,
> His steadfast face and sightless eyes, I gazed,
> As if admonished from another world.
> (7, lines 630–49)

As in "Resolution and Independence," Wordsworth confronts a victim of social injustice, but situates the encounter away from social turmoil in a moment of personal crisis. He establishes the blind man's social context clearly and with sincere feeling; he is "a sight not rare" on these streets. But Wordsworth at once moves this confrontation into a universal or cosmic context. His deepest feeling is that he has been "admonished from another world," not disturbed by the material facts of this one. This is the "more soothing" perspective than Crabbe's that characterizes some of Wordsworth's greatest lyrics.

Unlike his meeting with the leech gatherer in "Resolution and Independence," which resulted in a moment of revelation, there is no breakthrough or conversion experience in the London scene. When Wordsworth looks at the blind beggar, he feels himself at a dead end. The experience is rendered honestly, but the material and social particulars that would make sense of the blind man's story, which Crabbe would itemize in detail, are experienced by Wordsworth as troubling admonitions from another world. Though Wordsworth's desire to address men was a powerful and humane response to the genuine complexity of modern life, his poetic theory made it difficult to portray social reality as anything but a mystery.

Much of the 1802 preface is devoted to imagining an alternative to the existing social order. Wordsworth's urge to draw subjects from humble and rustic life is not so much the result of an egalitarian impulse as an attempt to escape the complex modern society represented by the city and to penetrate beneath social turmoil to a pure human nature. As Coleridge makes clear in chapter 17 of the *Biographia Literaria*, Wordsworth's conception of humble and rustic life had little to do with the actual rural conditions in England that Levinson so clearly describes and everything to do with the aspects of the social reality of his day that Wordsworth found threatening. The words he associated with rustic life—*essential, simplicity, plainer*—indicate a turn from chaos to order, artifice to nature, opaqueness to clarity, and the unknown to the familiar and domestic, not from city to country or from upper class to lower.

Wordsworth's contention that the "very language of men" (*Prose* 1:130) is preferable to the poetic diction of neoclassical poetry has the same motive as his theory about choosing subjects from low and rustic life. The theory seems republican, but it proceeds from Wordsworth's desire to oppose a complex and troubling reality with an imaginative world that is essential and plain. Wordsworth wanted to create a language that would be the universal poetic equivalent of that spoken by men in small, manageable, knowable communities: "The language, too, of these men has been adopted . . . because, from their rank in society and the sameness and narrow circle of their intercourse, being less under the influence of social vanity, they convey their feelings and notions in simple and unelaborated expressions. Accordingly, such a language, arising out of repeated experience and regular feelings, is a more permanent, and a far more philosophical language, than that which is frequently substituted for it by poets" (*Prose* 1:125). The language of rural men is privileged because it is not that of urban industrial society and therefore not corrupted. The association of the city with vice and the country with virtue is of course perennial, but Wordsworth adapted it to his nineteenth-century situation by equating linguistic vice not only with sophistication and pretension, the traditional sins of the city, but with the ambition, social climbing, and general instability characteristic of modern industrial society.

When in the *Biographia Literaria* Coleridge debunked Wordsworth's claim that he used the real language of real men (chap. 20), he missed the point of Wordsworth's project, which was to invent a language that suggested a knowable community to replace a social existence that appeared unknowable and threatening. Wordsworth tried to create a language that would unite rather than divide men, but in order to address all men he replaced their actual diversity with a concept of humanity that is privatized and abstract rather than social and concrete.

The abstract quality of "Man" in the 1802 preface is much more prominent in the 1815 "Essay, Supplementary to the Preface," where Wordsworth makes an aggressive distinction between his ideal reader and his actual audience:

> Still more lamentable is his error who can believe that there is any thing of divine infallibility in the clamour of that small though loud portion of the community, ever governed by factitious influence, which, under the name of the PUBLIC, passes itself, upon the unthinking, for the PEOPLE. . . . To the People, philosophically characterized, and to the embodied spirit of their knowledge, so far as it exists and moves . . . his devout respect, his reverence, is due. (*Prose* 3:84)

"The People" is an evident idealization intended to compensate for the difficulty Wordsworth experienced in his perceptive response to industrial society. He replaced his conception of the poet as a man speaking to men with a conception of the poet who controls his relationship to his audience by "*creating* the taste by which he is to be enjoyed" (*Prose* 3:80), reasserting control in a situation in which taste was varied and unpredictable. The 1802 definition implied the possibility of a dialogue with readers; by 1815 Wordsworth conceived of the poet as a recluse, authoritative and withdrawn, marking his turn to a more conservative political as well as poetic stance.[3]

The 1815 edition of Wordsworth's poems in which the "Essay, Supplementary to the Preface" appeared was issued in the middle of the poetry boom initiated by Scott and Byron. During this period, sales of poetry books, fees for authors, and profits for publishers were all unprecedentedly high. Wordsworth was well aware of the situation, as shown by his 1814 letter to Samuel Rogers concerning *The Excursion*: "I shall be content if the Publication pays its expenses, for Mr. Scott and your friend Lord B[yron] flourishing at the rate they do, how can an honest *Poet* hope to thrive?" (*Letters* 3:148). For Wordsworth, an "honest Poet" was one who addressed "the People" rather than the actual audience enthralled by Scott's and Byron's romances.

Wordsworth's solution, like Blake's, was to separate the ideal readers, the active, spiritually athletic ones, from the mass of readers who merely gratified tastes or sought diversion. The men he sought to address in 1802 became the mass he refused to gratify in 1815. By 1821 he was so disgusted that he wrote to Henry Crabb Robinson, "As to Poetry, I am sick of it—it overruns the Country in all the shapes of the Plagues of Egypt" (*Letters* 4:44). Wordsworth's exasperation reveals the conflict between the writer's nineteenth-century situation and the romantic response to that situation. He was a professional who could be hurt by a glutted market; in response, he idealized the poet as a solitary seer unappreciated by his contemporaries, but fundamentally unaffected by them. As Mary Moorman, one of Wordsworth's biographers, put it: "Wordsworth wished his friends to believe that he was unmoved by hostile criticism because he was living in a loftier and purer world" (2:261). But of course he was notoriously sensitive to criticism, even from those who admired his work (see below).

Wordsworth's 1815 supplementary essay included a tendentious "literary history" that sought to prove that great authors can never be popular and that popular authors can never be great; that is, to show that the great writer had throughout history been alienated from his audience and his society. To rationalize Shakespeare's popularity, Wordsworth asserted that he "stooped to accommodate himself to the People" and had to share his fame with unworthy pretenders (*Prose* 3:68). Of course, all writers must work within publicly understood conventions and coexist with other practitioners. It is arguable that great works like Shakespeare's plays or novels like *Tom Jones* or *Great Expectations* can be produced only during periods when an actively interested public stimulates the production of a number of works (of inevitably varying quality) that the great writer competes with, uses, and transforms. It is hard to imagine a society that could produce and support only great writers, yet Wordsworth implies that such a situation is ideal in his attack on the age that produced Shakespeare. By claiming that Shakespeare's age undervalued him by forcing him to collaborate with his players and to compete with other dramatists, Wordsworth justified his own distaste for the current literary institution and its network of writers, publishers, reviewers, and readers.

Wordsworth next had to counter Johnson's claim in the *Lives of the Poets* that Milton was sufficiently valued by his public because thirteen hundred copies of *Paradise Lost* were sold in two years. Since the genius of the work itself could not be questioned, the character of the public response to it had to be. Wordsworth claimed that the figure of thirteen hundred copies sold was "inflated" because it included so many people who bought the book for the wrong reasons: "Take, from the number of purchasers, persons of this class [Milton's political admirers], and also those who wished to possess the Poem as a religious work, and but few, I fear, would be left who sought for it on account of its poetical merits" (*Prose* 3:70). Wordsworth's discrimination among the readers of *Paradise Lost* projects onto the past his dissatisfaction with contemporary arrangements for publishing, reviewing, and reading. He imposed on seventeenth-century readers his idea of reading as an exclusively "literary," "poetical" activity in order to resist the politicized idea of reading held by the nineteenth-century working class and the moralistic idea of reading held by some of the bourgeoisie.

Wordsworth's observations on later writers were even more contradictory. In his discussion of James Thomson (1700–48) he begins by acknowledging that Thomson was both inspired and popular. But unlike Milton, who was popular for the wrong reasons, Thomson achieved popularity of the wrong sort: Thomson's "case appears to bear strongly against us:—but we must distinguish between wonder and legitimate admiration. . . . Wonder is the natural product of Ignorance; and as the soil was *in such good condition* at the time of the publication of the 'Seasons,' the crop was doubtless abundant" (*Prose* 3: 73–74). Here Wordsworth attacks a formation that resembled the coming mass reading public, which by definition responds only to fashion and novelty. He idealizes readers in previous "golden ages" of literature, exaggerates the faults of more recent readers, and refuses to investigate and account for the conditions that gave rise to the ignorance that did exist among eighteenth-century readers. Because Thomson was popular with this new group of inferior readers, Wordsworth is forced to conclude that he was in fact an inferior poet ("he could not work miracles"; "he writes a vicious style" [*Prose* 3:74]) who simply treated natural subjects in a novel way and more skillfully than Pope or Dryden.

In his discussion of Thomas Percy's *Reliques*, Wordsworth associates the artist's most severe creative problems with the rise of commercial publishing and the institution of reviewing in the eighteenth century:

> Dr. Percy was so abashed by the ridicule flung upon his labours from the ignorance and insensibility of the persons with whom he lived, that, though while he was writing under a mask he had not wanted resolution to follow his genius into the regions of true simplicity and genuine pathos . . . , yet when he appeared in his own person and character as a poetical writer, he adopted . . . a diction scarcely in any one of its features distinguishable from the vague, the glossy, and unfeeling language of his day. (*Prose* 3: 75–76)

Like Thomas Chatterton, Percy could not address his audience directly and still express himself authentically. Wordsworth characterized the new situation as one in which public institutions thwart private expression by ridiculing it or by channeling it into trite forms. Wordsworth found in Percy a historical precedent for his sense of being harshly reviewed and superseded by lesser poets who pandered to established taste.

For Wordsworth, the mask that the artist must adopt before he can communicate represents the way commercial and social forces reduce the true artist's insights to the merely conventional. Wordsworth's version of literary history is an ideological polemic that portrays great artists struggling for creative autonomy in a social context that taints their work, never invigorates it, and a professional polemic that shows the great artist being victimized by competition, never stimulated or rewarded by it.

But as John Hayden notes in his collection of reviews of the romantic poets, "Contrary to the popular view, the Romantic reviewers were on the whole very much in favor of the literature with which they were dealing. They had some serious qualifications to that approval, as well they might in an age of so much literary experimentation. They also provided an atmosphere of concern and interest which may have been an important stimulus to English Romantic literature" (xviii). The *Lyrical Ballads*, for example, had been favorably reviewed by both liberal and conservative publications, and by the standards of the time were fairly successful, going through three editions in four years (Moorman 1:486). According to Derek Roper, the *Lyrical Ballads* were particularly well received for a book that "came before the critics as a small anonymous volume of no particular prestige" (94–95, 110). Wordsworth's habit of considering himself and other great writers to be unappreciated and solitary voices indicates not only his uncertainty about literature's function in the new social order but his sense that the modern self is somehow lost in the arena of mass society. Wordsworth resorted to this posture even though reviewers were by no means ungenerous to his poetry and his growing reputation arguably benefitted from the treatment he received in the major reviews.[4]

Wordsworth's attitude toward the new reading publics and the literary market had been ambivalent from the beginning; he was never comfortable with publishing. In 1798, for example, he wrote to James Tobin, "There is little need to advise me against publishing; it is a thing which I dread as much as death itself" (*Letters* 1:211). And as late as 1842 he wrote to Aubrey de Vere, "Publication was ever to me most irksome; so that if I had been rich, I question whether I should ever have published at all" (qtd. in Jordan 24). But he adopted a professional attitude toward his career when necessary, and even came to equate literary value with market value in certain instances. *The Excursion* was published at two guineas and *The White Doe* in a guinea quarto edition, both very expensive. Wordsworth justified the price using the vocabulary of the literary market when, at a dinner party in 1820, he remarked to Sir Humphrey Davy, "Do you know the reason why I published *The White Doe* in quarto? To show the world my own opinion of it" (qtd. in Moorman 2:285). He also spent much effort in his later years lobbying members of Parliament about a new copyright law to protect literary property. Though he characterized the poet as a recluse, the move seems to have been a reaction to a literary institution that he found uncongenial.

The confident tone and public aspirations of the 1802 preface at first seem at odds with the private character of much of the poetry of the period, particularly the Lucy poems, *Michael*, and *The Ruined Cottage*. But Wordsworth's faith that the poet can speak to men may reflect the happiness of returning from exile in Germany and taking up residence at Grasmere.

In *The Ruined Cottage* Wordsworth placed an auditor for the story into the poem itself, the same technique used by Coleridge in "The Rime of the Ancient Mariner." By creating a surrogate reader the poet guarantees at least one sympathetic hearer for the poem, one person who will be affected the way the poet wants him to be. In *The Ruined Cottage* the actual reader overhears the poem instead of being directly addressed. In Wordsworth's imagination the poem is addressed to an ideal audience of one, who is taught how to respond to the poem as he listens to the story.

This skepticism about the poet's relationship to his audience is also evident in *Michael*, where Wordsworth's deference about his subject carries an implicit rebuke to his reader's sensibility:

> Nor should I have made mention of this dell
> But for one object which you might pass by,
> Might see and notice not. (lines 14–16)

Because *Michael* would not appear relevant to the contemporary urban audience even though it is written to meet its deepest needs, Wordsworth does not even address this audience. Instead, he directs the poem to a posterity that is an explicit self-projection:

> Therefore, although it will be a history
> Homely and rude, I will relate the same
> For the delight of a few natural hearts;
> And, with yet fonder feeling, for the sake
> Of youthful Poets, who among these hills
> Will be my second self when I am gone.
> (lines 34–39)

The ideal reader included in *The Ruined Cottage* is one who shares Wordsworth's faith that "the human mind is capable of being excited without the application of gross and violent stimulants" (*Prose* 1:128). Unlike the frantic novels and sickly tragedies preferred by contemporary readers, *The Ruined Cottage* is

> A tale of silent suffering, hardly clothed
> In bodily form, and to the grosser sense
> But ill adapted, scarcely palpable
> To him who does not think.
> (lines 233–36)

As in "Composed Upon Westminster Bridge," Wordsworth defines his ideal audience by rebuking his actual audiences. In *The Ruined Cottage*, drafted just before he fled to Germany, Wordsworth is as much preoccupied with those who will not or cannot appreciate his work as by those who do.

Paradoxically, Wordsworth excludes the unfit reader in order to achieve an imaginative unity with all men. In *The Ruined Cottage* the auditor achieves a feeling of brotherhood with Margaret, who is, as Jerome McGann points out, a victim of the social upheavals of the 1790s (*Romantic Ideology* 82 ff.). It is "with a brother's love" that the listener "blessed her in the impotence of grief" (lines 499–500). The tension in the 1802 preface between Wordsworth's awareness of social problems and his poetic strategy for combatting them is evident here as well. At the end of *The Ruined Cottage*, human suffering brought about by social and economic change is redeemed by an act of transcendent consciousness:

> What we feel of sorrow and despair
> From ruin and from change, and all the grief
> The passing shews of being leave behind,
> Appeared an idle dream that could not live
> Where meditation was. (lines 520–24)

There is great power in this conclusion, for meditation is the faculty against which Wordsworth sees modern life conspiring, and which he sets out to restore in his poetry. But the "secret spirit of humanity" that the listener discovers unites a living person and a dead one, not contemporaries. This paradox repeats the romantic sense that the only author who can reach an audience is a dead one, speaking to posterity. The spiritual union depicted can take place only in the contemplative mind because the embattled sufferer has no time for the meditation that redeems her.

Like "Tintern Abbey," *The Ruined Cottage* depends for its power on the reader's willingness to separate individual consciousness from social turmoil. Wordsworth's great gift is his ability to capture the particular historical experience of his contemporaries: their feeling of separation from social processes; their sense of private life as the only realm of freedom in an embattled society; their sense of other people as strangers who can be understood only in moments of ultimate or universal experience, such as solitude or death. These historical particulars are what make *The Ruined Cottage* so poignant and moving, not in spite of but because of Wordsworth's effort to transcend historical particulars.

It is very difficult not to dismiss the listener's empathy with Margaret as cold comfort when compared to the brute material circumstances of her destruction. In fact, Wordsworth seems to anticipate and preemptively refute the popular caricature of the poet as an idle dreamer:

> But we have known that there is often found
> In mournful thoughts, and often might be found
> A power to virtue friendly; were't not so
> I am a dreamer among men, indeed
> An idle dreamer. (lines 227–31)

But that caricature proceeds from the very separation of the spiritual from the material realm on which *The Ruined Cottage* depends. As in the Lucy poems, Wordsworth's model of human empathy and love in *The Ruined Cottage* is the feeling of an isolated man for a woman who is dead, as if the only true relationships are imaginary, private, and thus "absolute" ones existing outside of time and society. From a critical perspective, the poetic solution to social ills offered by Wordsworth differs very little from the conventional Christian response that he would embrace in his later years.

Wordsworth attempted to will a paradoxical community into being in his poetry. In the Lucy poems, *Michael*, or *The Ruined Cottage*, a community is imagined that includes the poet, his sensitive readers, and the representative characters in the poems. However, the experience that links these individuals is isolation, the single experience of modern life shared by all. The real bond of brotherhood that his readers achieve occurs when they recognize their shared isolation, as the auditor in *The Ruined Cottage* does when he feels fundamentally united with another isolated, destroyed soul.

The paradox that isolated readers form a community evokes a number of precise historical experiences, including the actual circumstances of reading that were common by the nineteenth century. The increase in book production and literacy was transforming reading from a largely public to an increasingly private activity. During much of the eighteenth century, there were more people listening to the printed word in coffeehouses and at work than there were readers. By Wordsworth's time, the middle- and upper-class purchasers or borrowers of polite literature were more likely to read at home or in libraries. Many early nineteenth-century readers are thus represented by the auditors built into Wordsworth's poems and implied by his intimate addresses: they are each alone.

It is clear from Wordsworth's diminishing poetic power as his career proceeded, and from his prickly relations with actual readers when he was at the height of his powers, that this experience of isolation was impossible to sustain as a basis for creative work. The ultimate value Wordsworth placed on private experience led him to see as compromising any sort of give-and-take with readers. He was notoriously impatient with anything less than complete acceptance of his work. In 1802 he wrote to Sara Hutchinson, his future sister-in-law, concerning "Resolution and Independence,"

> You say and Mary (that is you can say no more than that) the Poem is *very well* after the introduction of the old man; this is not true, if it is not more than very well it is very bad, there is no intermediate state. You speak of his speech as tedious: everything is tedious when one does not read with the feelings of the Author—"*The Thorn*" is tedious to hundreds; and so is the *Idiot Boy* to hundreds. It is in the character of the old man to tell his story in a manner which an *impatient* reader must necessarily feel as tedious. But Good God! Such a figure, in such a place, a pious self-respecting, miserably infirm Old Man telling such a tale! . . . it is of the utmost importance that you should have had pleasure from contemplating the fortitude, independence, persevering spirit, and the general moral dignity of this old man's character. (*Letters* 1:367)

In this letter Wordsworth is essentially demanding that Hutchinson precisely reproduce his experience, that she become Wordsworth while reading the poem. Characteristically, Wordsworth exaggerates the negative response to the *Lyrical Ballads* and blames the reader for her real or imagined failure to be moved by the poetry.

Wordsworth's notorious impatience with actual readers led him to replace the existing reading public with one created in his own image.[5] He cultivated the sort of attention he received from readers whom Coleridge described as "young men of strong sensibility and meditative minds," whose admiration was "distinguished by its intensity, I might almost say, by its *religious* fervor." Seventeen-year-old John Wilson had written to Wordsworth that the *Lyrical Ballads* was "the book which I value next to my Bible" (qtd. in Jacobus 10). Wordsworth, of course, liked this sort of response, and it seemed to support the romantic idea of the poet as an inspired prophet or oracle. Byron had this concept in mind when he called Wordsworth "this arch-apostle of mystery and mysticism" (qtd. in Moorman 2:267).

Coleridge sensed that even in the 1800 preface Wordsworth was in some ways attacking his readers, who must have been "wondering at

the perverseness of the man, who had written a long and argumenta-
tive essay to persuade them that 'Fair is foul, and foul is fair;' in other
words, that they had been all their lives admiring without judgement,
and were now about to censure without reason" (*Biographia* chap. 4,
72). Coleridge felt that the *Lyrical Ballads* themselves would have
caused no controversy, but that the preface antagonized readers with
its controversial theories of poetic language and subject matter. Thus
Wordsworth's ambitious effort to reach a larger audience for poetry
and to articulate a new relationship between that audience and the poet
was inhibited rather than advanced by the preface. Wordsworth failed
because his democratic hopes could not mask his skepticism about the
new reading publics and his feeling that they could neither judge nor
reason.

Yet Wordsworth's attempt to imagine a new bond between the poet
and his audience is one of the most valuable examples of the romantic
mental posture. The poet, in his important formulation, is "the rock of
defence for human nature; an upholder and preserver, carrying everywhere with him relationship and love. In spite of difference of soil and
climate, of language and manners, of laws and customs: in spite of
things silently gone out of mind, and things violently destroyed; the
Poet binds together by passion and knowledge the vast empire of human society, as it is spread over the whole earth, and over all time"
(*Prose* 1:141). In those "things silently gone out of mind, and things violently destroyed," Wordsworth evokes his age of confusing and terrible
social upheaval. His was the paradigmatic, deeply humane British romantic response to that upheaval. Wordsworth saw a society in which
people were growing alienated from each other and from the social
processes that affected them. He tried to reunite a fragmented society
by an act of individual will and to overcome specific social ills with a
general concept of human nature independent of society. By adopting
such a paradoxical response to social problems, however—by transfer-
ring social problems to the sphere of consciousness—Wordsworth reproduced the isolation of his contemporaries in the solitary figures of
his poems.

In his greatest poems, Wordsworth captured the deepest responses of his contemporaries to historical and material circumstances. As he revealed at the end of *The Prelude*,

> The last and later portions of this gift
> Have been prepared, not with the buoyant spirits
> That were our daily portion when we first
> Together wantoned in wild Poesy,
> But, under pressure of a private grief,
> Keen and enduring. (14, lines 415–20)

What spurred him to create his finest works was the feeling of loss in the face of rapid change that he shared with other men and women.

In order to write most authentically about suffering and grief, Wordsworth directly addressed his contemporaries, perhaps more directly than ever before in his poetry, in the last line of "Elegaic Stanzas": "Not without hope we suffer and we mourn." Though "Elegiac Stanzas" was prompted by the private grief that Wordsworth mentions in *The Prelude*, namely, the death of his brother, the startling shift of pronoun to the first-person plural represents what may be Wordsworth's greatest attempt to become a man speaking to men. But this magnificent act of self-criticism marks the end of Wordsworth's career as a major poet. Afterward, in bidding farewell to "the heart that lives alone, / Housed in a dream, at distance from the Kind" (lines 53–54), Wordsworth abandoned the only stance from which he could write great poetry.

In *The Recluse*, Wordsworth no longer saw himself as a man speaking to men, but as the author of a poem "having for its principal subject the sensations and opinions of a poet living in retirement" (*Prose* 3:5). A tendency evident in the 1802 preface thus became the ruling principle of one of his major works. As Marilyn Butler notes, *The Excursion* represents a transformation of Wordsworth's earlier social commitment, for "the poem's admirable men and women—especially its central figure, the Pedlar—have found in the mountains and in solitude a fulfillment that schemes to change society could not give" (*Romantics* 140). However, in the preface to *The Excursion*, Wordsworth still tried to assert a social function for literature. Even as a poet in retirement he wanted "to please and, he would hope, to benefit his countrymen" (*Prose* 3:6).

But the year after this preface was written, Wordsworth defined poetry in the 1815 "Supplementary Essay" as "ethereal and transcendent, yet incapable to sustain her existence without sensuous incarnation" (*Prose* 3:65). Wordsworth now equates poetry and religion, and in his reluctance to admit poetry's dependence on the material world we see the result of Wordsworth's representative and admirable desire both to transform the world and to transcend it.

CHAPTER THREE

Religious Vocation and Blake's Obscurity

William Blake was reintroduced to English readers in 1863 by Alexander Gilchrist and Dante Gabriel Rossetti as a genius neglected in his own time. It is true that Blake's works reached few contemporaries, but Blake had been on the verge of attracting a very visible living audience. Wordsworth and Coleridge read the *Songs of Innocence and of Experience* and admired them greatly. Blake's work was being circulated among leading romantic intellectuals by Crabb Robinson and other interested purchasers of the illuminated books. Hazlitt, Lamb, Landor, and perhaps Dorothy Wordsworth were among those who knew of Blake's work. He is referred to by contemporaries almost invariably as a man of genius. Leopold Damrosch wonders why such readers did not "conclude that a great poet was living in their midst and hasten to seek him out" (308), but it is also possible to wonder why Blake himself did not seek the attention of his potentially sympathetic contemporaries and through them the wider audience to whom he addressed, but did not send, his visions.

To begin to answer this question, one must acknowledge that Blake was not a literary man in any sense that his contemporaries could recognize. His art was an expression of his religious vocation. "Mark well my words!" he says repeatedly in *Milton,* "they are of your eternal salvation" (2: 25; 96).[1] As William Butler Yeats noted in the introduction to his 1893 edition of Blake, the 1780s were "the only purely literary and purely artistic period of [Blake's] life; for in a very short time he came to look upon poetry and art as a language for the utterance of conceptions, which, however beautiful, were none the less thought out more for their visionary truth than for their beauty. The change made him a greater poet and a greater artist; for 'He that findeth his life shall lose it, and he that loseth his life for My sake shall find it'" (Wittreich 259). Blake worked against the tradition of the classical epic, which was "set up by artifice against the Sublime of the Bible," and presented himself as recovering the truth of the "holy Lamb of God," in visions that would enable him to build Jerusalem "in Englands green & pleasant Land" (1: 3, 15–16; 95–96).

Blake's religious purposes were obvious to Coleridge, as a letter of February 1818 reveals: "P.S. I have this morning been reading a strange publication—viz. Poems with very wild and interesting pictures, as the swathing, etched (I suppose) but it is said—printed and painted by the Author, W. Blake. He is a man of Genius—and I apprehend, a Swedenborgian—certainly, a mystic *emphatically*. You perhaps smile at *my* calling another Poet, a *Mystic*; but verily I am in the very mire of common-place common-sense compared with Mr Blake, apo- or rather ana-calyptic Poet, and Painter!" (Bentley, *Records* 251). Coleridge locates the difference between his work and Blake's in the religious content of the *Songs*. Blake is "a mystic *emphatically*," so much so that even Coleridge seems down-to-earth by comparison. The difference is not one of degree, but of kind, for the form of Blake's work is as strange as its content. Coleridge used conventional publication methods to distribute his work to an audience, however much he objected to certain features of the system. By contrast, Blake was not producing literature but doing something different, "very wild" and "strange." His unconventional method of illustrating and printing his own work was not intended to create a new type of literature, but to distinguish his work from the literature of his day.

As Kay and Roger Easson write in their commentary on *The Book of Urizen*, "Blake thought that the book, because of its abstract and static form, had become the vehicle of error, the adversary of transformation, in culture. He felt he had to renovate the book, therefore, in order to renovate culture" (88). "He conceived of his material as sanctified," writes Mark Schorer, "hence not to be tampered with, but copied directly" (7). "Blake's divine dictation," continues Schorer, "is not so close to literary convention as to the habit of those stages in religious mysticism which identify inspiration with revelation" (13). Blake modeled his work on the medieval illuminated manuscript, which unlike modern mass-produced books was individually crafted and sacred. He associated printed books with the "books formd of metals" and the "book of iron" written by Urizen, the repressive god of reason in Blake's mythology (*Urizen* 4: 24; 72; *Ahania* 3: 64; 86), while he conceived of his own engraved and hand-colored books as works of liberation rather than repression, in both their form and their content.[2]

Though other romantics also conceived of poetry as a private, inspired, even quasi-religious activity, they usually were willing to publish their work and thus acknowledge its social dimension, however grudgingly. Blake would not publish through normal channels because his idea of visionary responsibility prevented him from entering into temporal or material arrangements that would compromise his vision. Benjamin Malkin, a contemporary biographer, noted in 1806 that "enthusiastic and high flown notions on the subject of religion have hitherto, as they usually do, prevented his general reception, as a son of taste and of the muses" (Wittreich 25).

Blake's early thinking about the artist's relationship to his audience was different in tone and practice from that he adopted in later years. In the 1780s and early 1790s, Blake was a member of the radical group that met at publisher Joseph Johnson's home. The influence of Paine, Priestley, Godwin, and Wollstonecraft has been noted frequently in the content of Blake's early works (Ferber 140–41). Radical ideas also influenced their form, as we can see in one of Blake's earliest addresses to the public, from 1793:

> The Labours of the Artist, the Poet, the Musician, have been proverbially attended by poverty and obscurity; this was never the fault of the Public, but was owing to a neglect of means to propagate such works as have wholly absorbed the Man of Genius. Even Milton and Shakespeare could not publish their own works.
>
> This difficulty has been obviated by the Author of the following productions now presented to the Public; who has invented a method of Printing both Letter-press and Engraving in a style more ornamental, uniform, and grand, than any before discovered, while it produces works at less than one fourth of the expense.

> If a method of Printing which combines the Painter and the
> Poet is a phenomenon worthy of public attention, the Author is
> sure of his reward. (692)

Blake's method of printing was politically as well as religiously motivated, as this romantic literary history reveals. David Bindman notes,
"Through Blake's invention the artist could by-pass the publishers,
who invariably exploited artists and prevented the publication of anything critical of the nation's godless rulers" (14). Blake was also trying
to reach the people directly rather than through the traders in art that
he attacked with increasing vehemence in the 1800s. Consistent with
his radical sympathies, he here blames the system of publishing and
distribution for depressing the artist, not the people who would support the artist if they could.

However, the new printing method resulted in books that were as
expensive as conventional books and thus available only to wealthier
patrons and collectors rather than to "the people." The *Songs of Innocence* cost five shillings at a time when the average weekly wage for a la-
borer was 10 to 12 shillings.[3] Even if Blake had reached the people, his
political sympathies and his religious purposes were pulling him in opposite directions: toward a community of liberty, equality, and frater-
nity on the one hand, and toward a private salvation available only to
the true believer on the other. His radical sympathies were obvious
though increasingly obscured by the religious symbolism of his prophetic books. Obvious too were his religious purposes, announced at
once to the contemporary public by the form of his illuminated books,
which indicated the "extremism and anti-rationality of the petty craftsman" (Bindman 14).

By the early 1800s, Blake defined his work in direct opposition to the
public's standards and expectations. He wrote to Thomas Butts in 1803,
"But if all the World should set their faces against This [his "Poetic pursuits"]. I have Orders to set my face like a flint. Ezekiel iii C 9v. against
their faces & my forehead against their foreheads" (730). Here Blake
defined himself as an Old Testament poet-prophet, but in the course of
his career he withdrew from the public role of the prophet and devoted
his energies to increasingly private and obscure religious visions.

In spite of its price and the limited number of copies he could produce, Blake clearly intended the *Songs of Innocence* to be "a book that all may read" ("Introduction" 7). In this work, he has perhaps his clearest sense of his audience and his relationship to them. *Songs of Innocence* is a book to be read to the children of upper- and upper-middle-class parents who could afford it. When the chimney sweep says, "So your chimneys I sweep & in soot I sleep" (10), the line poses an uncomfortable moral question to privileged children and at the same time confronts their parents with the social consequences of their economic status: other people serve them and yet live in misery. But "The Chimney Sweeper" also provides an image of social reconciliation and renovation. The final line, "So if all do their duty, they need not fear harm"—and the endless debate over whether the word *duty* is used ironically and the whole line is subversive or, rather, the word is to be taken in its moral, Christian sense—presents the upper-class audience with a lower-class boy who is doing his duty. By extension, the poet asks his polite readers to do their duty, including the work of redefining social duty in Christian terms of selflessness and concern for others.

At the end of "Holy Thursday" Blake cautions his upper-class readers to "cherish pity, lest you drive an angel from your door" (13). The line alludes to Christ's story about those who gain salvation by feeding the hungry, aiding the sick, and clothing the naked. "Inasmuch as ye have done it unto one of the least of these my brethren, ye have done it unto me" (Matthew 25:40). The direct address to the comfortable reader ("from *your* door") reminds him that the charity school children, like the chimney sweep, are angels or images of Christ, and thus present the reader with an opportunity for salvation. In "The Chimney Sweeper," Tom Dacre's dream of liberation from earthly suffering is meant to include the reader. The poems are thus more than attacks on upper-class complacency, though this is where they begin.

In *Vision and Disenchantment*, Heather Glen makes a powerful case for Blake's *Songs of Innocence* as his most advanced and potentially redemptive vision of a human community (see esp. chap. 4 and the conclusion). The *Songs of Experience*, on the other hand, present a divided society and represent Blake's increased feeling of separation from his readers. The *Experience* version of "The Chimney Sweeper" concludes:

And because I am happy, & dance & sing,
They think they have done me no injury:
And are gone to praise God & his Priest & King
Who make up a heaven of our misery. (23)

The reader is now implicated as "they," not addressed as "you," and the
sense of "our misery" as opposed to "their" comfort does not hold out
much hope of reconciliation. When the reader is addressed directly in
the *Songs of Experience*, it is with irony, as in "The Human Abstract":
"Pity would be no more, / If we did not make somebody Poor" (27).
Glen argues that the *Songs of Experience* represent Blake's criticism of
radical protest, which polarizes society into oppressors and oppressed
and offers no alternative vision, only conflict (chap. 5). But this reading
deemphasizes Blake's growing resolve to "set my face like a flint against
their faces" and his increasing bitterness against the ruling classes for
their self-interested war policy and their corrupt methods of patroniz-
ing the arts.

In *The Marriage of Heaven and Hell*, Blake maintained some of his
confidence that he could reach an audience. The penultimate Proverb
of Hell is "Truth can never be told so as to be understood, and not be
believed" (10: 69; 38). But the statement, like *The Marriage* itself, is
strident and problematic. In his subsequent career, Blake grew more
aggressive toward his audience, insisting that his works contained the
Truth. Yet he also grew more unwilling to tell the Truth in forms that
his readers could understand or in works that they could obtain.

Blake alludes to his personal and professional dissatisfaction in the
unpublished work *The Four Zoas*:

What is the price of Experience do men buy it for a song
Or wisdom for a dance in the street? No it is bought with the price
Of all that a man hath his house his wife his children
Wisdom is sold in the desolate market where none come to buy
(35: 11–14; 325)

He may be referring to his failure to reach the public with his *Songs of
Experience*, though his claim that "none come to buy" is misleading,
considering the few copies Blake produced and his occasional reluc-

tance to fill orders he did receive.[4] However, he clearly blames the public for rejecting him, a self-isolating posture that would increasingly characterize Blake's attitude toward his potential audience.

In the minor prophecies, Blake characterizes his audience as stunted and self-enclosed. *The Book of Urizen* presents the consequence of the fall as the loss of visionary power:

> The Senses inward rush'd shrinking
> Beneath the dark net of infection
>
> Till the shrunken eyes clouded over
> Discernd not the woven hipocrisy
> But the streaky slime of the heavens
> Brought together by narrowing perceptions
> Appeard transparent air; for their eyes
> Grew small like the eyes of a man.
> (25: 29–36; 82)

Blake's joke is that the fallen angels are like the English public whom he cannot reach because they are "bound down / To earth by their narrowing perceptions" (27: 46–47; 83). But the satiric tone disappears on the last plate of the work. When the sons of Urizen realize their fallen condition, a group led by Fuzon (Moses) tries to warn their fellow citizens to escape. But

> Perswasion was in vain;
> For the ears of the inhabitants
> Were wither'd, & deafen'd, & cold:
> And their eyes could not discern,
> Their brethren of other cities.
> (28: 14–18; 83)

This is Blake's sense of his situation as a writer addressing a deafened public. Because the people "are not capable of a firm perswasion of any thing," they are doomed and the writer cannot save them. They have created an impenetrable barrier between themselves and the prophet.

But Blake was creating a formidable barrier between himself and his readers. With every work he addressed a smaller or a less clearly defined audience. As John Howard has demonstrated, *The Marriage of Heaven and Hell* seems to be addressed to members of the Swedenborgian New Church. The work refers elaborately and particularly to controversies within the New Church, and is structured so "Blake can speak so that only initiated Swedenborgians can understand the trenchant attack" (Howard 36). To modern readers, who often read the work in a context provided by Nietzschean transvaluation, the work is relatively accessible, but to contemporaries the context was intentionally obscure. As Howard remarks, "it seems addressed to no one" (20).

The *Songs of Experience* seem to be addressed to like-minded radicals and to the disaffected who by 1794 were an isolated and harassed group. The introduction to *Experience* is aggressive and millenarian:

Hear the voice of the Bard
Who Present, Past, & Future sees;
Whose ears have heard
The Holy Word
That walk'd among the ancient trees.
(18)

In the minor prophecies Blake began constructing his private mythology, which, with the partial exceptions of *America* and *Europe*, is more concerned with the psychosexual diagnosis of mankind's fall than with the social and political renovation pursued in the *Songs of Innocence*. *The Book of Los*, the last of the minor prophecies to be engraved, concentrates almost exclusively on the trials of the poet-prophet in a fallen world.

A passage in *The Four Zoas* presents an allegory of Blake's turn from a social to a private vision of art:

Enitharmon spread her beaming locks upon the wind & said
O Lovely terrible Los wonder of Eternity O Los my defence
    & guide
Thy works are all my joy. & in thy fires my soul delights
If mild they burn in just proportion & in secret night
And silence build their day in shadow of soft clouds & dews
Then I can sigh forth on the winds of Golgonooza piteous forms

That vanish again into my bosom but if thou my Los
Wilt in sweet moderated fury. fabricate forms sublime
Such as the piteous spectres may assimilate themselves into
They shall be ransoms for our Souls that we may live.
(90: 15–24; 370)

The passage presents Blake's artistic manifesto. His works will fuse energy and order as they "burn in just proportion" and express "sweet
moderated fury." Blake is also defining artistic salvation as private
rather than public. Here it seems to include only the artist and his one
adoring hearer. Enitharmon resembles Wordworth's Dorothy, and the
listener in *The Ruined Cottage*, in her unquestioning affirmation of the
artist's vision, which she internalizes completely. By the end of the sev-
enth night of *The Four Zoas*, in which this passage occurs, Blake has discovered the strategy of transforming corporeal into mental strife used
by Wordsworth. He places mental rather than material struggle at the
center of human existence.

As in Wordsworth's work and in Shelley's *Prometheus Unbound*, the
strategy of internalization is motivated by love and a deeply humane
feeling for the suffering of others:

Startled was Los he found his Enemy Urizen now
In his hands. he wonderd that he felt love & not hate
His whole soul loved him. (90: 64–66; 371)

Yet Blake had trouble resolving the conflict between his message of
Christian love and forgiveness and the form he used to express it, the
obscure prophetic epic. Late in his life he would write, "The Beauty of
the Bible is that the most Ignorant & Simple Minds Understand it
Best" ("Annotations to Thorton," 667). But when he was working on
The Four Zoas, or perhaps shortly after, he wrote to the Rev. Dr. John
Trusler, who had commissioned a painting from Blake, "You say that I
want somebody to Elucidate my Ideas. But you ought to know that
What is Grand is necessarily obscure to Weak men. That which can be
made Explicit to the Idiot is not worth my care. The wisest of the An-
cients considerd what is not too Explicit as the fittest for Instruction
because it rouzes the faculties to act" (Aug. 1799, 702). Modern critics

sometimes quote this passage as an example of romantic artistic integrity and of Blake's refusal to compromise his vision. But the statement is also, and most immediately, an unmistakable personal insult. It marks the beginning of Blake's conscious turn in his work from egalitarian to increasingly private and even solipsistic intentions. He now advances obscurity as a measure of artistic value.

Every reader of Blake notices this change, though each values it differently. Marilyn Butler notes that, "true to the reticence of the counter-revolutionary period, Blake began to value the mystery and secrecy which in his revolutionary period he denounced as the characteristic of priestcraft." She goes on to observe that "many of Blake's subsequent admirers have not merely preferred the later work, but seen its mystery and compensatory world-building as the heart of this great artist" (*Romantics* 51). On the other hand, in *Blake's Sublime Allegory*, Stuart Curran and Joseph Wittreich assembled a collection of essays by critics who consider *The Four Zoas*, *Milton*, and *Jerusalem* to be Blake's supreme achievements. Their defense of this judgment resembles Enitharmon's response to Los: "The interests of the contributors [to this volume] are generous in their diversity. . . . Such varied interests and perspectives, of course, preclude a definitive statement on the major prophecies. But the prophecies are themselves, in the fullest sense of the word, their own and only definitive statement" (xvi). It has been characteristic of Blakeans since Gilchrist and Rossetti to place Blake's works beyond criticism, as holy books that need not reveal determinate meanings because they are what they are.[5] But every text ever written is in some sense its own and only definitive statement. That fine critics put this tautology forward as proof of a work's supreme value demonstrates the extent to which modern Blakeans not only accept but value the mystifications presented in Blake's late works.

When Blake turned to the prophetic mode, he hoped to undertake a more extensive analysis of social injustice, with a corresponding increase in poetic power and social efficacy. In a number of passages in the major prophecies, Blake used the freer line and wider scope to achieve tremendous rhetorical effects, and the famous opening lyric to *Milton* testifies that Blake's deepest hopes for social change persisted:

Bring me my Bow of burning gold:
Bring me my Arrows of desire:
Bring me my Spear: O clouds unfold!
Bring me my Chariot of fire!

I will not cease from Mental Fight,
Nor shall my Sword sleep in my hand:
Till we have built Jerusalem,
In Englands green & pleasant Land.
(1: 9–16; 95–96)

But *Jerusalem* itself was intended to be "incomprehensible / To the Vegetated Mortal Eye's perverted & single vision" (53: 10–11; 202), a phrase that recalls *The Book of Urizen* and the insult to Trusler. The profundity of *Jerusalem* is bought at the cost of willfully excluding contemporary readers.

Blake dramatized his turn away from the audience in *Jerusalem*, and attempted to justify it:

And Los shouted with ceaseless shoutings & his tears poured
  down
His immortal cheeks, rearing his hands to heaven for aid Divine!
But he spoke not to Albion: fearing lest Albion should turn his
  Back
Against the Divine Vision: & fall over the Precipice of Eternal
  Death. (71: 56–59; 226)

Here Blake presents himself as the prophet who separates himself from other men in order to save them, the posture Wordsworth adopted in placing "meditation" and contemplation above social activism. Blake wrote in his notebook: "Great things are done when Men & Mountains meet / This is not Done by Jostling in the Street" (511). Blake's response to his excruciatingly difficult times is understandable, and in some ways heroic and full of integrity. But for an artist intent on addressing the public, as Blake claimed to be as late as the "Public Address," it represents an evasion and a loss:

The Visions of Eternity, by reason of narrowed perceptions,
Are become weak Visions of Time & Space, fix'd into furrows of
    death;
Till deep dissimulation is the only defence an honest man has left.
(*Jerusalem*, 49: 21–23; 198)

In *Jerusalem* Blake completely rejects his contemporary audience. David Erdman has noted that he deleted the word *dear* from the phrase "Dear Reader" in his preface to the poem, and also erased a reference to the "love and friendship" of those who accepted his "Giants & Fairies" (Erdman 384–85). He also added the inscriptions "sheep" and "goats" to the third plate of *Jerusalem*, over the address "To the Public." Blake was winnowing out his readers like the Christ who separated the saved from the damned, by speaking in a manner increasingly inaccessible to corporeal hearing.

In *The Everlasting Gospel* Blake would write,

The Vision of Christ that thou dost see
Is my Visions Greatest Enemy
Thine has a great hook nose like thine
Mine has a snub nose like to mine
Thine is the Friend of All Mankind
Mine speaks in parables to the Blind.
(524)

The passage implies that vision is radically subjective, an insight that could provide a basis for tolerance and a community based on agreement among the inevitably diverse people of a free society. Instead, Blake appeals to the fearsome version of the Christ who speaks in parables in order to damn his hearers: "That seeing they may see, and not perceive; and hearing they may hear, and not understand; lest at any time they should be converted, and their sins should be forgiven them" (Mark 4:12; also Matt. 13:13). Blake's late work is not intended to save the reader, but to exclude him; Blake in effect invites the reader to be damned. He put it crudely in his notebook when he wrote, "He's a Blockhead who wants a proof of what he Can't Perceive / And he's a Fool who tries to make such a Blockhead believe" (507). Like other romantics in moments of frustration, Blake demanded instant, uncritical assent to his work. He no longer conceives of his work as a potential dialogue; the relationship between writer and reader is that of priest and initiate.

As his letter to Trusler shows, Blake in some ways courted oblivion, although Suzanne Hoover has discovered through her study of posthumous references to Blake that "he never was in actual danger of being forgotten" (311). However, *Jerusalem* was probably preserved only because of its striking designs. Allan Cunningham, whose biography kept Blake's name before the public until Gilchrist's edition, wrote of *Jerusalem* that its "crowning defect was obscurity," but that "if the work be looked at for form and effect rather than for meaning, many figures may be pronounced worthy of Michael Angelo" (Wittreich 166–67). Gilchrist, the man responsible for Blake's entrance into the canon of English poetry, found the text of *Jerusalem* to be "words empty of meaning to all but him who uttered them," a judgment echoed by Swinburne and William Michael Rossetti (Gilchrist 184; Swinburne 276). After *Jerusalem*, Blake no longer expressed his visions in prophetic books, though he continued to be active as an artist until the end of his life. The work in some ways represents a dead end for Blake as well as for his readers.

In his letter to Trusler, Blake denied that this was so: "But I am happy to find a Great Majority of Fellow Mortals who can Elucidate My Visions & Particularly they have been Elucidated by Children who have taken a greater delight in contemplating my Pictures than I even hoped. . . . There is a vast Majority on the side of Imagination or Spiritual Sensation" (Aug. 1799, 703). This statement is evidence of growing personal pressure on Blake to justify his vocation and his stance toward the audience. The appeal to his fellow mortals resembles Wordsworth's distinction between the public and the people in the 1815 "Essay, Supplementary to the Preface." Even if Blake's comment about the "Great Majority" is interpreted as a metaphorical statement about mankind's potential, it still reveals him casting about for some basis for his work in contemporary society.

In his prophecies Blake imagines an ideal audience, just as Wordsworth did in *The Ruined Cottage*. Blake responded to an even smaller audience than Wordsworth's with a correspondingly greater imaginative compensation. In *Milton*, Blake replaced his small earthly audience with a vast heavenly one:

> The Bard ceased. All consider'd and a loud resounding murmur
> Continu'd round the Halls; and much they question'd the
> immortal
> Loud voicd Bard. and many condemn'd the high tone'd Song
> Saying Pity and Love are too venerable for the imputation
> Of Guilt. Others said If it is true! if the acts have been perform'd
> Let the Bard himself witness. Where hadst thou this terrible Song.
>
> The Bard replied. I am inspired! I know it is Truth! for I Sing
> According to the inspiration of the Poetic Genius
> Who is eternal all-protecting Divine Humanity
> To whom be Glory & Power & Dominion Evermore
> Amen. (13: 45–54; 107–8)

He then imagined that the heavenly response to his utterance would be transmitted to earth, where it would transform the world, "Shaking the roots & fast foundations of the Earth in doubtfulness" (14: 4–8; 108).

Blake's self-isolation led to the severe personal crisis he experienced at Felpham, where he moved in 1800 to accept the patronage of William Hayley, a well-known literary man. During this period, Blake felt torn between his responsibility to his private vision and his public duty to "the People," whom he still sought to address. In September 1801 Blake wrote about his visionary power in an uncharacteristically negative way:

> Time flies faster, (as seems to me), here than in London I labour incessantly & accomplish not one half of what I intend because my Abstract folly hurries me often away while I am at work, carrying me over Mountains & Valleys which are not Real in a Land of Abstraction where Spectres of the Dead wander. This I endeavour to prevent & with my whole might chain my feet to the world of Duty & Reality. but in vain! the faster I bind the better is the Ballast for I so far from being bound down take the world with me in my flights. . . . Alas wretched happy ineffectual labourer of times

moments that I am! who shall deliver me from this Spirit of Abstraction & Improvidence. (Letter to Butts 716)

Blake presents himself as an unwilling visionary who laments his prophetic powers because they tear him away from the earthly duties that he would perform if he could. Though he went to Felpham to make money as an engraver and to have a pleasant setting in which to work on his own projects, within a year he began to experience these two objectives as mutually exclusive; he would write later, "Where any view of Money exists Art cannot be carried on, but War only (Read Matthew CX. 9 & 10 v)" (*The Laocoon* 275).

At Felpham, Blake would convert his "Abstract folly" into a higher form of insight, and in the late prophetic books transform the "Mountains & Valleys which are not Real" into the geography of spiritual truth. Such transformations require great spiritual integrity, but cannot be sustained without some personal cost. At Felpham the cost proved harrowing for Blake and for his wife, Catherine. One of Blake's early nineteenth-century biographers, Frederick Tatham, recounted in 1832 that Blake at Felpham "was a subject of much temptation & mental suffering & required sometimes much soothing" (Bentley, *Records* 525). Tatham elaborated in an evocative letter to Gilchrist: "[Catherine] would get up in the night, when he was under his very fierce inspirations, which were as if they would tear him asunder, while he was yielding himself to the Muse, or whatever else it could be called, sketching and writing. And so terrible a task did this seem to be, that she had to sit motionless and silent; only to stay him mentally, without moving hand or foot: this for hours, and night after night" (Bentley, *Records* 526). What Tatham describes is creativity in response to a terrible compulsion. Leopold Damrosch discusses Blake's psychological condition at Felpham and its relationship to his works, and notes that "Blake scholars, anxious not to be identified with those who 'dare to mock with the aspersion of Madness,' [*Milton*, 41: 8; 142] have been hesitant to speculate about the terrible psychic pressure which Blake evidently experienced in the late 1790s and which came to a head at Felpham in the early 1800s" (310 ff.). Yet Blake's correspondence gives ample evidence that he was on the borderline between sanity and insanity, capable of carrying on his work but still feeling divided from himself and his earthly existence (Damrosch 311, n.16; Letter to Butts, November 1802, 720).

The most powerful and detailed account of the pressures Blake faced occurs in his January 1803 letter to Butts:

> My unhappiness has arisen from a source which if explord too narrowly might hurt my pecuniary circumstances. As my dependence is on Engraving at present & particularly on the Engravings I have in hand for Mr. H. & I find on all hands great objections to my doing anything but the meer drudgery of business & intimations that if I do not confine myself to this I shall not live. this has always pursud me. . . . that I cannot live without doing my duty to lay up treasures in heaven is Certain & Determined & to this I have long made up my mind . . . I am not ashamed afraid or averse to tell You what Ought to be Told. That I am under the direction of Messengers from Heaven Daily & Nightly but the nature of such things is not as some suppose. without trouble or care. Temptations are on the right hand & left behind the sea of time & space roars & follows swiftly he who keeps not right onward is lost & if our footsteps slide in clay how can we do otherwise than fear & tremble. . . . But if we fear to do the dictates of our Angels & tremble at the Tasks set before us. if we refuse to do Spiritual Acts. because of Natural Fears or Natural Desires! Who can describe the dismal torments of such a state!—I too well remember the Threats I heard!—If you who are organized by Divine Providence for Spiritual communion. Refuse & bury your Talent in the Earth even tho you should want Natural Bread. Sorrow & Desperation pursues you thro life! & after death shame & confusion of face to eternity . . . You will be calld the base Judas who betrayd his Friend!— Such words would make any Stout man tremble & how could I then be at ease? But I am now no longer in That State & now go on again with my Task Fearless. and tho my path is difficult. I have no fear of stumbling while I keep it. (724)

Blake expresses here his sense that the prophet is set apart from other men and that prophetic vision exacts a terrible cost, whatever its ultimate glory. He now conceives of his talent as a terrifying religious responsibility. Blake's sense of the word *talent* is that given by the parable of the talents, which threatens the possessor with damnation should he fail to use it, just as Milton mentions in his sonnet the one talent that is death to hide. Blake heard this threat and concluded that his work could not coexist with pecuniary considerations or the drudgery of business, both represented by Hayley. In the Laocoon engraving he later fused his artistic activity and his religious vocation, and separated them from material and temporal considerations: "Christianity is Art & not Money / Money is its Curse" (274).

After the Felpham crisis, Blake addressed and criticized this world from the perspective of another, and felt justified in putting the burden of understanding on the public that he had once sought to reach. Of *Milton*, or perhaps *Jerusalem*, he wrote to Butts in July 1803, "I consider it as the Grandest Poem that This World Contains. Allegory addressd to the Intellectual powers while it is altogether hidden from the Corporeal Understanding is My Definition of the Most Sublime Poetry" (730). In this letter Blake reproduced his attack on Trusler with Hayley as his sacrificial goat: "I regard Fashion in Poetry as little as I do in Painting. so if both Poets & Painters should alternately dislike (but I know the majority of them will not) I am not to regard it at all but Mr. H approves of My Designs as little as he does of my Poems and I have been forced to insist on his leaving me in both to my Own Self Will. for I am determind to be no longer Pesterd with his Genteel Ignorance & Polite Disapprobation" (730). As in the letter to Trusler four years earlier, Blake dismissed his actual audience (Hayley) and replaced him with an imaginary audience of approving artists who reward his labors with the true understanding that few real people had yet demonstrated.

This sort of compensation recurs often in Blake's writing after Felpham. For the most part he seemed content to dismiss the idiots and the goats who are beneath his contempt, but every so often the need for public approval surfaced in a half-acknowledged manner, as in the parenthetical qualification, "but I know that the majority will not [dislike his work]." Blake emerged from Felpham as the most uncompromising of artists and the truest to his own experience. But he achieved this integrity by elevating the artist and denigrating the audience, a difficult stance from which to create.

In a letter to Hayley written after he returned to London, Blake hinted at the direction his own career was taking. He mentions an encounter with another artist, a Mr. Spilsbury, who

> says that he relinquished Painting as a Profession. for which I think he is to be applauded. but I concieve that he may be a much better Painter if he practises secretly & for amusement than he could ever be if employd in the drudgery of fashionable dawbing for a poor pittance of money in return for the sacrifice of Art & Genius. he says he will never leave to Practise the Art because he loves it & This Alone will pay its labour by Success if not of money yet of True Art. which is All. (September 1804, 755)

This is a buried and disingenuous rebuke to Hayley, for the sacrifice of "Art & Genius" to "fashionable dawbing" is precisely what Blake felt Hayley had demanded of him. Like Spilsbury, who functions here as Blake's surrogate, Blake abandoned public art for a "True Art" carried on secretly for the private benefit of the artist. Blake here announces the possibility that the artist can be authentic only by withdrawing entirely from the contemporary world.

In his imaginative world Blake confronted his opponents boldly. In *Milton*, Hayley is Satan, the Accuser, whom the Bard overcomes. In his notebook Blake demanded of Hayley, "Do be my Enemy for Friendships sake" (506), echoing his assertion in *The Marriage* that "Opposition is true Friendship" (42). But in his letters to Hayley, Blake expressed gratitude that verges on fulsomeness, especially when compared to the contempt for Hayley he expressed in letters to Butts and James Blake (766, 725). The correspondence with Hayley seems to have filled Blake with self-disgust: "I write the Rascal Thanks till he & I / With Thanks & Compliments are quite drawn dry" (506). This notebook entry and the letters to Hayley belie the view of Blake as a man who knew his own mind and could assert it with confidence against opposition. In his imaginative world Blake carried on his mental fight. But in the actual world, as he later said of himself, "I am hid" ("Annotations to Reynold's *Discourses*" 636).

Blake emerged from hiding in 1809 and 1810 with a series of writings intended for the public: the *Descriptive Catalogue*, which was printed and sold at the 1809 exhibition of his paintings, and "A Vision of the Last Judgment" and the "Public Address," both discovered in Blake's notebooks and assembled by later editors. These documents demonstrate Blake's awareness of how the industrial revolution was affecting artistic work in the early nineteenth century. Blake's religious vocation gave him a language with which to criticize his commercial and industrial age. He felt that his imperialistic and increasingly secular society was a threat to art: "Rome & Greece swept Art into their maw & destroyed it a Warlike State never can produce Art. It will Rob & Plunder & accumulate into one place, & Translate & Copy & Buy & Sell & Criticise, but not Make" ("On Virgil" 270). Blake's analysis of the economic situation of the arts in England emerged from personal and professional frustration: "Resentment for Personal Injuries has had some share in this Public Address But Love to My Art & Zeal for my Country a much Greater" (574).[6] Blake's personal financial crisis led him to a powerful analysis of the general situation in English arts. His struggle for economic survival led him to feel his exclusion from the English artistic establishment as an economic sanction: "The Enquiry in England is not whether a Man has Talents. & Genius? But whether he is Passive & Polite & a Virtuous Ass: & obedient to Noblemens Opinions in Art & Science. If he is; he is a Good Man: If Not he must be Starved" ("Annotations to Reynold's *Discourses*" 642). In the "Public Address" Blake repeats his claim that the artist's creative power transcends his financial condition: "It is Nonsense for Noblemen & Gentlemen to offer Premiums for the Encouragement of Art when such Pictures as these can be done without Premiums let them Encourage what Exists Already & not endeavour to counteract by tricks" (577). But finally Blake's feelings about his personal situation were ambivalent: "I demand therefore of the Amateurs of art the Encouragement which is my due if they continue to refuse theirs is the loss not mine & theirs is the Contempt of Posterity I have Enough in the Approbation of fellow labourers this is my glory & exceeding great reward I go on & nothing can hinder my course" ("Public Address" 580). Blake at once demands his earthly reward and claims that the compensations offered by posterity and the idealized audience of his "fellow labourers" are sufficient.

At times Blake analyzed the commercialization of the arts in England with force and precision and called for new arrangements; at other times he simply accepted the existing arrangements and attempted to survive within them. Gilchrist noticed how this split affected the tone of Blake's *Descriptive Catalogue*: "It is a literary composition which halts between the monologue of a self-taught enthusiast and the circular of a competing tradesman" (228). Gilchrist precisely captured Blake's situation as a man caught between two worlds, an inspired prophet who must make a living in the world as he finds it. At times Blake called on other artists to join him in resisting the effects of commerce and industrialization on their work; at other times, like Coleridge in the *Biographia*, he simply asserted his genius against the lesser talents of other artists in order to compete with them in the marketplace. Blake responded to his professional crisis with a fierce individualism that reproduced the competitive conditions he objected to rather than subverting them. Blake's assertion of his own genius was often a commercial claim on behalf of his works against the works of other artists.

Like Wordsworth during this decade, Blake intended to use the documents of 1809 and 1810 to appeal to "the people" over the heads of the critics who represent contemporary standards tainted by commerce and manufacture: "Mr. B. appeals to the Public, from the judgment of those narrow blinking eyes, that have too long governed art in a dark corner. The eyes of stupid cunning never will be pleased with the work any more than with the look of self-devoting genius" (preface to *Descriptive Catalogue* 529).[7] Blake's hope even as late as the "Public Address" is that there is a real audience for his work:

It has been said of late years The English Public have no Taste for Painting This is a Falshood The English are as Good Judges of Painting as of Poetry & they prove it in their Contempt for Great Collections of all the Rubbish of the Continent brought here by Ignorant Picture dealers an Englishman may well say I am no Judge of Painting when he is shewn these Smears & Dawbs at an immense price & told that such is the Art of Painting I say the English Public are true Encouragers of real Art while they discourage & look with Contempt on False Art (581–582).[8]

Blake characterizes his audience much as he did during the 1790s; the people are the source of true standards, which tyrannical critics and aristocratic patrons try to corrupt or repress. The passage repeats Blake's earlier hopes that the people would overthrow existing institutions, including false canons of art.

The predominant mood in the "Public Address" is confident and democratic, but that mood is expressed in a document that Blake never published. It seems almost as if Blake was compensating for his inability to reach an actual audience by aggressively refusing to try to reach one: "When I tell any Truth it is not for the sake of Convincing those who do not know it but for the sake of defending those who Do" ("Public Address" 578). For the remainder of Blake's career he addressed only initiates: first a small group of patrons, then at the end of his life the group of disciples led by Samuel Palmer and George Richmond. The economic crisis of 1809–10 ended just as the psychological crisis at Felpham had ended. Blake was determined to reject the available audience and deny them his prophetic gifts.

Blake's late stance toward public issues, whether political, economic, or social, was that the only lasting solutions are private ones: "I am really sorry to see my Countrymen trouble themselves about Politics. If Men were Wise the Most arbitrary Princes could not hurt them If they are not Wise the Freest Government is compelld to be a Tyranny Princes appear to me to be Fools Houses of Commons & Houses of Lords appear to me to be fools they seem to be something Else besides Human Life" ("Public Address" 580). Like Godwin before him and Shelley and Emerson after him, Blake came to feel that social reform was dependent on individual spiritual renovation. Like Emerson in *Self-Reliance*, Blake's feeling about individuals and government is compatible with the Victorian ethos of individualism. In his influential Victorian manual, *Self-Help* (1859), Samuel Smiles echoes Blake's sentiment almost exactly: "Even the best institutions can give a man no active help. Perhaps the most they can do is to leave him free to develop himself and improve his individual condition" (35). Both Blake and Smiles were representative in their advocacy of self-realization, which in Blake's case is explicitly religious.

Blake posits an inner freedom independent of external constraints and, in the "Public Address," an inner weakness that the best government could not relieve. Political life is recast as salvation and damnation. In "A Vision of the Last Judgment" he gives over social and political reform as futile:

> Many Persons such as Paine & Voltaire with some of the Ancient Greeks say we will not Converse concerning Good & Evil we will live in Paradise & Liberty You may do so in Spirit but not in the Mortal Body as you pretend till after the Last Judgment for in Paradise they have no Corporeal & Mortal Body that originated with the Fall & was calld Death & cannot be removed but by a Last judgment while we are in the world of Mortality we Must Suffer
>
> The Whole Creation Groans to be deliverd there will always be as many Hypocrites born as Honest Men & they will always have superior Power in Mortal Things. (564)

Blake is like Wordsworth and Coleridge when they appeal to the domestic virtues and adopt personal, fundamentally religious solutions to public problems.

Blake's Victorian readers, even those confused by the obscurity of his late works, acknowledged this tendency and valued it more than Blake's early radicalism. Gilchrist reports the following reminiscence of John Thomas Smith, an acquaintance of Blake: "He loved liberty, . . . yet no man less resembled the vulgar radical. His sympathies were rather with Milton, Harrington, and Marvell—not with Milton as to his puritanism, but his love of a grand ideal scheme of republicanism; though I never remember him speaking of the American institutions: I suppose Blake's republic would always have been ideal" (qtd. in Gilchrist 331). Blake's political hopes and his conception of the poet's essentially religious vocation were in constant tension. Swinburne's study of Blake emphasizes that art cannot coexist with social or moral activism, even if the artist intended to unite them (87 ff.).[9]

Like Shelley's, Blake's view of the self was easily incorporated into the Victorian ideology of individualism. His first readers noticed this at once, and not always with approval. In 1839 J. J. Garth Wilkinson published an edition of the *Songs of Innocence and of Experience*. He was the first to compare Blake and Shelley in print: "Self-will in each, was the centre of the Individual, and self-intelligence, the 'Anima Mundi' of the Philosopher, and they both imagined, that they could chop and change the Universe, even to the confounding of Life with Death, to suit their own creative fancies" (qtd. in Bentley, *Critical Heritage* 59). Wilkinson noted that the poets support the concept of individual autonomy, which allows one to "chop and change" the spiritual world just as it challenged one to manipulate material reality for personal gain in the real world. But he valued Blake because the poet elevated the self above the turmoil that self-will was creating in the social world: "If the Volume gives one impulse to the New Spiritualism which is now dawning on the world;—if it leads one reader to think, that all Reality for him, in the long run, lies out of the limits of Space and Time; and that Spirits, and not bodies, and still less garments, are men; . . . it will have done its work in its little day" (qtd. in Bentley, *Critical Heritage* 60). Wilkinson put Blake before the public as a religious writer, typical and exemplary of the romantic stance, and Gilchrist followed Wilkinson in recovering Blake for explicitly religious purposes:

> Blake was, in spirit, a denizen of other and earlier ages of the world than the present mechanical one to which chance had rudely transplanted him. It is within the last century or so, that 'the heavens have gone further off,' as Hazlitt put it. The supernatural world has during that period removed itself further from civilized, cultivated humanity than it was ever before—in all time, heathen or Christian. There is, at this moment, infinitely less practical belief in an invisible world, or even apprehension of it, than at any previous historical era, whether Egyptian, classic, or medieval. It is *only* within the last century and a half, the faculty of seeing visions could have been one to bring a man's sanity into question. (326)

Gilchrist enlists Blake in the war against industrialism and seculariza-
tion that was fought on a number of fronts during the Victorian period, fronts as diverse as the socialism of William Morris and the popular interest in spiritualism and the occult. Blake was fighting this same
war and, as the quote from Hazlitt shows, so were the other romantics.
Blake became for Gilchrist what Wordsworth was for Mill, an answer
to the Victorian crisis of faith.

In offering Blake to Victorian readers as a religious visionary, Gilchrist, the Rossettis, and Swinburne undertook a paradoxical critical
enterprise. They made great claims for the uncompromising artist despite the fact that they could not understand many of his works, especially the later prophecies now considered major. Deborah Dorfman
reports that "to a Blake analyst willing . . . to try [to understand *Jerusalem*], William Rossetti suggested that after a few years in solitary con-
finement devoted to reading the prophetic books one might possibly
'piece together their myths, trace their connection, reason out their
system'" (191). Swinburne also qualified his admiration, at least for
Jerusalem, by noting, "It were a mere frenzy of discipleship that would
undertake by force of words to make straight those crooked ways"
(276).

In *Milton* Blake denounced "the idiot Questioner who is always
questioning / But never capable of answering" (41: 12–13; 142). At the
end of the Gilchrist biography, Dante Gabriel Rossetti was more conciliatory but finally no more compromising in his apology for Blake:
"Now perhaps no poet ever courted a public with more apparent need
for some smoothing of the way, or mild forewarning, from within,
from without, or indeed from any region whence a helping heaven and
four bountiful winds might be pleased to waft it, than does Blake. . . .
Yet, on the other hand, there is the plain truth that such aid will not be
at all needed by those whom these writings *will* impress, and almost
certainly lost upon those whom they *will not*" (qtd. in Gilchrist 383).
Rossetti acknowledges that Blake's work requires elucidation, but asserts that criticism is finally useless before it since Blake's readers are
from the beginning either "sheep" or "goats." He thus established a
tradition in Blake criticism that is comfortable with mystery and de-

pendent on paradox, a tradition whose concepts and vocabulary are religious.[10]

Blake himself invited such responses when he wrote to Butts in 1803, after leaving Felpham,

> Now I may say to you what perhaps I should not dare to say to any one else. That I can alone carry on my visionary studies in London unannoyd & that I may converse with my friends in Eternity. See Visions, Dream Dreams, & prophecy & speak Parables unobserv'd & at liberty from the Doubts of other Mortals. perhaps Doubts proceeding from Kindness. but Doubts are always pernicious Especially when we Doubt our Friends Christ is very decided on this Point: "He who is Not With Me is Against Me" There is no Medium or Middle state. (728)

Here and elsewhere Blake repudiated critical reading and condemned his "idiot questioners" in advance. Blake's first readers were true to his sense of himself as an inspired prophet who commanded unquestioning assent, and most modern Blakeans treat the poet as Yeats did when he called him "one of those great artificers of God who uttered mysterious truths to a little clan" (qtd. in Wittreich 271). After Felpham, Blake sought disciples rather than readers, and for the most part he achieved his aim.

CHAPTER FOUR

Private Poet, Public Man: Shelley and Romantic Self-Division

Shelley responded to the political events of his day with more precision and fervor than any romantic poet except Blake. In the great years in Italy, 1819 and 1820, he produced *Prometheus Unbound*, *The Cenci*, *The Mask of Anarchy*, and *A Philosophical View of Reform*, as well as superb political songs and sonnets such as "Men of England" and "England in 1819." This intensely creative period was a direct response to social and political turmoil: the trials for libel and forged paper money in England; the agitation for parliamentary reform and the increasing government reaction, culminating in the Peterloo massacre; and the revolutionary movements in Spain and Greece.

In *A Philosophical View of Reform* Shelley called on writers and intellectuals to use their talents to advance the struggle. The tactics he advocated were the same used by men like William Cobbett and Francis Burdett; such tactics eventually resulted in a freer press in England: "For public opinion in England ought first to be excited to action, and the durability of those forms within which the oppressors intrench themselves brought perpetually to the test of its operation. . . . For this purpose government ought to be defied, in cases of questionable result, to prosecute for political libel" (Clark 258). Shelley's early poem *Queen Mab* was being circulated in a pirated version by radical publishers, and directly after Peterloo he composed *The Mask of Anarchy*, the greatest social protest poem of this or perhaps any other period. It would certainly have drawn the attention of a government willing to fine Burdett two thousand pounds and jail him for three months for condemning Peterloo in a letter to the newspapers. Shelley seemed to be abandoning the solitary stance of *Alastor* and the obscure style of *The Revolt of Islam* and preparing to address the English public directly.

The Cenci and *Peter Bell the Third*, the latter being an accessible satiric attack on Wordsworth's politics, were intended for middle- and upper-class readers. *The Cenci* had some success and went into a second edition. *The Mask of Anarchy*, a ballad, and *A Philosophical View of Reform*, the most sustained and impressive political treatise written by a romantic poet, were directed to the working class and liberal intellectual sympathizers. At this crucial point in his career, Shelley considered the poet as a worker alongside other workers, as this list from *A Philosophical View of Reform* reveals: "Every man whose scope in society has a plebeian and intelligible unity, whose personal exertions are more valuable to him than his capital; every tradesman who is not a monopolist, all surgeons and physicians and those mechanics and editors and literary men and artists, and farmers, all those persons whose profits spring from honorably and honestly exerting their own skill and wisdom or strength in greater abundance than from the employment of money" (qtd. in Clark 250). Here Shelley was thinking about the poet as a member of society, not as a Wordsworthian solitary or a Blakean prophet howling in the wilderness.

But Shelley's career was a remarkable sequence of balked intentions. *A Philosophical View of Reform* was left unfinished and remained unpublished until 1920. *The Mask of Anarchy* was not published until 1832, when the first Reform Bill made it more historical than topical. *Peter Bell the Third* was not published until 1839. The proposed volume of *Popular Songs* for workers was never assembled. And Shelley's response to the pirating of *Queen Mab* was ambivalent at best. The poem was just the sort of production that Shelley advocated circulating, daring the government to prosecute for libel. In some of his letters he expressed a certain pleasure that *Queen Mab* had resurfaced, but in others he said that the work should be suppressed on the grounds that it was "perfectly worthless in point of literary composition" and "in the subtler discriminations of metaphysical and religious doctrine, it is still more crude and immature" (*Complete Works* 854).[1] He finally had his publisher apply for a legal injunction against the pirates, though *Queen Mab* was eventually published by Richard Carlile and became known as the Chartists' Bible (Holmes 660 ff.).[2]

Shelley biographer Richard Holmes explains that Leigh Hunt, editor of *The Examiner* and Shelley's close friend, and Charles Ollier, Shelley's publisher, feared prosecution and so withheld Shelley's more controversial works. This is understandable enough, especially since Hunt was a liberal who preferred less confrontational tactics than those advocated by Shelley in his radical phases.[3] But Holmes concludes that this simple explanation is insufficient:

> One cannot blame Hunt if his author was not in England. Shelley was not there to stand by his editor, and to take legal responsibility on his own shoulders; or indeed to choose alternative means of publication. It was Shelley's own self-exile in Italy, his failure to be on the spot, that provided the ultimate cause of the critical sequence of failed publications in late 1819 and early 1820. This in turn was to dictate the obscure fortunes of the remaining works printed in his lifetime. (Holmes 541)

Holmes's account of this period in Shelley's life, in which the poet possessed "a consciousness of formidable active powers that it is difficult to conceive on ordinary terms," is indispensable for an understanding of the works of these years (556). But in tracing Shelley's "obscure fortunes" to his failure to see his works of 1819 and 1820 published, Holmes downplays the extent to which ambivalence about publishing was characteristic of Shelley throughout his career.

Despite its radicalism, the 1813 edition of *Queen Mab* was intended for a polite audience. Shelley wrote to a friend, "Like all egotists, I shall console myself with what I may call, if I please, the suffrages of the chosen few" (*Letters* 1:352). He made little effort to circulate the poem in a form appropriate to working-class or radical readers. Shelley's treatment of *Queen Mab* is representative not only of his ambivalence toward his work and its role in society but of the remarkable variety of attitudes his culture held (and ours holds) toward him. In his own time he was praised as a genius and condemned as an atheist, celebrated as a great poetic craftsman and dismissed for his obscurity. After his death he was hailed as a social revolutionary and condescended to as an ineffectual angel. It is hard to think of another poet about whom so many opposing assertions have been made. Yet only a poet who was himself self-divided could provoke such contradictory responses.

In his *Memoir of Shelley*, Thomas Love Peacock wrote that many readers had confused the poet represented in *Alastor, or, The Spirit of Solitude* with Alastor, the spirit who pursues him (56). Like the frequent confusion of Frankenstein with the monster he creates, the popular error reveals something significant about the work: it expresses Shelley's ambivalence about a poet's relationship to mass society, which he calls in the preface to *Alastor* "the unforseeing multitudes" (*Complete Works* 2). His claim, like Wordsworth's, is that the poet's solitude is distinctive and important because it possesses a redemptive social force.

Shelley's radical sympathies prevented him from completely dismissing the public as a mass or the mob, but his view of the poet in *Alastor* tends toward such a conception. The narrator laments that the poet dies,

> The brave, the gentle, and the beautiful,
> The child of grace and genius. [while] Heartless things
> Are done and said i' the world, and many worms
> And beasts and men live on. . . . (lines 689–92)

The poet of *Alastor* is not a fellow worker, but a feared seer:

> The cottagers,
> Who ministered with human charity
> His human wants, beheld with wondering awe
> Their fleeting visitant. . . .
> the infant would conceal
> His troubled visage in his mother's robe
> In terror at the glare of those wild eyes . . .
> (lines 254–57, 262–64)

Shelley was at this time repudiating Wordsworth's politics, but the concept of the poet as a powerful but solitary priest held by Wordsworth and Coleridge continued to influence him.

Shelley apparently repudiated the idea of the poet as a solitary in *A Philosophical View of Reform* and in the political poetry of 1819 and 1820. Yet just after he heard about Peterloo, in September 1819, he wrote to Ollier, "The ill account you give of the success of my Poetical attempts sufficiently accounts for your silence; but I believe the truth is, I write less for the public than for myself" (*Letters* 2:116). It may never be clear why Shelley did not seek other means of publishing his work when it became apparent that Hunt and Ollier were in effect suppressing it. The resignation and the search for compensatory definitions of his work ("I write . . . for myself") are almost impossible to reconcile with the direct address to the working class in *The Mask of Anarchy*. Yet the fact remains that he acquiesced in Hunt's and Ollier's inactivity and gave himself over to romantic conceptions of the poet's relationship to the public.

In *A Defence of Poetry* Shelley made this claim for the social efficacy of poetry:

> The most unfailing herald, companion, and follower of the awakening of a great people to work a beneficial change in opinion or institution, is poetry. At such periods there is an accumulation of the power of communicating and receiving intense and impassioned conceptions respecting man and nature. . . . Poets are the hierophants of an unapprehended inspiration; the mirrors of the gigantic shadows which futurity casts upon the present; the words which express what they understand not; the trumpets which sing to battle and feel not what they inspire; the influence which is moved not, but moves. Poets are the unacknowledged legislators of the world. (Brett-Smith 59)

Shelley was similar to Wordsworth and Blake in his view of the poet as a quasi-religious influence whose province is spiritual, private, and personal reform rather than material reform. But when Shelley claimed in the 1821 *Defence* that poets are unacknowledged legislators, he was taking a more exalted view of the poet than when he made the same statement in the 1820 *A Philosophical View of Reform*.

The "unacknowledged legislator" passage is identical in both documents, but it means something quite different in each. In *A Defence of Poetry* the passage concludes the essay as it now exists. It is a rhetorical flourish intended to summarize Shelley's view of poetry's social role and of the poet's power. In *A Philosophical View of Reform* the passage comes near the end of the first chapter, and is sharply qualified in the next paragraph: "But, omitting these more abstracted considerations, has there not been and is there not in England a desire for change arising from the profound sentiment of the exceeding inefficiency of the existing institutions to provide for the physical and intellectual happiness of the people?" (qtd. in Clark 240). In *A Philosophical View of Reform* Shelley's concern is political change and the tactics for achieving it, not defenses of the poet's practice. The poet is one worker among many and asserting his power is less important than effecting social change.

In *A Defence of Poetry*, however, Shelley separated the poet's work from social issues: "A poet therefore would do ill to embody his own conceptions of right and wrong, which are usually those of his place and time, in his poetical creations, which participate in neither" (Brett-Smith 33–34). The statement deconstructs some of Shelley's greatest works, such as *Prometheus Unbound* and *The Mask of Anarchy*, which of course embody Shelley's conceptions of right and wrong. In the *Defence* Shelley differentiated between a higher, eternal morality that the poet by definition embodies and immediate questions of right and wrong, which in Shelley's day were urgent and intractable. In dismissing didactic poetry, Shelley claimed that great poets like Homer penetrate to the essence of morality while lesser poets simply affect "a moral aim" (Brett-Smith 34), but he did not make it clear how one can separate any particular value expressed in a poem (such as the code of vengeance in Homer or the repudiation of vengeance in *Prometheus Unbound*) from the "poetry" in a great work.

In his life and work, Shelley was torn between his engagement with the issues of his place and time and his sense of himself as a poet who should escape place and time. As he wrote to Peacock in 1819, "I consider Poetry very subordinate to moral & political science, & if I were well, certainly I should aspire to the latter" (*Letters* 2:71). Shelley would retract this admission by making vast claims for poetry in the *Defence*, but those claims emerged from Shelley's painful sense that his talents were not suited to the issues that most concerned him.

Shelley's next major work after the *Defence* was *Adonais*, a poem that makes explicit the self-division evident in *Alastor* and the *Defence*. Shelley described himself in these lines:

> he, as I guess,
> Had gazed on Nature's naked loveliness,
> Actaeon-like, and now he fled astray
> With feeble steps o'er the world's wilderness,
> And his own thoughts, along that rugged way,
> Pursued, like raging hounds, their father and their prey.
> (lines 274–79)

The isolation of the poet from society that Wordsworth's narrators represent is here completely internalized by Shelley. The lines describe Shelley's rejection of Wordsworth's view of the poet's relationship to nature as opposed to society, but when the poet turns to society he is ineffectual ("With feeble steps") and finally thrown back on his own thoughts. Instead of redeeming the world, the poet's thoughts are thwarted, directed inward, and transformed into hounds that pursue and tear him. While working on *Adonais* in the summer of 1821, Shelley told Claire Clairmont that "in writing poetry he found the only real form of mental *relief* which lifted him above 'the stormy mist of sensations'" (Holmes 656), even though *Adonais* is a poem about Keats as a poet being destroyed by contact with the uncomprehending world. The solace he found in composing the elegy on Keats's death was ambiguous. He told Horace Smith that when he composed *Adonais*, "I wrote, as usual, with a total ignorance of the effect that I should produce" (*Letters* 2:349). Clearly Shelley was uncertain about the impact his work would have on the various reading audiences.[4]

Adonais represents the first full-blown instance of the myth of the romantic poet: unappreciated by vulgar contemporaries, acutely sensitive, too good for this world, destined to be understood only by other poets and by posterity. Shelley invented and believed the story that

Keats was killed by the review of his work in the *Quarterly*: "The savage criticism on his *Endymion*, which appeared in the *Quarterly Review*, produced the most violent effect on his susceptible mind; . . . a rapid consumption ensued, and the succeeding acknowledgements from more candid critics of the true greatness of his powers were ineffectual to heal the wound thus wantonly inflicted. It may be well said that these wretched men know not what they do" (*Complete Works* 484). Here, in the preface to *Adonais*, the poet is explicitly linked to Christ, and the whole configuration of Shelley's late thoughts about the poet becomes clear. Christ was a reformer who was misunderstood and crucified, just as Shelley was a reformer who failed to reach the public that he wished to save.

As Richard Holmes makes clear, in *Adonais* Shelley was writing about his own poetic career as well as about Keats's, particularly the savage but in some ways apt review of Shelley's work by John Taylor Coleridge in the *Quarterly* in 1819. Shelley was unconsoled by the appreciations of his poetry that were beginning to appear in 1820 and 1821. In Holmes's words, Shelley

> forc[ed] the myth of Keats's death to express his own almost unbearably bitter feelings. More and more, the extent to which his great poetry and writing of the autumn and winter of 1819–20 had been suppressed or ignored or turned aside was borne in on him. The prospect of renewed friendship with Byron, outstandingly the most successful English poet of the age, had especially brought this home. . . . His claims to be "morbidly indifferent" to praise or blame rang almost painfully false. (Holmes 658–59)

In *Adonais* Shelley attacked reviewers with more contempt than Coleridge had, but for the same reasons:

> The herded wolves, bold only to pursue;
> The obscene ravens clamorous o'er the dead;
> The vultures to the conquerer's banner true
> Who feed where Desolation first has fed.
> (lines 244–47)

The rage against critics proceeded not simply from political disappointment but from the professional frustration that Shelley, like Wordsworth and Coleridge, was undergoing.

Like the older writers, Shelley perceived that reviews were gaining power in the literary institution. He protested against the change in the 1817 preface to *The Revolt of Islam*: "It is the misfortune of this age that its Writers, too thoughtless of immortality, are exquisitely sensible to temporary praise or blame. They write with the fear of Reviews before their eyes. This system of criticism sprang up in that torpid interval when Poetry was not. Poetry, and the art which professes to regulate and limit its powers, cannot subsist together" (*Complete Works* 38). Shelley was right that his was an age of reviews, but he sentimentalized past ages when writers wrote under pressure from patrons or coteries rather than from a middle-class audience whose tastes were both consulted and formed by magazines. Shelley obscures the fact that all writers write with an audience in mind, and instead argues that writers should appeal to the permanent standards of their craft, not to current fashions. In his view, current criticism represents a failure of imagination, a spiritual deadness, and therefore critics cannot judge the work of writers, who themselves set the standards for true poetry. The Shelleyan twist is that criticism is a tyrannical practice that poets must overthrow, but otherwise his argument for the writer's professional rights is in accord with Wordsworth's and Coleridge's earlier polemics.

In *Peter Bell the Third*, which lampoons the political apostasy of Wordsworth, Shelley nonetheless links himself to the older poet as a practicing writer dissatisfied with the current arrangements governing literary work. When Peter reads the current reviews of his work, Shelley presents his response sympathetically:

"What!" cried he, "this is my reward
For nights of thought, and days of toil?
Do poets, but to be abhorred
By men of whom they never heard,
Consume their spirits' oil?"
(lines 493–97)

When in the next stanza Peter finds that he has been attacked for immorality, it is clear that he is a composite of Wordsworth, Shelley, and other contemporary writers, whom Shelley sees as united in this one respect: their hostile relationship with an impersonal literary institution composed of incompetent reviewers and an uncomprehending and vulgar public.

Mary Shelley recognized the problems this stance posed for Shelley. In her note to *The Witch of Atlas* in the 1839 edition of Shelley's poems, she wrote,

> The surpassing excellence of *The Cenci* had made me greatly desire that Shelley should increase his popularity by adopting subjects that would more suit the popular taste than a poem conceived in the abstract and dreamy spirit of the *Witch of Atlas*. It was not only that I wished him to acquire popularity as redounding to his fame; but I believed that he would obtain a greater mastery over his own powers, and greater happiness in his mind, if public applause crowned his endeavours. . . . Shelley did not expect sympathy and approbation from the public; but the want of it took away a portion of the ardour that ought to have sustained him while writing. He was thrown on his own resources, and on the inspiration of his own soul; and wrote because his mind overflowed, without the hope of being appreciated. . . . I felt sure that, if his poems were more addressed to the common feelings of men, his proper rank among the writers of the day would be acknowledged. . . . But my persuasions were in vain, the mind could not be bent from its natural inclination. (*Complete Works* 462)

Shelley could not sustain creative work in isolation, and Mary Shelley's insight is corroborated by the frustration Shelley himself felt at the end of his career, and by the increasing diffuseness of his writing evident in the *Defence of Poetry*.

Shelley wrote in 1822 to John Gisborne:

> I write little now. It is impossible to compose except under the strong excitement of an assurance of finding sympathy in what you write. . . . Lord Byron is in this respect fortunate. He touched

a chord to which a million hearts responded, and the coarse music which he produced to please them disciplined him to the perfection to which he now approaches. I do not go on with "Charles the First." I feel too little certainty of the future, and too little satisfaction with regard to the past, to undertake any subject seriously and deeply. (*Letters* 2:436)

Of all the romantic writers, Shelley was most aware of how self-defeating the posture of isolation could be, politically and personally. Yet he fell back on that posture with increasing stridency in the 1820s, as his dedication to *The Witch of Atlas* reveals:

> To Mary
> (ON HER OBJECTING TO THE FOLLOWING POEM, UPON THE
> SCORE OF ITS CONTAINING NO HUMAN INTEREST)
> How, my dear Mary,—are you critic-bitten
>   (For vipers kill, though dead) by some review,
> That you condemn these verses I have written,
>   Because they tell no story, false or true?

This verse, and the faint note of condescension and envy in his remarks about Byron, represent Shelley's discouraged retreat from actual readers and their needs, standards, and expectations.

The reviewers who were beginning to recognize Shelley's poetic talent in the early 1820s sensed that this retreat was in some ways characteristic. In 1820 the reviewer in *The Honeycomb* wrote, "we think Mr. Shelley has never been duly appreciated. This neglect, for it almost amounts to that, is, however, entirely owing to himself. He writes in a spirit which people do not comprehend: there is something too mystical in what he says—something too high or too deep for common comprehensions. He lives in a very remote poetical world, and his feelings will scarcely bear to be shadowed out in earthly light" (Barcus 36). This reviewer confirmed Mary Shelley's feeling that there was a public available to Shelley if he had overcome his "natural inclination" to abstraction. Other reviewers admitted Shelley's genius but objected to his radical politics. In *The Album*, in 1822, a critic wrote, "There is Mr. Shelley; who possesses the powers of poetry to a degree, perhaps, superior to any of his distinguished contemporaries. The mixing of his unhappy philosophical tenets in his writings has prevented, and will prevent, their becoming popular. His powers of thought, too, equally subtle and profound, occasionally lead him beyond the capability of expression, and in those passages he, of course, becomes unintelligible" (Barcus 329). In his combination of great praise with rueful censure, this critic prefigured much of the Victorian response to Shelley. More important, in separating Shelley's poetry from his politics, the reviewer repeats a separation that Shelley himself unconsciously acknowledged, a separation between the private, quasi-spiritual self and the public arena that is hostile to it.

In Thomas Love Peacock's critique of Shelley, Peacock senses this contradiction between Shelley's political hopes and his attempt to use poetry to accomplish them. In *Nightmare Abbey*, first published in 1818, Peacock based the character Scythrop Glowry on Shelley, with whom he had been friends since 1812. Scythrop is a social revolutionary, but a mystical one:

> Knowledge is power [said Scythrop]; it is in the hands of a few, who employ it to mislead the many, for their own selfish purposes of aggrandisement and appropriation. What if it were in the hands of a few who should employ it to lead the many? What if it were universal, and the multitude were enlightened? No. The many must always be in leading-strings; but let them have wise and honest conductors. A few to think, and many to act; that is the only basis of a perfect society. . . . So thinks the sublime Kant, who delivers his oracles in language which none but the initiated can comprehend. (*Abbey* 15)

Peacock here lampoons the romantic tendency to express egalitarian sentiments in obscure language and private forms. Other critics also noticed this problem of style in Shelley's works. As the reviewer in *The Honeycomb* commented on *The Revolt of Islam*, "So well did Mr. Shelley imagine this poem qualified to accomplish the philanthropic object for which it was written, that we have heard, he actually wished that a cheap edition of it should be printed in order that it might be distributed amongst all classes of persons; certainly one of the wildest of his imaginations. He should have written intelligibly to common understandings if he wished to become popular" (Barcus 273). Shelley grasped the tactics necessary to reach his audience, as he showed in *A Philosophical View of Reform*, but could not consistently accommodate his poetic practice to them.

Peacock noted that Shelley shared Coleridge's difficulties with the existing audience. In *Nightmare Abbey* Scythrop is best friends with Mr. Flosky, a take-off on Coleridge's Germanic and Christian obscurantism. Flosky constantly attacks "the reading public," a phrase Peacock uses for its novelty and its leveling connotations, thus reminding us that the phrase originated during the early nineteenth century along with the phenomenon it described. Flosky laments, "How can we be cheerful when we are surrounded by a *reading public*, that is growing too wise for its betters?" (110). He also reproves a reader of light fiction: "I am sorry to find you participating in the vulgar error of the reading public, to whom an unusual collocation of words, involving a juxtaposition of antiperistatical ideas, immediately suggests the notion of hyperoxysophistical paradoxology." The reader replies, understandably, "Indeed, Mr Flosky, it suggests no such notion to me" (74). Shelley embraced the democratic potential of the reading public in theory, as Coleridge decidedly did not, but when Peacock linked him to Coleridge's obscurity, it was not an arbitrary hit. Shelley's handling of the first edition of *Queen Mab*, the form of *The Revolt of Islam* and *Prometheus Unbound*, and even later pieces, such as *Ode to Liberty* and *Ode to Naples* where the radical content is tempered by austere classical forms, all make him vulnerable to Peacock's attack.

Peacock also satirized the abstract and universalizing character of much romantic thought, such as Shelley's assertion in the *Defence*: "A poet participates in the eternal, the infinite, and the one; as far as relates to his conceptions, time and place and number are not" (Brett-Smith 27). In passages such as these Shelley separated the poet from social and political affairs in the way that Peacock had anticipated in *Nightmare Abbey*. Peacock saw that conservatives like Wordsworth and Coleridge and radicals like Shelley all tried to alter social and political reality by transcending it. In his parody of *Biographia Literaria*, Peacock has Mr. Flosky say,

> Sir, the great evil is, that there is too much commonplace light in our moral and political literature; and light is a great enemy to mystery, and mystery is a great friend to enthusiasm. Now the enthusiasm for truth is an exceedingly fine thing, as long as the truth, which is the object of the enthusiasm, is so completely abstract as to be altogether out of the reach of the human faculties; and, in that sense, I have myself an enthusiasm for truth, but in no other, for the pleasure of metaphysical investigation lies in the means, not in the end; and if the end could be found, the pleasure of the means would cease. . . . The beauty of this process is, that at every step it strikes out into two branches, in a compound ratio of ramification; so that you are perfectly sure of losing your way, and keeping your mind in perfect health, by the perpetual exercise of an interminable quest. (*Abbey* 49)

Shelley would write in *Prometheus Unbound* that "the deep truth is imageless," a conception of man's relationship to "ultimate reality" perfectly compatible with Flosky's sense of intellectual endeavor. Like the other romantics, including Byron, Shelley often thought of the poet as an insatiable quester searching for an absolute reality that could be approached only through poetry.

After reading *Nightmare Abbey* Shelley acknowledged Peacock's criticism of this tendency, accepting it graciously and with characteristic openness. He wrote to Peacock, "I suppose the moral is contained in what Falstaff says 'For Gods sake talk like a man of this world'." But he qualified his acknowledgment with a comment recalling the ambivalence of *Alastor*: "and yet looking deeper into it, is not the misdirected enthusiasm of Scythrop what J[esus] C[hrist] calls the salt of the earth?" (*Letters* 2:98). Shelley could see enthusiasm for what it was as well as Peacock, but apparently he could discover only "misdirected" means for accomplishing his social and political ends.

Peacock renewed his dialogue with Shelley on the writer's social function in *The Four Ages of Poetry*, published in *Ollier's Miscellany* in 1820. Peacock's work is known to modern readers mainly as the essay that prompted *A Defence of Poetry*, but it shares important ideas about the social function of poetry with more familiar romantic polemics. Peacock's essay must be considered in any analysis of Shelley's, not only because, as Marilyn Butler notes, they form "a philosophic dialogue" about the romantic writer's social role, but because Peacock's essay reveals and criticizes the contradictions in Shelley's position (*Peacock Displayed* 293).

In *Peacock Displayed* Marilyn Butler shows how "Peacock's desired ideal [is] a campaigning literature of ideas, a comic vehicle containing a wholly serious purpose" (286). This seriousness of purpose informs *The Four Ages of Poetry*, despite its abusive satire. Throughout the essay Peacock attacks the idea shared by Wordsworth and Shelley that poetry is a superior, indeed an ultimate mode of knowing:

> intellectual power and intellectual acquisition have turned themselves into other and better channels, and have abandoned the cultivation and the fate of poetry to the degenerate fry of modern rhymsters, and their olympic judges, the magazine critics, who continue to debate and promulgate oracles about poetry, as if it were still what it was in the Homeric age, the all-in-all of intellectual progression, and as if there were no such things in existence as mathematicians, astronomers, chemists, moralists, metaphysicians, historians, politicians, and political economists. (Brett-Smith 19)

This is a rich passage for what it shares with romanticism as well as for what it attacks. For all his cynicism, the ideal of poetry held by Peacock differs little from that held by Wordsworth or Shelley: he says that poetry was once "the all-in-all of intellectual progression." Peacock simply tried to understand the relationship of this ideal to the contemporary social and historical situation of poetry.

Peacock treats poets as one professional group among many, knowing full well that the poets did not acknowledge this intellectual division of labor in their theories, though they were forced to come to grips with it in their careers. What troubled Peacock about romantic defenses of poetry was their anachronistic and mystifying character. When he called poets "semi-barbarians in a civilized community" living in "the days that are past" (Brett-Smith 16), he was referring to the reactionary quality of romantic polemics that justified the poet's function as priestly or vatic or defined poetry as a mode of retreat from modern social arrangements into nature or the past. Peacock's satire was an attempt to force defenses of literature's social function to be mounted in terms of current social arrangements, without appeals to "golden ages" that could easily be dismissed as ideologically motivated fantasies.

In *The Four Ages* Peacock makes the half-serious claim that poetry as an important human activity is dead because other, more valuable social activities now occupy the best minds. But the thrust of Peacock's criticism is not that poetry is an inherently useless anachronism; he feels that writers render themselves useless by abdicating their social role. Poetry now, "consisting merely of querulous, egotistical rhapsodies, to express the writer's high dissatisfaction with the world and every thing in it, serves only to confirm what has been said of the semibarbarous character of poets, who from singing dithyrambics and 'Io Triumphe,' while society was savage, grow rabid, and out of their element, as it becomes polished and enlightened" (Brett-Smith 18). If the writer withdraws from contemporary social conflicts, poetry can no longer make an essential and recognized contribution to social life, and Peacock holds the romantics accountable for failing to define a concrete function for poetry in the current social order. Peacock attacked the romantic response to social crisis in which the poet separates himself from society in order to save it.

In *A Defence of Poetry* Shelley was responding to an attack that was not only cogent and relevant, but one for which he had provided the ammunition. In the January 1819 letter to Peacock written just before *The Four Ages*, Shelley said, "I consider Poetry very subordinate to moral & political science, & if I were well, certainly I should aspire to the latter; for I can conceive a great work, embodying the discoveries of all ages, & harmonising the contending creeds by which mankind have been ruled" (*Letters* 2:71). In *The Four Ages* Shelley's own ambivalence about poetry was turned against him in the witty and aggressive polemic of an admired friend. He was thus stung into claiming a greater social role for poetry than his theory or practice could bear.

Shelley confronted social problems that seemed too complex to be solved but that were too evident to be ignored or plausibly transcended. The poet could not retreat from them and still claim to have a significant place in human affairs. In the 1802 preface to the *Lyrical Ballads*, Wordsworth shifted the arena of conflict from society to the human mind, where the poet could provide a service that still counted as a social one, even if it was private and therapeutic rather than public and ameliorative. In the *Defence* Shelley attempted to put the poet back into the social arena, but as a divine agent rather than as a man working with and for other men. At certain points in the essay the poet is not even imagined as human: "A poet is a nightingale, who sits in darkness and sings to cheer its own solitude with sweet sounds; his auditors are as men entranced by the melody of an unseen musician, who feel that they are moved and softened, yet know not whence or why" (Brett-Smith 31). Here poetry is no longer addressed to men, but is a radically private activity incidentally overheard by them.

In this passage Shelley reverses in fantasy the actual relationship between writers and readers in the early nineteenth century, for in fact it was the audience that was "unseen," not the poet, and it was the poet's job to move and soften a group of people without being certain of who they were or why they read. Shelley exacerbated an already difficult situation by trying to address an English audience from Italy, and by eliminating readers from his theory of poetry. Other authors felt exposed to the reading public, not hidden from it, but Shelley acted as an "unseen musician" in relation to his English readers.

In his poetry Shelley sometimes imagined himself making contact with an audience, though that contact is usually expressed as a paradox:

> Like a Poet hidden
>   In the light of thought,
> Singing hymns unbidden,
>   Till the world is wrought
> To sympathy with hopes and fears it heeded not.
> ("To a Sky-Lark," lines 36–40)

The audience is converted to the poet's beliefs, but the poet himself effects that conversion in the most indirect manner. Characteristically, the poet is described as hidden, and the world does not ask for his song; he sings unbidden, and his song transforms the world as if by magic.

Furthermore, the poet is not like a skylark; the skylark is like a poet, and represents a power that the poet does not yet have:

> Teach me half the gladness
>> That thy brain must know,
> Such harmonious madness
>> From my lips would flow
> The world would listen then—as I am listening now.
> ("Sky-Lark," lines 101–5)

In Shelley's view, it would take an entirely new kind of poetry to reach the contemporary audience, which appears in this poem (as in Wordsworth's "Composed Upon Westminster Bridge") as heedless and deaf. The poet is the only one who can hear poetry because it has a divine rather than a human source and is thus beyond the faculties of the average reader. The images of the writer as one of another species in "To a Sky-Lark" and in the *Defence* express Shelley's alienation from his audience in its most extreme form.

Shelley's claim that poetry creates social and historical reality is subverted throughout the *Defence* by his metaphors for the poet himself, who is imagined as a vulnerable and transitory agent of a superhuman power—"the mind in creation is like a fading coal"—and as essentially separate from other men, not linked in common cause with them: "But in the intervals of inspiration, and they may be frequent without being durable, a poet becomes a man, and is abandoned to the sudden reflux of the influences under which others habitually live" (Brett-Smith 57). Rather than presenting a social theory of poetry in the *Defence*, Shelley opposes the poet to the man and transforms poetry from a human production to a divine mystery.

Despite the power of poetry itself, Shelley describes the actual human production of poems as an ineffable and futile business: "but when composition begins, inspiration is already on the decline, and the most glorious poetry that has ever been communicated to the world is probably a feeble shadow of the original conceptions of the poet" (Brett-Smith 54). Shelley almost never used the word *poetry* to refer to the writing of poems or to published work. He felt that true art is barely involved with the material world, and then only tragically so, because he was himself almost completely divorced from the literary institution in England. He was living in Italy and unaware of what Ollier and Hunt were doing with his work. In consequence, he elevated the conception of poems over the publication of poetry for actual readers; and he argued that private inspiration was more rewarding than actual composition, with its inevitable links to the reading public. In his theory, Shelley made composing for an audience incidental to the poet's real work.

Shelley's theory reproduced the separation of men from each other and from the products of their labor that is characteristic of industrial society. In his discussion of Dante and Milton in the *Defence*, Shelley makes a statement that reveals the unwitting connection of romantic poetry with the reigning social ideology: "Milton's poem [*Paradise Lost*] contains within itself a philosophical refutation of that system of which, by a strange and natural antithesis, it has been a chief popular support" (Brett-Smith 46). Consciously, Shelley is using *Paradise Lost* to confirm his belief that all great poetry advances the cause of social liberation. But he acknowledges that *Paradise Lost* has in fact upheld orthodox Christianity. The poem thus supports a real-world ideology that the poet (in Shelley's reading) intended to subvert. In the *Essay on Christianity* Shelley argued that the reformer is inevitably misunderstood by his society; here he describes the relationship between the poet and his culture as "a strange and natural antithesis." The phrase is so odd that it seems like a slip of the pen. The conflict between the poet and his readers is strange to Shelley the idealist, who feels that the poet represents the true spirit of the people, but it seems natural to Shelley the writer, who feels that the poet's beliefs will rarely coincide with the public's. What we have is a buried reference to the fate of Shelley's own poetry, which, like Milton's, upholds the dominant ideology despite his efforts to transform it.

The compatibility of Shelley's views with capitalist ideology is confirmed by the history of Shelley's reception in Victorian England. In an 1841 review of several recently published Shelley collections, G. H.

Lewes saw the poet as an exponent of Victorian liberal values: "The vital truth Shelley everywhere enforced, although treated as a chimaera by most of his contemporaries, and indulged as a dream by some others, has become the dominant Idea—the philosophy and faith of this age, throughout Europe—it is progression, humanity, perfectability, civilization, democracy—call it what you will—this is the truth uttered unceasingly by Shelley, and universally received by us" (qtd. in Duerksen 25–26). For Lewes, Shelley was neither the prophet of radical social change adopted by the Chartists nor the escapist dreamer of Arnold and Tennyson. But most Victorian readers incorporated Shelley by lining up on either side of the division between his social and political radicalism and his theory that poetry connects private consciousness with a divine realm.

Shelley's early readers were for the most part Chartists attracted to his social and political views. As John Guinn puts it, "the story of Shelley's literary reputation between the time of his death in 1822 and the publication of his collected poems in 1839 is, by and large, the story of the popularity of *Queen Mab* with radical journalism" (101). However, by 1833, Edward Bulwer-Lytton had already begun the Victorian reclamation of Shelley by emphasizing how the religious character of his work contradicted his professed beliefs: "despite the young audacity which led him into denying a God, his poetry is of a remarkably ethereal and spiritualizing cast. It is steeped in veneration—it is forever thirsting for the Heavenly and the Immortal—and the Deity he questioned avenges Himself only by impressing His image upon all that the poet undertook" (2:69). With the publication of Mary Shelley's edition in 1839, her view of Shelley as an angel too good for this world began to win adherents. They could point to *Alastor, Adonais*, and the famous lyrics like "To a Sky-Lark" and "The Cloud," in addition to Mary Shelley's extensive notes that argued her view.

The split between the reformer and the poet was noticed, but it became increasingly possible and common to follow Bulwer-Lytton in dismissing the political Shelley as immature or misguided and finding his true value in his inspired poetry. According to Roland Duerksen, "early Victorian liberal criticism, which showed an apologetic appreciation of Shelley, fostered the later critical view that Shelley was among the great poets of England but that he was 'dead wrong' in virtually all the beliefs that really mattered to *him*" (25).

Shelley's poetry reinforces the connection between literature and the private rather than public life created for Victorian readers by romantic literature. Modern arguments that attempt to rehabilitate Shelley as a practical and coherent political thinker depend almost exclusively on works he left unpublished, such as *A Philosophical View of Reform* and *The Mask of Anarchy*, and on statements made in private correspondence. When these documents are placed in their historical and biographical context, they confirm Shelley's ambivalence about his social and political activities and, to my mind, justify the Victorian separation of the poet from the athiest reformer more than they support the twentieth-century efforts to unify the two.[5]

The Victorian response to Shelley kept the actual contradictions in his work in the foreground, if only to dismiss that part of the work judged unacceptable. The split between what Miriam Allott calls the aesthetic and the extra-aesthetic Shelley began very early in the nineteenth century, as Allott's account of an 1821 review of *Queen Mab* shows: the reviewer "left Shelley's 'palpably absurd and false' opinions for others to judge, seeing the 'prominent features' of his poetical character to be 'energy and depth' and . . . finding that 'All Mr. Shelley's thoughts are feelings. He certainly communicates to a reader the impression made in his own mind, and gives it . . . all the vividness and strength with which it struck his own fancy'" (Allott 4). In an 1829 letter to his mother, Thackeray asserted that "Shelley's 'strong and perhaps good feelings' had been perverted by an 'absurd creed', and that conceit and false religion had misguided his 'high powers'" (qtd. in Duerksen 23). Thackeray rehabilitated Shelley in exactly the same way that Shelley had rehabilitated Dante and Milton: as great poets who had been forced to accommodate themselves to the creeds of their benighted times. Ironically, Shelley contributed to the cultural ideology that permitted Thackeray's separation of political events from the private consciousness that creates poetry and gives individuals access to "eternal" values. By removing the offensive ideas from the sublime art and the propagandist from the genius, the Victorians found in Shelley a poet in their own image. But it was an image fostered by Shelley himself, even in a document such as the *Defence*, where his conscious intention was to connect art with society and politics.

The Shelley Society, which met from 1886 to 1895, was a perfect emblem of the unresolved contradictions in the poet's political and social views and his poetic practice. Its members were socialists attracted to Shelley's politics and aesthetes interested in his personality and his tragic life, a combination that inevitably led to controversy. In one of the last addresses to the Society, A. G. Ross attempted to prevent the socialists, most prominently George Bernard Shaw, from using Shelley's political ideas for their own purposes, to the detriment of the poetry. His formulation echoes a number of passages in the *Defence* and elsewhere, and accurately reproduces Shelley's ambivalence: "when the blatant and cruel socialism of the street endeavours to use the lofty and sublime socialism of the study for its own base purposes, it is time that with no uncertain sounds all real lovers of the latter should disavow any sympathy with the former" (qtd. in Smith 271). His statements were rebutted by Chairman Rossetti and of course by Shaw, who called Ross's "the most astonishing [address] he had ever heard" (qtd. in Smith 271), but this final debate testifies to the odd combination so often found in romantic work of great power and great ambivalence about how that power is to be applied to social and historical affairs.

The final irony of *A Defence of Poetry* was that it too was left unfinished and was not published until 1840. Even a brief document such as the preface to *Prometheus Unbound* contains most of Shelley's contradictory attitudes toward art's social function. In the preface Shelley admits to "a passion for reforming the world," the phrase Peacock applied to Scythrop in *Nightmare Abbey*. But his qualification of this reforming impulse is immediate and characteristic: "But it is a mistake to suppose that I dedicate my poetical compositions solely to the direct enforcement of reform, or that I consider them in any degree as containing a reasoned system on the theory of human life. Didactic poetry is my abhorrence" (*Complete Works* 228). Shelley's distrust of system, of direct efforts at reform, and of the socialism of the street was echoed by romantic writers such as Blake and Emerson. It proceeded from the recalcitrance of contemporary social problems, which Shelley called in

A Philosophical View of Reform "the difficult and unbending realities of actual life" (Clark 254).

Raymond Williams found the end of the *Defence* "painful to read" (*Culture and Society* 63), but it seems to me harder to read remarks like the following prefaced to a great poem such as *Prometheus Unbound*:

> let the uncandid [readers] consider that they injure me less than
> their own hearts and minds by misrepresentation. Whatever tal-
> ents a person may possess to amuse and instruct others, be they
> ever so inconsiderable, he is yet bound to exert them: if his at-
> tempt be ineffectual, let the punishment of an unaccomplished
> purpose have been sufficient; let none trouble themselves to heap
> the dust of oblivion upon his efforts; the pile they raise will betray
> his grave which might otherwise have been unknown. (*Complete
> Works* 228)

The form of this address is the modest eighteenth-century plea to the reader to consider the writer's offering, a form appropriate to commercial publishing arrangements. The tone of address is that of a man deeply wounded by alienation from his audience, who anticipates rejection in advance and who introduces his work to the reader as *already* buried in "the dust of oblivion." In a letter to Godwin written in 1812, Shelley revealed that this ambivalent attitude toward his readers was characteristic: "I shall address myself no more to the illiterate. I will look to events in which it will be impossible that I can share, and make myself the cause of an effect which will take place ages after I have mouldered in the dust" (*Letters* 1:277). In the *Defence* Shelley will make vast claims for poetry, but here in 1812, and when actually presenting a poem to the public in 1819, he imagines the artist as a dead man.

CHAPTER FIVE

Romantic Conceptions of the Writer in Hawthorne and Poe

In an 1821 letter to his mother, Nathaniel Hawthorne described the vocational choices facing a gifted young man of the period:

> I have not yet concluded what profession I shall have. The being a minister is of course out of the question. I should not think that even you could desire me to choose so dull a way of life. Oh, no, mother, I was not born to vegetate forever in one place, and to live and die as calm and tranquil as—a puddle of water. As to lawyers, there are so many of them already that one half of them (upon a moderate calculation) are in a state of actual starvation. A physician, then, seems to be "Hobson's choice"; but yet I should not like to live by the diseases and infirmities of my fellow creatures. . . . Oh that I was rich enough to live without a profession! What do you think of my becoming an author, and relying for support upon my pen? . . . How proud you would feel to see my works praised by reviewers, as equal to the proudest productions of the scribbling sons of John Bull. But authors are always poor devils, and therefore Satan may take them. (qtd. in Bell 127)

Hawthorne felt that each professional opportunity presented intolerable limits and frustrations. A culture that seemed to offer each individual many choices in fact offered few acceptable or realizable ones. Hawthorne's letter precisely reflects its period and the difficulties a wide-open culture imposed on each individual.

Tocqueville noted and described these difficulties:

When all the privileges of birth and fortune are abolished, when all professions are accessible to all, and a man's own energies may place him at the top of any one of them, an easy and unbounded career seems open to his ambition and he will readily persuade himself that he is born to no common destiny. But this is an erroneous notion, which is corrected by daily experience. The same equality that allows every citizen to conceive these lofty hopes renders all the citizens less able to realize them; it circumscribes their powers on every side, while it gives freer scope to their desires. . . . they have opened the door to universal competition. . . . This constant strife between inclinations springing from the equality of condition and the means it supplies to satisfy them harasses and wearies the mind. (2:146)

Hawthorne's letter is one symptom of the exhausting paradox of democratic life: his confidence in his abilities was undercut by a deep uncertainty about how he could use them. Hawthorne's desire to be "rich enough to live without a profession" was a fantasy he shared with almost every American of his time (and perhaps of any subsequent time). In a rapidly expanding market society, all young men had to find or create a place for themselves, but this was a process fraught with turmoil, uncertainty, and intense pressure on the individual.

After the success of *The Scarlet Letter*, Hawthorne wrote to his friend Horatio Bridge that the "only sensible ends" of a literary career were, "First, the pleasurable toil of writing; second, the gratification of one's family and friends; and, lastly, the solid cash" (qtd. in Mellow 314). It was possible to balance creative satisfaction with professional success in nineteenth-century America, but, as with any professional venture, this balance was difficult for any one writer to maintain. The variety and vitality of the antebellum literary scene served readers and the cause of literature well, but this variety and vitality made it difficult to achieve or maintain preeminence. Hawthorne even admitted late in his career that if his novels had been written by someone else, he probably would not have read them through (Mellow 527).

Like other romantics, Hawthorne tried to give the appearance of living above trade, even though he was dependent on it. In his prefaces he habitually portrayed himself as a gentleman author without ties to the reading public:

> the public—if my limited number of readers, whom I may venture to regard rather as a circle of friends, may be termed a public. ("The Old Manse," *Tales* II49)

> nor was it until long after this period, if it even yet be the case, that the Author could regard himself as addressing the American Public, or, indeed, any Public at all. He was merely writing to his known or unknown friends. (preface to *Twice-told Tales* II51)

But early in his career he wrote plaintively to his wife-to-be: "Other persons have bought large estates and built mansions with such little books as I mean to write; so perhaps, it is not unreasonable to hope that mine may enable me to build a little cottage—or, at least, to buy or hire one. . . . Dearest, how much depends on these little books!" (qtd. in Mellow I88). Hawthorne's awareness of his competitors and his urgent sense of the connection between his work and his livelihood belie his later self-presentations. Ironically, Hawthorne presented himself as a nonprofessional "addressing a very limited circle of friendly readers, without much danger of being overheard by the public at large," in the prefaces to collections of tales he was reissuing to take advantage of the success of *The Scarlet Letter* (preface to *The Snow-Image* II54).

As Milton Stern writes, "Hawthorne had a considerable and appreciative select audience at the time he thought himself 'the obscurest man of letters in America'" (33). After his isolated apprenticeship and the anonymity of his early career as a sketch writer, the pose of neglected author had become habitual for Hawthorne. In the I851 preface to *Twice-told Tales*, Hawthorne presented himself as imprisoned by an earlier self-conception gone out of control. Having come "to be regarded as a mild, shy, gentle, melancholic, exceedingly sensitive, and not very forcible man," on the basis of his tales and sketches, Hawthorne was "by no means certain, that some of his subsequent productions have not been influenced and modified by a natural desire to fill up so amiable an outline, and to act in consonance with the character assigned him" (II53). Richard Brodhead's heartbreaking account of

Hawthorne's frustrating last years suggests that Hawthorne was one of the first American public figures to be victimized by his own celebrity, for celebrity is just as Hawthorne describes it here, the often unwilling substitution of a public image for a private sense of oneself.[1]

From the late 1830s on, Hawthorne's career was marked by a struggle between his romantic conception of the artist as a doomed solitary and his efforts to "open an intercourse with the world" (1152). In three stories from 1844, the year in which the birth of his first child triggered an intense crisis in his professional life, Hawthorne seems to have been extremely tempted by high romantic conceptions of the artist's role.[2] In "The Artist of the Beautiful," "Drowne's Wooden Image," and "A Select Party," he lamented the need for the artist to embody his vision at all, much as he had lamented the need to choose a profession at the beginning of his career. The stories express Hawthorne's desire to separate his work from commercial and professional pressures and to live above trade. The artists in these stories are trapped between their visions of themselves as inspired artists and their functional roles in society as craftsmen: Owen Warland is a watchmaker by trade, Drowne is a figurehead carver. Both find the commercial aspects of their work deadening; for Drowne, genius is only a source of frustration because it unfits him for his place in society. Drowne's one inspired creation is opposed to his ordinary figureheads, whose wooden appearance and allegoric tendencies recall Hawthorne's self-deprecating conception of his own work. Drowne recognizes that he lacks inspiration, and when he does achieve it, it only serves to expose the dull ordinariness of the rest of his work.

For Hawthorne, as for Shelley (whom Owen Warland strongly resembles), true works of art are contaminated when they are rendered in material form; "literature" is what happens in the author's mind and soul, not published work that he offers to the public. As Hawthorne wrote in "A Select Party," "it would not be too much to affirm that every author has imagined, and shaped out in his thought, more and far better works than those which actually proceeded from his pen" (955).[3] The narrator of "The Artist of the Beautiful" laments, "Alas, that the artist, whether in poetry or whatever other material, may not content himself with the inward enjoyment of the Beautiful, but must chase the flitting mystery beyond the verge of his ethereal domain, and crush its frail being in seizing it with material grasp" (916). Owen Warland must produce work, of course, but the narrator presents his "impulse to give external reality to his ideas" as a mysterious inner necessity, not as a response to professional or commercial pressure.

In "The Artist of the Beautiful" Hawthorne revealed how difficult it was for him to reconcile the claims of the democratic audience and literary professionalism with romantic conceptions of literary greatness: "It is requisite for the ideal artist to possess a force of character that seems hardly compatible with its delicacy; he must keep his faith in himself, while the incredulous world assails him with its utter disbelief; he must stand up against mankind and be his own sole disciple, both as respects his genius, and the objects to which it is directed" (913). In this story the sense of personal fortitude gives way to an arrogant judgment on the reading public. Hawthorne echoes Shelley's *Alastor* in this typical romantic opposition between artist and public: "The prophet dies; and the man of torpid heart and sluggish brain lives on" (924).[4] Even when the audience enjoys the artist's work it is not worthy of it: War- land "knew that the world . . . whatever praise might be bestowed, could never say the fitting word, nor feel the fitting sentiment which should be the perfect recompense of an artist who, symbolizing a lofty moral by a material trifle—converting what was earthly, to spiritual gold—had won the Beautiful into his handiwork. Not at this latest moment, was he to learn that the reward of all high performance must be sought within itself, or sought in vain" (928). Though later Haw- thorne would write to Bridge about the satisfactions of "solid cash," here "perfect recompense" can never take the form of "earthly gold," and the audience is criticized not because they are indifferent to the ar- tist's work, but because they buy it as they would any commodity.

American romantic writers were caught between their sense of themselves as an elite group and their dependence for a livelihood on the reading public. Hawthorne reflected this anxiety in "The Artist of the Beautiful":

"How strange it is," whispered Owen to himself, leaning his head upon his hand, "that all my musings, my purposes, my passion for the Beautiful, my consciousness of power to create it—a finer, more ethereal power, of which this earthly giant [Danforth] can have no conception—all, all, look so vain and idle, whenever my path is crossed by Robert Danforth! He would drive me mad, were I to meet him often. His hard, brute force darkens and confuses the spiritual element within me. (912)

Hawthorne's anxiety about the public led him to caricature it in Danforth, who represents Hawthorne's idea of the democratic public's utilitarian common sense and materialism. Aware that authors were directly dependent on the public's expectations, Hawthorne felt himself forced to walk an uneasy line between his romantic self-conception and the public appeal required for his professional survival.[5]

In his Preface to *Twice-told Tales*, Hawthorne argued that his tales were "his attempts, and very imperfectly successful ones, to open an intercourse with the world" (1152). But his attempt was an ambivalent one, undertaken in the wake of *The Scarlet Letter*'s unexpected success. Hawthorne's later creative collapse is prefigured in "The Custom House," when he discussed his sense of the emptiness of the literary career: "It is a good lesson—though it may often be a hard one—for a man who has dreamed of literary fame, and of making for himself a rank among the world's dignitaries by such means, to step aside out of the narrow circle in which his claims are recognized, and to find how utterly devoid of significance, beyond that circle, is all that he achieves, and all he aims at" (*Novels* 141). Hawthorne was skeptical of the romantic conceptions of literary work that he had advanced in the 1840s, but he could not reconcile himself to literary professionalism either. His final creative breakdown ironically coincided with his achievement of secure literary fame.

Hawthorne was one of the first American writers to be canonized, and his work was used to mark the separation between high and popular literature. As Evert and George Duyckinck noted in their 1855 *Cyclopaedia of American Literature*, "the whole retinue of literary reputation-makers fastened upon the genius of Hawthorne" (504). But as Hawthorne's work was elevated, his sense of detachment from his career and his period grew. His famous complaint in the preface to *The Mar-*

ble Faun that the United States had no past and no institutions for the novelist to work with has unaccountably been taken as an accurate description of the "thinness" of American antebellum life, when it is clearly the complaint of a man willfully insulated from the events of his times. Hawthorne wrote to George Ticknor in 1860, "Are times so terribly bad as people say? I have left off reading the newspapers and only know by hearsay that the Union is falling asunder" (qtd. in Ticknor, *Hawthorne* 253). In an 1864 *North American Review* retrospective on Hawthorne's career, George William Curtis found it odd that Hawthorne could find so little to write about during the "fierce debate" preceding the Civil War, and wondered that "our great romancer . . . looked at the American life of his time . . . and could see only monotonous sunshine," apparently unable to "see a Carolina slave-pen" or finding in it "only a tame prosperity" (Crowley 418–19). Behind Hawthorne's complaint was a deep creative impasse. He lacked a sense of being connected to an audience and had no feeling of being an active participant in the arrangements governing literary production in his time.

In a grateful letter to Fields, written when his career as a novelist was over (though he did not yet know it), Hawthorne expressed his continuing mystification about the terms of his success and his essentially passive attitude toward his professional career: "My literary success, whatever it has been, or may be, is the result of my connection with you. Somehow or other you smote the rock of public sympathy on my behalf, and a stream gushed forth in sufficient quantity to quench my thirst, though not to drown me" (qtd. in Ticknor, *Hawthorne* 254). Hawthorne was giving shape to the now-common idea that a publisher mediates between the literary genius and the public that threatens him. The public is seen as a mysterious force to be manipulated, not a set of human beings whose responses are necessary to the writer's work. Hawthorne could no longer write for this abstract audience, despite several attempts (one a romance about the elixir of life, which Hawthorne was clearly searching for in his own career). His late breakdown makes it appear that his habitual pose of solitary author addressing a small circle of friends was more than a wry conceit; it was a creative necessity that sustained him during his long apprenticeship and his brief period of success as a professional author.

Hawthorne revealed the precariousness of this pose and the pressures that made it necessary in a letter to Ticknor written when *The Marble Faun* was in press:

> I feel that I shall come before the public, after so long an interval, with all the uncertainties of a new author. If I were only rich enough, I do not believe I should ever publish another book, though I might continue to write them for my own occupation and amusement. But with a wing of a house to build, and my girls to educate, and Julian to send to Cambridge, I see little prospect of the "dolce far niente," as long as there shall be any faculty left in me. (qtd. in Ticknor, *Glimpses* 35)

At the end of his career Hawthorne invoked the same fantasy of independent wealth that he had invoked at the beginning, in the 1821 letter to his mother. In the preface to *The Marble Faun*, Hawthorne spoke one last time of addressing "that one congenial friend,—more comprehensive of his purposes, more appreciative of his success, more indulgent of his shortcomings, and, in all respects, closer and kinder than a brother,—that all-sympathizing critic, in short, whom an author never actually meets, but to whom he implicitly makes his appeal whenever he is conscious of having done his best" (*Novels* 853). Hawthorne now had a "sad foreboding" that this ideal reader was dead, and replaced by a mysterious Public: "The Gentle Reader, in the case of any individual author, is apt to be extremely short-lived; he seldom outlasts a literary fashion, and, except in very rare instances, closes his weary eyes before the writer has half done with him. If I find him at all, it will probably be under some mossy grave-stone, inscribed with a half-obliterated name, which I shall never recognize" (854). The tone is perhaps wry and self-disparaging, but the frustration underlying this passage was real: Hawthorne never completed another novel. No other American writer's career, including Melville's, ended so abruptly or dramatically.

Hawthorne's romantic stance became tragic when he turned readers into an abstract and hostile force whose tastes could not be discerned and whose pressure had to be resisted. If the audience is made into an abstraction, then addressing that audience becomes a barely sustainable performance in which the belief in the democratic potential of the audience is countered by a barely masked sense of futility about addressing them at all. The careers of romantic authors were often brief because it is difficult to address an audience whose importance—indeed, whose very reality—one has come to doubt. Hawthorne's premature burnout could have been predicted when he wrote, "What is the mystery of these innumerable editions of the 'Lamplighter,' and other books neither better nor worse?" (qtd. in Ticknor, *Hawthorne* 141). The key word here is *mystery*, for Hawthorne was puzzled throughout his career by the public and his relationship to it.

In 1847, Edgar Allan Poe criticized Hawthorne for his sense of isolation from the reading public: "But the simple truth is, that the writer who aims at impressing the people, is *always* wrong when he fails in forcing the people to receive the impression. How far Mr. Hawthorne has addressed the people at all, is, of course, not a question for me to decide. His books afford strong internal evidence of having been written to himself and his particular friends alone" (qtd. in Bank 177). Poe could pose this challenge to other American writers, because, as Lewis Simpson has written, Poe "lived more intimately in the America where literature was product and commodity than any other major writer of the nineteenth century" (147). But Poe was himself a self-divided figure caught between romantic conceptions of the artist and his professional functions as editor, writer, and critic. The strain of maintaining these competing self-conceptions marked Poe's life and work, and in part explains the irascibility of his criticism and the combination of melodrama and formal brilliance in his fiction and poetry.

Poe's critical stance shifted between that of the high romantic and the hard-headed professional craftsman. In the Drake-Halleck review of 1836, Poe replaced the confusion of professional life with an ordered, if marginal, space that the poet could rule: "If, indeed, there be any one circle of thought distinctly and palpably marked out from amid the jarring and tumultuous chaos of human intelligence, it is that evergreen and radiant Paradise which the true poet knows, and knows alone, as the limited realm of his authority—as the circumscribed Eden of his dreams" (*Complete* 864). Like Shelley, Poe tried to define a space in which the poet's power was unquestioned even if its actual effectiveness was small. The phrase "knows alone" is ambiguous in the same way that Shelley's phrase "unacknowledged legislator" is ambiguous: Poe's poet may have sole power over his realm only because it is a realm of one, just as Shelley's poet may legislate only insofar as he is unacknowledged. Yet Poe also accepted the claims of the market on the writer's work. In an 1841 review he argued, "is this an age—is this a day—in which it can be necessary even to advert to such considerations as that the book of the author is the property of the public, and that the issue of the book is the throwing down of the gauntlet to the reviewer?" (*Complete* 928). But Poe could also, like Blake, view the market as an environment "of the most virulent indignity, . . . untraceable slanders, . . . ruthless assassination in the dark," most of it directed against him.[6]

In the end, Poe took refuge, as Blake had, in the concept of genius, as this selection from the *Marginalia* reveals: "I have sometimes amused myself by endeavoring to fancy what would be the fate of any individual gifted, or rather accursed, with an intellect very far superior to that of his race. Of course, he would be very conscious of his superiority; nor could he . . . help manifesting his consciousness. Thus he would make himself enemies at all points" (*Complete* 1053). Poe, of course, succeeded in making numerous enemies, even though as late as 1846 he could pronounce this unintentionally ironic judgment on a fellow writer, Laughton Osborn: "He has no doubt been misapprehended, and therefore wronged by the world; but he should not fail to remember that the source of the wrong lay in his own idiosyncracy—one altogether unintelligible and unappreciable by the mass of mankind" (*Godey's Lady's Book*, June 1846; qtd. in Long 30). As Poe must have sensed, the concept of genius was growing increasingly difficult to use as an oppositional or consoling self-definition.

On the one hand, it was becoming domesticated. As E. J. Hobsbawm writes, the genius in bourgeois society was coming to represent "a non-financial version of individual enterprise, 'the ideal', which complemented and crowned material success and, more generally, the spiritual values of life" (*Age of Capital* 285). On the other hand, the concept was becoming a veil for the general inability to define literary greatness in a market environment or to explain why particular works succeeded or failed in the marketplace. In a review of Hawthorne's career, Henry Tuckerman revealed how unhelpful the concept could be: "There is a charm also essential to all works of genius which for want of a more definite term we are content to call the ineffable" (Bank 279). Tuckerman asserted that genius was beyond reason and accessible only to the "appreciative mind," but he succeeded only in revealing his professional anxiety about the arbitrariness of the literary marketplace.

Poe's sententious judgments and ad hoc theorizing were responses to this arbitrariness. In April 1849 he wrote in his *Marginalia*,

> Are our most deserving writers to be *forever* sneered down, or hooted down, or damned down with faint praise, by a set of men who possess little other ability than that which assures temporary success to *them*, in common with Swaim's Panaceas or Morrison's Pills? The fact is, some person should write, at once, a magazine paper . . . [on] why it is that ubiquitous quack[s] in letters can always "succeed," while *genius*, (which implies self-respect, with a scorn of creeping and crawling,) must inevitably succumb. (*Complete* 1053)

In the opposition between hack writers and geniuses, Poe's criticism explicitly unites what seemed separate in the polemics of Wordsworth and Coleridge: theory and invective. Poe wrote that the critic must have "a talent for analysis and a solemn indifference to abuse," a combination that reflected a market situation where professional disputes were disguised as philosophical arguments over the nature of literature. The formalism of Poe's literary theory and his isolation of an aesthetic realm were responses to a professional situation marked by intense competition for the existing audience. As David Long has written, Poe "privately craved a large audience," but in public he tried "to distinguish himself from British critics, from underqualified American authors, from the 'aristocracy of talent' that he sometimes celebrated— but most of all from the 'man of the crowd' that his occupation required him to be." Poe became obsessed with trying "to deny his affiliation with the mob and to differentiate himself from the democratic mass audience upon which he subsisted" (18, 36–37).

Poe tried to conciliate the mass audience with literary theories aimed at busy readers largely occupied with other pursuits. Many of Poe's famous critical pronouncements—that there is no such thing as a long poem, that the tale is preferable to the novel because its brevity promotes unity of effect—are of a piece with his sense of the age as an age of journalism in which people read magazines because they had no time for books. Yet his reader-centered theories of literature coexisted with a venom and snobbery that, like Coleridge's, was born of personal frustration.

Despite his immersion in the business of literature, Poe often idealized literature as unconnected to commercial or material concerns. In 1842 he defined poetry in Shelleyan fashion:

> It is the desire of the moth for the star. It is not the mere appreciation of the beauty before us. It is a wild effort to reach the beauty above. It is a forethought of the loveliness to come. It is a passion to be satiated by no sublunary sights, or sounds, or sentiments, and the soul thus athirst strives to ally its fever in futile efforts at *creation*. . . . the result of such effort, on the part of souls fittingly constituted, is alone what mankind have agreed to denominate Poetry. (*Complete* 939)

As Leslie Fiedler has remarked, the pathos of Poe's career and premature death was "not that [he] nobly refused to provide what the marketplace demanded, but that [he] tried to do so and failed" (30). Poe followed Shelley and Emerson in dealing with his frustration by separating the magnificent conception from the inevitably bungled execution.[7] Poe also followed Shelley in attempting to separate the didactic elements of a work from its literary elements; both men were attempting to create a specialized sphere that the poet could inhabit and dominate.

CHAPTER SIX

Emerson as a Cultural Spokesman

On the lecture platform and in his essays, Ralph Waldo Emerson exemplified the romantic writer for his American audience. He was an oracle, a sage, a prophet of the self against a confusing and hostile social order. At the same time, Emerson popularized this romantic conception in the United States by making it a paradigm for his work and that of later writers. For example, one of the first reviewers of Emily Dickinson in the 1890s alluded to Emerson to describe the poet's work: "That is an orphic utterance, no doubt; and such is all of this poet's work. She is, like Emerson, a companion for solitude, a stimulating comrade in the arduous intellectual ways" (Carman 66).

Considered radical early in his career, Emerson soon became a cultural spokesman. As the reviewer of Dickinson's poetry remarked, "it is quite true that he [Emerson] who was hailed as a sceptic and destroyer in his early career, was in reality a prophet and a founder" (Carman 66). What was it that Emerson founded? We have many reports of Emerson's charisma as a speaker. James Russell Lowell observed that "like all original men, [he] has his peculiar audience, and yet I know none that can hold a promiscuous crowd in pleased attention so long as he" (Konvitz 44). On the lyceum and lecture circuit, Emerson forged a style based on the sermon, aphorism, and proverb. His style was instantly recognizable, as this delightful send-up in the *Ohio State Journal* from January 1857 reveals:

> If a man has three friends, he will have four by counting himself one, and the same rule of addition would hold good if he had half a dozen. I called on a distinguished chemist the other day, and found him in the act of converting chicken salad into oyster pat-

ties. He told me it may easily be done by means of a leather retort and a guttapercha gridiron. Yet there are not more than sixty men in a century, or maybe sixty-five, who are seven feet nine, and half of those live in Boston. (Mead 40–41)

The parodist captures Emerson's transitionless style, his weave of homely anecdote and Orphic pronouncement, and his habit of leaving the reader with a sententious maxim to puzzle over.[1] By the 1850s Emerson's style was as popular as its sources, the sermon and proverb. One newspaper reviewer even praised Emerson with this complaint: "Ralph Waldo Emerson's lecture greatly disappointed all who listened. It was in the English language instead of the Emersonese in which he usually clothes his thoughts, and the thoughts themselves were such as any plain common-sense person could understand and appreciate" (*Hampshire and Franklin Express*, 18 Dec. 1857; qtd. in Sewall 115). However, many of Emerson's listeners could barely recollect what they heard of Emerson's actual thoughts. It was not what Emerson said but what he *was* that impressed listeners, and the way that his persona made them feel.

Emily Dickinson's sister-in-law had this to say about the same lecture that allegedly disappointed the Yankee reviewer: "I remember very little of the lecture except a fine glow of enthusiasm on my own part. . . . I felt strangely elated to take his transcendental arm afterward and walk leisurely home" (qtd. in Sewall 115). Hers was a typical response. In Lowell's view, "we do not go to hear what Emerson says so much as to hear Emerson" (Konvitz 45). Margaret Fuller agreed: "Many were satisfied to find themselves excited to congenial thought and nobler life, without an exact catalogue of the thoughts of the speaker" (Konvitz 22). Lowell said of Emerson's audiences, "what they do not fully understand they take on trust" (Konvitz 43). Emerson's peculiar genius was his ability to reach his audience by maintaining a gulf between himself and them.

William Dean Howells reported that, though he had not read much of Emerson, he nevertheless "had this sense of him, that he was somehow beyond and above my ken, a presence of force and beauty and wisdom, uncompanioned in our literature" (Howells 56). The young Abner Doubleday wrote to Emerson in 1845 to thank him for his *being*, not for his work: "why do I write to you at all—you who are way up there on that platform breathing a purer air than any to which I have attained. . . . But I still have a strong desire to thank you for existing" (*Collected Works* 3:xli). Audiences responded to Emerson because he gave the impression of being detached from the world and from them. Emerson had the aloofness befitting a wise man speaking to a culture of self-subsistent individuals.

Bronson Alcott spoke of Emerson's "pains to be impersonal or discreet, as if he feared any the least intrusion of himself were an offense offered to self-respect, [to] the courtesy due to intercourse and authorship." O. B. Frothingham elaborated on Alcott's remarks:

> To others this exquisite reserve, this delicate withdrawal behind his thought, has seemed not only one of Emerson's peculiar charms, but one of his most subtle powers. . . . in an age of personalities, voluntary and involuntary, the man who keeps his individual affairs in the background, tells nothing of his private history, holds in his own breast his petty concerns and opinions, and lets thoughts flow through him, as light streams through plate glass, is more than attractive—is noble, is venerable. To his impersonality in his books and addresses, Emerson owes perhaps a large measure of his extraordinary influence. (Konvitz 58)

Frothingham captured the way Emerson transformed his detachment from his audiences into spiritual power: "In the lecture room, he seems to be so completely under the spell of his idea, so wholly abstracted from his audience, that he is as one who waits for the thoughts to come, and drops them out one by one, in a species of soliloquy or trance. He is a bodiless idea. When he speaks or writes, the power is that of pure mind. The incidental, accidental, occasional, does not intrude" (Konvitz 58). The power Emerson held over his audiences resulted from the link between the effect he most wanted to create—that of presenting a fully formed and autonomous self to the public—and the feeling his public most wanted confirmed—that their alienation from each other and from the social forces that determined their lives was in fact liberating and not debilitating, power and not impotence.

When Doubleday thanked Emerson not for writing but for existing, he exemplified the striking coincidence between the romantic conception of the artist as someone whose consciousness was more important than his material work and the desire of the American public for writers and books to inspire them but not to alter the structure of their lives.[2]

Emerson's early criticism of religious and social practices rested on a deep agreement with his culture about the sanctity of private life and the necessity to protect the individual from contamination by society. *Contamination* is not too strong a word. When Emerson wrote to President Martin Van Buren to protest the removal of the Cherokee Indians from their land, he wrote in his journal that "this stirring in the philanthropic mud, gives me no peace" and spoke of other reformers with visceral disgust as men who "warm each other's skin and lubricate each other's tongue" at their misguided gatherings (*Journals* 5:479). Other members of the Transcendental Club, such as Theodore Parker, Orestes Brownson, and George Bancroft, felt compelled by the logic of their investigations to participate in politics or to call for new social arrangements, while Emerson maintained that a reformed society could proceed only from the renovated individual, the whole man.

This belief was fostered by capitalist culture and was already widespread in nineteenth-century American society in various versions: self-culture, individualism, the ideology of freedom and opportunity. The feeling of being separated from other men, from the forces that determine one's life, and from one's very self is the feeling that Emerson justified to his culture, on the lecture platform and in his essays, as "the infinitude of the private man" (*Journals* 7:342). The most celebrated observers of nineteenth-century American life all noted the conflict between the American belief in individualism, freedom, and opportunity, and the widespread feeling of helplessness and detachment from social reality that American social arrangements seemed to inspire. Tocqueville wrote: "When the inhabitant of a democratic country compares himself individually with all those about him, he feels with pride that he is the equal of any one of them; but when he comes to survey the totality of his fellows and to place himself in contrast with so huge a body, he is instantly overwhelmed by the sense of his own insignificance and weakness" (2:11). Later in the century, the Englishman James Bryce corroborated Tocqueville's observation, describing the United States as

> an enormously large and populous country, where the governing votes are counted by so many millions that each individual feels himself a mere drop in the ocean, the influence which he can exert privately, whether by his personal gifts or by his wealth, being confined to the small circle of his town or neighbourhood. On all sides there stretches round him an illimitable horizon; and beneath the blue vault which meets that horizon there is everywhere the same busy multitude with its clamour of mingled voices which he hears close by. In this multitude his own being seems lost. He has the same insignificance which overwhelms us when at night we survey the host of heaven, and know that from even the nearest fixed star this planet of ours is invisible. (2:349)

Both men remarked on the feeling that the nineteenth-century social environment was inhuman and hostile.

In the first chapter of *Nature* Emerson transformed this feeling of insignificance into a feeling of power by using the stars as a metaphor for a realm that is hospitable *because* it is solitary:

> To go into solitude, a man needs to retire as much from his chamber as from society. . . . if a man would be alone, let him look at the stars. The rays that come from those heavenly worlds, will separate between him and vulgar things.
>
> The stars awaken a certain reverence, because though always present, they are always inaccessible. (*Collected Works* 1: 8, 9)

The feeling of separation from the world and the detached perspective forced on individuals by capitalist social arrangements was the very perspective that Emerson recommended to his audience as the solution to social problems caused by those arrangements.

In *The American Scholar* Emerson argued that the scholar knows the world only when he sees that social upheavals such as war and economic dislocation are ephemera:

[I]t becomes him to feel all confidence in himself, and to defer never to the popular cry. He and he only knows the world. The world of any moment is the merest appearance. Some great decorum, some fetish of a government, some ephemeral trade, or war, or man, is cried up by half mankind and cried down by the other half, as if all depended on this particular up or down. The odds are that the whole question is not worth the poorest thought which the scholar has lost in listening to the controversy. Let him not quit his belief that a popgun is a popgun, though the ancient and honorable of the earth affirm it to be the crack of doom. (*Collected Works* 1:63)

In the panic year of 1837, when *The American Scholar* was delivered, Emerson's argument for the solidity of the spiritual world had force because the commercial world indeed appeared to be crumbling. In contrast to the irrational realm of trade, Emerson could offer to his public spiritual laws for the creation of a private self. Emerson's exhilaration at this coincidence between his deepest beliefs and the economic crisis pervades the journals of this period.

In a later essay, "The Poet," Emerson responded to the divisiveness of industrial capitalism as Wordsworth had, by positing an order to which the poet has access through his understanding of the whole man. Like Wordsworth in his later career, Emerson made this argument in spiritual terms:

For as it is dislocation and detachment from the life of God that makes things ugly, the poet, who re-attaches things to nature and the Whole,—re-attaching even artificial things and violation of nature, to nature, by a deeper insight,—disposes very easily of the most disagreeable facts. Readers of poetry see the factory-village and the railway, and fancy that the poetry of the landscape is broken up by these; for these works of art are not yet consecrated in their reading; but the poet sees them fall within the great Order not less than the beehive or the spider's geometrical web. (*Collected Works* 3: 11–12)

Elsewhere Emerson protested against the psychic fragmentation and material violence accompanying the progress of capitalism in nineteenth-century America, but in this passage his awareness of material dislocation and the pain it caused is "disposed of." The poet is no longer the man who protests but the man who "consecrates" social upheaval by subsuming it under a larger order, which is finally natural rather than social, divinely ordained rather than man-made.

Emerson found a receptive audience for this message because capitalist arrangements were far advanced in America. People already regarded the self as the cause of growth and change, while they thought of society as an external realm with its own incomprehensible laws. The unrestricted expansion of the American economy put severe pressure on individuals: not simply the pressure of seemingly inexplicable setbacks such as the panic of 1837, but the pressure to succeed in an impersonal competitive arena in which every man was forced to create himself. Austrian diplomat Baron von Hubner put more succinctly than Tocqueville or Bryce the paradox of opportunity and the psychic and material violence it inflicted on individuals: "North America offers an unlimited field of liberty to the individual. It does not only give him the opportunity: it forces him to employ all the faculties with which God has endowed him. The arena is open—as soon as he enters it he must fight, and fight to the death" (23). The Orwellian character of von Hubner's observation that freedom was coercion and self-creation in fact self-immolation makes clear the extent to which the paradoxes of Emerson's career were cultural paradoxes. The oscillation in his journals between exhilaration and self-doubt, his radical individualism and his desire to be subsumed in the One Mind, his detached perspective on society and his desire to merge with all men and the universe—all were representative reactions of individuals forced to accept the capitalist transformation of the concept of freedom.

As Tocqueville noted, "it is extremely difficult to obtain a hearing from men living in democracies, unless it is to speak to them of themselves" (2:274). In an early lecture, Emerson sounded the note that ensured his growing popularity: he described his times as "the Age of Severence, of Dissociation, of Freedom, of Analysis, of Detachment . . . the age of the first person singular" (*Early Lectures* 3: 188–89). Emerson's appeal to the Whole Man, like Wordsworth's before him, coincided with the general sense that the individual could achieve freedom only by escaping mass society and finding some private realm in the contemplation of Nature or the Self.[3]

In *The American Scholar* Emerson opposed the One Man to man's partial and crippling social functions, just as Wordsworth had done in the preface to the *Lyrical Ballads*. Yet, in his address, Emerson exposed a connection between his ideal and the culture's ideology and also revealed the tragic consequences that both imposed on the individual: "Another sign of our times, also marked by an analogous political movement, is the new importance given to the single person. Every thing that tends to insulate the individual,—to surround him with barriers of natural respect, so that each man shall feel the world is his, and man shall treat with man as a sovereign state with a sovereign state,— tends to true union as well as greatness" (*Collected Works* 1:68). The hopes Emerson expressed here are at once deconstructed by the language he used to express them: the insulated individual, surrounded by barriers, treating with his neighbors not as members of the same community but as foreign nations. Emerson's metaphors are infected by the brutalities of his times: nationalism, the growing antebellum threats to "true union," and the international tensions of the quest for national "greatness."

Emerson agreed with "the melancholy Pestalozzi" that "no man in God's wide earth is either willing or able to help any other man" (*Collected Works* 1:69), but he turned this utter social failure into a strength, the call for self-reliance and spiritual independence that so inspired his contemporaries. But those contemporaries haunt this passage of the address: they are the "Young men of the fairest promise . . . hindered from action by the disgust which the principles on which business is managed inspire, and turn drudges, or die of disgust, some of them suicides" (*Collected Works* 1:69). It is a terrible vision of disappointment and waste, all the more because of Emerson's silent complicity in these thwarted lives. For "the principles on which business is managed" were the same that Emerson outlined in this very passage: sovereign individuals competing for self-fulfillment in an ideological atmosphere where human arrangements and decisions were subsumed beneath the "natural laws" of capitalist society.

In Emerson, as in Wordsworth, the poet's work is to unite men isolated by current social and economic arrangements, but both writers found that they could effect such unions only through an imaginative act, not through actual social reform. In *The Ruined Cottage* Wordsworth imagined a brotherhood among men linked by the shared experience of isolation, a union that Wordsworth suggests can only come about within the imaginative structure of his poem. In "New England Reformers" Emerson raised a Wordsworthian paradox into a social principle:

> The union is only perfect, when all the uniters are isolated. It is the union of friends who live in different streets or towns. Each man, if he attempts to join himself to others, is on all sides cramped and diminished of his proportion; and the stricter the union, the smaller and more pitiful he is. But leave him alone, to recognize in every hour and place the secret soul, he will go up and down doing the works of a true member, and, to the astonishment of all, the work will be done with concert, though no man spoke. (*Collected Works* 3:157)

This is an apt if unwitting description of the mystified character of social relations under capitalism.

Emerson's greatest struggle as a writer was to keep himself separate from a social organization to which he was hostile and yet to define his work as of fundamental social importance. In Wordsworth, who had undertaken the same struggle, Emerson found a vocabulary he could use to argue that his private self-explorations possessed an unquestionable public validity. In *The American Scholar* Emerson echoed Wordsworth's preface to the *Lyrical Ballads* in order to claim that the poet "learns that in going down into the secrets of his own mind he has descended into the secrets of all minds. He learns that he who has mastered any law in his private thoughts, is master to that extent of all men whose language he speaks, and of all into whose language his own can be translated. The poet in utter solitude remembering his spontaneous thoughts and recording them, is found to have recorded that which men in crowded cities find true for them also" (*Collected Works* 1:63). The poet's ability to discover general feelings in his solitary state is not a mystery at all, for the pervasive individual experience under capitalist social arrangements is precisely that of feeling isolated and of experiencing isolation as power and independence from social constraints. The American poet could look into his own heart and discover secrets common to all men because in early nineteenth-century America, one feeling common to many was that of feeling alone in the mass society represented by the crowded city.

Emerson described the feeling of being alone in the crowd, which Hawthorne had chronicled so powerfully in "Wakefield," as a choice one could and should make, not as a social condition imposed on the individual. In "Self-Reliance" he wrote, " It is easy in the world to live after the world's opinion; it is easy in solitude to live after our own; but the great man is he who in the midst of the crowd keeps with perfect sweetness the independence of solitude" (*Collected Works* 2:31). Emerson's ideal, to carve out a private life in the midst of a social world that conspired against it, appealed to the nineteenth-century public because the "independence of solitude" was precisely the condition being experienced by men and women in a rapidly growing market economy, with its impersonal exchange relations and its emphasis on economic and cultural self-improvement.

Emerson defused the potentially subversive insight that the contemporary social order thwarted men by isolating them from each other by replacing it with the paradoxically soothing notion that the human condition is one of mutual isolation.[4] In 1837 he wrote in his journal under the heading "Society an imperfect Union," "Is it not pathetic that the action of men on men is so partial? We never touch but at points. Man is insular and cannot be touched. Every man is an infinitely repellent orb, and holds his individual being on that condition" (*Journals* 5:328). Tocqueville also saw that men in America only touched "at points," but he described this situation as the result of social relations that prevailed in an industrial economy, not as man's "natural" condition: "Not only are the rich not compactly united among themselves, but there is no real bond between them and the poor. Their relative position is not a permanent one; they are constantly drawn together or separated by their interests. The workman is generally dependent on the master, but not on any particular master; these two men meet in the factory, but do not know each other elsewhere; and while they come into contact at one point, they stand very far apart on all others (2:170). Emerson himself experienced this feeling of being cut off from other men ("Baulked soul!" *Journals* 5:328), but transformed the feeling into an affirmation of individual being that was humane in its defense of human wholeness yet tragic in its recapitulation of the experience of isolation.

Like Wordsworth, Emerson was a member of a cultural elite that felt itself threatened by the new industrial society. As William Charvat noted, Emerson's *American Scholar* "was essentially a plea to his own class to recapture cultural power and leadership by reforming its education and vitalizing its ideals" (*Profession* 65). In that address and in "The Poet" Emerson struggled to transform the literary man from someone with an increasingly marginal social function into a hero in the realm of consciousness, Life, and Power: "The poet alone knows astronomy, chemistry, vegetation and animation, for he does not stop at these facts, but employs them as signs. . . . By virtue of this science the poet is the Namer or Language-maker, naming things sometimes after their appearance, sometimes after their essence, and giving to every one its own name and not another's, thereby rejoicing the intellect, which delights in detachment or boundary" ("The Poet," *Collected Works* 3:23). Like Wordsworth, Emerson opposed Life to life lived in society and the poet's Power to the growing helplessness felt by individuals under the current social arrangements. He claimed to encompass all human life while diminishing the importance of particular social trends that were difficult to diagnose and ameliorate.

Perhaps Emerson's most explicit indictment of capitalist arrangements is to be found in the 1841 lecture "Man the Reformer," delivered to an audience of young members of the Mechanics' Apprentices' Library Association: "I do not charge the merchant or the manufacturer. The sins of our trade belong to no class, to no individual. One plucks, one distributes, one eats. Every body partakes, every body confesses,—with cap and knee volunteers his confession, yet none feels himself accountable. He did not create the abuse; he cannot alter it; what is he? an obscure private person who must get his bread. That is the vice,—that no one feels himself called to act for man, but only as a fraction of man" (*Collected Works* 1:148). In this lecture Emerson noted and criticized class strife, the division of labor, and the way a commercial society sunders man's "primary relations" with the world, his own work, and other men. His solution to these problems resembles the Jacksonian ideal of the yeoman farmer, but it also draws much from Wordsworth's 1802 preface to the *Lyrical Ballads*: "The power, which is at once spring and regulator in all efforts of reform, is faith in Man, the conviction that there is an infinite worthiness in him which will appear at the call of worth, and that all particular reforms are the removing of some impediment" (*Collected Works* 1:156). Here society is defined as a constraint that must be removed to allow Man to flourish, not as the only field in which human liberation can take place. In "Man the Reformer," Man is essentially the virtues of Emerson's Brahmin class writ large. Man is neither vulgar and grasping, like the members of the commercial class, nor duped by democratic ideology, like the members of the lower class: "The finished man should have a great prospective prudence, that he may perform the high office of mediator between the spiritual and actual world" (*Collected Works* 1:159). Like the Wordsworthian poet, Emerson spoke for Man by adopting a detached and contemplative perspective on social turmoil.[5]

Emerson's conception of Man finally posed little threat to his audience of rising men because his call to solve social ills through "self-help" and the restoration of "Faith and Hope," though spiritually moving, was finally conservative: a return to "absolute" values beneath social appearances (*Collected Works* 1: 155, 156). R. J. Wilson renders this harsh judgment: "What made the radicalism safe—and made it possible for Emerson to become a genteel institution in his own right after a time—was its civil inconsequence" (4). The "sublime prudence" advocated by Emerson was to subordinate social reform to individual self-culture, to postpone "always the present hour to the whole life" (*Collected Works* 1:160). Ironically, "Man the Reformer" ends with an image of capitalist practice invading the spiritual realm: "As the merchant gladly takes money from his income to add to his capital, so is the great man very willing to lose particular powers and talents, so that he gain in the elevation of his life" (*Collected Works* 1:160). The romantic abstraction Life is bought at the cost of leaving the diminished lives actually lived in society to run their course.

Emerson's relationship to his culture was an odd mixture of criticism and complicity, radical hostility and evident approval. As Carolyn Porter asserts, "taking an offensive rather than a defensive position in support of the whole man, [Emerson] was to end by sanctioning the actions of those very businessmen whose interests were served by the dominant culture" (112). Emerson reproduced in his very rejection of contemporary society the competitive and divisive social ideology that he attacked. In *The American Scholar* he wrote,

> Men in history, men in the world of to-day are bugs, are spawn, and are called "the mass" and "the herd." In a century, in a millenium, one or two men; that is to say, one or two approximations to the right state of every man. All the rest behold in the hero or the poet their own green and crude being,—ripened; yes, and are content to be less, so *that* may attain to its full stature. What a testimony, full of grandeur, full of pity, is borne to the demands of his own nature, by the poor clansman, the poor partisan, who rejoices in the glory of his chief. The poor and the low find some amends to their immense moral capacity, for their acquiescence in a political and social inferiority. They are content to be brushed aside like flies from the path of a great person, so that justice shall be done by him to that common nature which it is the dearest desire of all to see enlarged and glorified. (*Collected Works* 1:65)

Efforts have been made to rehabilitate this authoritarian strain in Emerson's thought, but it proceeds inevitably from his distinction between the individual and the mass. Emerson here reproduced the commonplace American belief that the successful man need not be trapped in a social order that diminishes everyone else; instead, the social order serves the successful man by providing the arena in which he rises above the masses by manipulating their desires. Emerson could never have become a man speaking to men on the lecture platform if this brutal scenario were not a generally accepted vision of American society. Far from hearing themselves condemned as mass society, Emerson's listeners felt themselves included in his descriptions of the individual struggling to free himself from its constraints.

By the time he wrote *Representative Men*, Emerson was using the ro-

mantic view propounded by Coleridge in the *Biographia Literaria* that
the writer had once been a sacred lawgiver but was now forced to ped-
dle his wares to the public:

> There have been times when [the writer] was a sacred person: he
> wrote Bibles; the first hymns; the codes; the epics. . . . Every word
> was true, and woke the nations to new life. He wrote without lev-
> ity, and without choice. Every word was carved before his eyes,
> into the earth and the sky. . . . But how can he [now] be honored,
> when he does not honor himself; when he loses himself in the
> crowd; when he is no longer the lawgiver, but the sycophant,
> ducking to the giddy opinion of a reckless public. (*Representative
> Men* 265)

Here the authoritarian wish beneath the democratic program surfaces.
If making contact with an actual audience on its own terms is syc-
ophancy, then the democratic wish to speak to all men has to be transformed into the romantic wish to speak as an unquestioned oracle.

The romantic conception of literature appealed to Emerson because
it confirmed his own conception of the artist as fundamentally detached from his society yet capable of altering it profoundly. In 1837 he
quoted Shelley with approval in his journal:

> The man of genius—Swedenborg or Carlyle, or Alcott, is ever, as
> Shelley says of his skylark,
>> "Like a Poet hidden
>>> In the light of thought,
>> Singing hymns unbidden
>>> Till the world is wrought
> To sympathy with hopes & fears it heeded not." (*Journals* 5:293)[6]

In "The Poet" Emerson continued to develop the romantic view of the
poet as one who is hidden yet heard, isolated but representative:

> the poet is representative. He stands among partial men for the
> complete man, and apprises us not of his wealth, but of the com-
> mon wealth. The young man reveres men of genius, because, to
> speak truly, they are more himself than he is. They receive of the

soul as he also receives, but they more. . . . . He is isolated among his contemporaries by truth and by his art, but with this consolation in his pursuits, that they will draw all men sooner or later. For all men live by truth and stand in need of expression. (*Collected Works* 3:4)

In Emerson the romantic faith in an audience of the future compensates for his feeling of separation from the current audience.

Emerson found it difficult to reconcile the demands facing the American writer with his romantic ideas about the nature of great literature. During one of his lecture tours he admitted that "the people are always right (in a sense) & . . . the man of letters is to say, these are the new conditions to which I must conform" (26 Jan. 1856, *Emerson in His Journals* 465). But he could never overcome his visceral disgust for mass society. He wrote in *Representative Men*, "enormous populations, if they be beggars, are disgusting, like moving cheese, like hills of ants, or of fleas—the more, the worse" (20). Emerson could never make up his mind about the social conditions of literary work. In *Representative Men* he wrote, "It is easy to see that what is best written or done by genius, in the world, was no man's work, but came by wide social labor, when a thousand wrought like one, sharing the same impulse" (197). But in "Culture" he wrote, "'T is very certain that Plato, Plotinus, Archimedes, Hermes, Newton, Milton, Wordsworth, did not live in a crowd, but descended into it from time to time as benefactors" (*Collected Works* 6:156). He tried to resolve the conflict by arguing a paradox familiar from Wordsworth and Shelley: "The saint and poet seek privacy to ends the most public and universal" (*Collected Works* 6:157). But in *Representative Men* he lamented the fact that Shakespeare, the world's greatest poet, "led an obscure and profane life, using his genius for the public amusement" (215). Emerson was appalled by the possibility that the greatest writer in English owed his achievement as well as his livelihood to his relationship with a vital contemporary audience.

In opposing great literature to popular work, Emerson repeated the conventional romantic abstraction of literature from its contemporary existence in books and magazines. True books "are not to be held by letters printed on a page, but are living characters translatable into every tongue and form of life. These are Scriptures which the missionary might well carry" ("Books," *Collected Works* 7:219). The tension between the American writer's responsibility to address the people and the romantic desire to recast the writer as a powerful oracle is built into the very conception of *Representative Men*: all but one of Emerson's "great men" are writers. The work is a fantasy of undisputed cultural hegemony, of Shelley's unacknowledged legislators finally receiving their due. In his essay "Books," Emerson defined great literature ("all books that get fairly into the vital air of the world") as "the majestic expressions of the universal conscience, . . . more to our daily purpose than this year's almanac or this day's newspaper. But they are for the closet, and to be read on the bended knee" (*Collected Works* 6: 195, 219). Emerson imagined the scholar as free of time and circumstance, "the man of ages" who "must also wish with other men to stand well with his contemporaries" (*Representative Men* 261). He is in the crowd but not of it.

Rather than resign himself to participating in a profession that demanded some degree of engagement with the mass audience, Emerson defined himself (and all true intellectual work) as apart from professional arrangements:

> Law of copyright and international copyright is to be discussed, and in the interim we will sell our books for the most we can. Expediency of literature, reason of literature, lawfulness of writing down a thought, is questioned; much is to say on both sides, and, while the fight waxes hot, thou, dearest scholar, stick to thy foolish task, add a line every hour, and between whiles add a line. . . . Life itself is a bubble and a skepticism, and a sleep within a sleep. . . . heed thy private dream; thou wilt not be missed in the scorning and skepticism; there are enough of them; stay there in thy closet and toil until the rest are agreed what to do about it. ("Experience," *Collected Works* 3: 37–38)

Like Longfellow, Emerson was a successful professional who pretended to be above professional debates. In *Representative Men* he described the literary life in Shakespeare's time as a golden age of authorship free from marketplace demands:

Shakspeare knew that tradition supplies a better fable than any invention can. . . . at that day, our petulant demand for originality was not so much pressed. There was no literature for the million. The universal reading, the cheap press, were unknown. A great poet, who appears in illiterate times, absorbs into his sphere all the light which is any where radiating. . . . He is therefore little solicitous whence his thoughts have been derived; . . . from whatever source, they are equally welcome to his uncritical audience. (*Representative Men* 194)

Emerson's targets are literary professionalism and the mass reading public. He did not trust the mass audience and resented its demands (even when it demanded the originality that he demanded of himself). He imagined a passive and uncritical audience in place of the existing reading public, and replaced the professional arrangements of the nineteenth century, such as copyright and literary property, with an idealized situation in which literature was not mediated by commerce.

Like so many romantic thinkers, Emerson "liberated" men from social programs and from the historical and even personal ties to other men that we often view as giving human life meaning, and then claimed to be embarked on a quest for the meaning of life. Emerson's vision of poetry and his vision of history were responses to a social order that promised unlimited freedom to all while imposing on each the hidden constraints of a competitive system. Because the individual must aspire to the unattainable goals that the ideology of freedom promises, the most common experience available to individuals will be that of being thwarted.

Tocqueville could see that many nineteenth-century Americans were afflicted by the contradiction between the ideology of opportunity and the frustrations imposed by "universal competition" and the "constant strife" that "harasses and wearies the mind" by defining as unsatisfactory any goal that might be realized. Success, he wrote,

perpetually retires from before them, yet without hiding itself from their sight, and in retiring draws them on. At every moment they think they are about to grasp it; it escapes at every moment from their hold. They are near enough to see its charms, but too far off to enjoy them; and before they have fully tasted its delights, they die.

In democratic times enjoyments are more intense than in the ages of aristocracy, and the number of those who partake in them is vastly larger; but, on the other hand, it must be admitted that man's hopes and desires are oftener blasted, the soul is more striken and perturbed, and care itself more keen. (2:147)

In *Nature* Emerson counseled each person to build his own world, while redefining the actions of men in the existing world as irrelevant follies. In "Spiritual Laws" he elaborated on this advice by putting forward his apparent inaction as true action: "We call the poet inactive, because he is not a president, a merchant, or a porter. . . . But real action is in silent moments. . . . I see action to be good, when the need is, and sitting still to be also good. . . . Why should we be busy-bodies and superserviceable? Action and inaction are alike to the true" (*Collected Works* 2: 93, 94). Yet in "Experience," which could be described as an essay about being thwarted, Emerson lamented the consequences of inactivity: "Very mortifying is the reluctant experience that some unfriendly excess or imbecility neutralizes the promise of genius. We see young men who owe us a new world, so readily and lavishly they promise, but they never acquit the debt; they die young and dodge the account; or if they live they lose themselves in the crowd" (*Collected Works* 3:30). Though the experience of being thwarted was a general one, Emerson blames the young men for their individual failures, repeating his culture's refusal to recognize that the current social structure guaranteed frustration for most.

That irony eventually returned to haunt Emerson in a famous passage from his eulogy for Thoreau:

Had his genius been only contemplative, he had been fitted to his life, but with his energy and practical ability he seemed born for great enterprise and for command; and I so much regret the loss of his rare powers of action, that I cannot help counting it a fault in him that he had no ambition. Wanting this, instead of engineering for all America, he was the captain of a huckleberry-party. Pounding beans is good to the end of pounding empires one of these days; but if, at the end of years, it is still only beans! (*Complete Works* 10:480)

The passage contradicts all of Emerson's major pronouncements on the sanctity of the private self and contemplation as a kind of action; it can thus be interpreted as a sharp if unconscious self-criticism. Emerson put forward Thoreau's virtues—"great enterprise" and "command"—as the virtues befitting a captain of industry. In doing so Emerson revealed the link between the very values that thwart the "young men of fairest promise" mentioned in *The American Scholar* and the self-contradictory cultural values that Emerson himself upheld, "the principles on which business is managed": individualism, self-fulfillment, and the competition that prevented the majority of citizens from being either whole or fulfilled. In the eulogy for Thoreau, one of the young men who owed us a new world, Emerson explicitly refuted his own contention that the scholar's inaction is a higher action. The private fruit is at last only beans.

In the face of the new social order, Emerson articulated a powerful fantasy already shared by the members of his culture: that the face-to-face relations of private domestic life were the highest social good because they were apart from society as it was currently constituted. The act of "tending one's garden" was transfigured by common consent into the highest form of social responsibility. In this respect Emerson was like other Victorian spokesmen and critics such as Dickens.[7] "Self-Reliance," Emerson's most positive assertion of the power of self, was also his most confident call to keep it independent of society: "At times the whole world seems to be in conspiracy to importune you with emphatic trifles. Friend, client, child, sickness, fear, want, charity, all knock at once at thy closet door and say,—"Come out unto us." But keep thy state; come not into their confusion. The power men possess to annoy me I give them by a weak curiosity. No man can come near me but through my act. 'What we love that we have, but by desire we bereave ourselves of the love'" (*Collected Works* 2:41). This message strongly appealed to a culture of individualists who felt detached from each other's common fate. But the freedom of the self to create its own world could give way without warning to its twin, the despair of being trapped in an impersonal world.

The conflict between Emerson's passivity toward the social world and his status as a public figure led him to some of his most tortured formulations of social responsibility. Stephen Whicher has pointed out how the reform movements posed a challenge to Emerson's belief that the private self could transform society (72). But far from altering his fundamental thinking, the reformers drove Emerson to more and more strenuous restatements of his belief in the inviolability of the private self.

For example, in his 1844 address on "New England Reformers," he stated, "If therefore we start objections to your project, O friend of the slave, or friend of the poor, or of the race, understand well, that it is because we wish to drive you to drive us into your measures. We wish to hear ourselves confuted. We are haunted with a belief that you have a secret, which it would highliest advantage us to learn, and we would force you to impart it to us, though it should bring us to prison, or to worse extremity" (*Collected Works* 3:163). Emerson's claim that by resisting the reformers he was really aiding them reveals the tremendous inertia beneath his spiritual radicalism. In this passage Emerson internalized all society's resistance to change. He pretends that reformers "have a secret" that they should reveal to him, though they were acting on issues that Emerson understood perfectly well and basing their actions on principles that he himself articulated. He claims to be willing to risk prison or worse if this secret is revealed, though the thrust of the passage is to shift responsibility for social change to others. Emerson's attitude toward reform in this passage is precisely that of his culture. The individual's duty when faced with a moral challenge is merely to challenge others to goad him out of his inertia if they can. This passage represents Emerson's difficulty in acting on social issues, even those about which he felt strongly.

Emerson's war with himself is evident in the famous journal passage describing his refusal to join Brook Farm:

> I wished to be convinced, to be thawed, to be made nobly mad by the kindlings before my eyes of a new dawn of human piety. And

not once could I be inflamed, but sat aloof and thoughtless; my
voice faltered and fell. . . . It was not the cave of persecution which
is the palace of spiritual power, but only a room in the Astor
House hired for the Transcendentalists. I do not wish to remove
from my present prison to a prison a little larger. I wish to break all
prisons. I have not yet conquered my own house. (*Journals* 7:407)

Emerson admits to the "cold selfpossession" that he had once lamented, then begins to compensate for it with theory and apocalyptic
fantasy. Ironically, he found himself voiceless when confronted with an
actual plan of action. His weak objection that the Brook Farm plan was
"merely" a group of his friends in a hotel room leaves the actual transformation of society, for good or ill, to other people in other hotel
rooms, boardrooms, or capitols. But the deeper tragedy of the passage
is that, by opposing the hotel room to the realm of the mind that he
wished to inhabit, Emerson repressed his actual instincts, which were
"to be convinced, to be thawed, to be made nobly mad," in favor of his
theory of withholding himself from society, which left him aloof, passive, and silent. Just as the criticism of Thoreau was a buried self-criticism, here the desire to break all prisons is an admission that actual
prisons are unassailable on Emersonian terms.

Much of Emerson's appeal to his audience was the air he possessed
of transcending social and historical turmoil. A German reader, Her-
mann Grimm, recorded a typical response to Emerson: "I look on with
wonder to see how the hurly-burly of modern life subsides, and the elements gently betake themselves to their allotted places" (Konvitz 51). It
may be that few writers have achieved so precisely the effect they intended to create, for Emerson recommended his perspective on the
world for the reasons cited by Grimm:

As soon as a man is wonted to look beyond surfaces, . . . he settles
himself into serenity. He can rely on the laws of gravity, that every
stone will fall where it is due; the good globe is faithful, and carries
us securely through the celestial spaces, anxious or resigned: we
need not interfere to help it on, and he will learn, one day, the mild
lesson they teach, that our own orbit is all our task, and we need

not assist the administration of the universe. ("New England Reformers," *Collected Works* 3:166)

Emerson's detached perspective on events minimized the importance
of social conflict by claiming to put it "in proper perspective," even
while affirming as progress the economic expansion that led to conflict.
Inaction came to seem like mature, reasoned contemplation rather
than indecisiveness or acquiescence, and by the time Emerson wrote
"Fate," his vocation as a writer was inseparable from his admission that
"we are incompetent to solve the times" (*Complete Works* 6:3).

Emerson himself seems to have recognized how complicity with his
culture haunted his attacks on it. In a startling journal passage from
1839 he wrote, "Am I a hypocrite who am disgusted by vanity everywhere, & preach self trust every day? We give you leave to prefer your
work to the whole world so long as you remain in it" (*Journals* 7:191).
The paradox of Emerson's relationship to his culture is explicit here: by
advocating that each person build his own world, he in fact affirmed
the existing world, which did not simply tolerate him but accepted him
as its sage. The asocial quality of his thought was itself a product of
bourgeois culture, in which the individualism that Emerson celebrated
and the vanity that disgusted him were aspects of the same self viewed
in two moods. In an eerie dream recorded in his journal, Emerson confronted the degree to which his protest was itself informed by the culture he criticized: "In my dream I saw a man reading in the library at
Cambridge, and one who stood by said, 'He readeth advertisements,'
meaning that he read for the market only and not for truth. Then I
said—Do I read advertisements?" (*Journals* 7:327). Emerson the poet-
preacher searching for absolute truth and Emerson the platform
speaker justifying his culture to itself here recognize that they are one
and the same.

CHAPTER SEVEN

Melville as a
Professional Writer

During Melville's working lifetime, two conceptions of literary work were common: the American writer could be either a professional working for the growing reading public or a romantic genius working to satisfy his own impulses. Every student of Melville knows that he felt pressed to choose one conception or the other: "What I feel most moved to write, that is banned, it will not pay. Yet, altogether write the *other* way I cannot. So the product is a final hash, and all my books are botches" (*Letters* 128). What Melville laments here as a weakness was in fact his great strength. I do not mean that he refused to give in to the public's demand to write "the other way." His great strength was to refuse to give in completely to the idea of romantic genius that he found powerfully tempting. Melville did not stop thinking of himself as a professional writer after *Mardi* and *Moby-Dick*, though his romantic ideas about critics, publishers, and readers made thinking of himself as a professional more difficult.

The most interesting phase of Melville's career for the present purpose is the three years he spent writing for magazines. Melville began writing magazine stories the year after publishing *Pierre* (1852), a bitter attack on the female reading public and on Melville's friends in the New York publishing world. The period ends when Melville began work on *The Confidence-Man* (1857), a novel that assaults contemporary readers' tastes and expectations, and yet one that contains several chapters of apologia (chaps. 14, 33, 44) and a plea for understanding that seems heartfelt: "Though every one knows how bootless it is to be in all cases vindicating one's self, never mind how convinced one may be that he is never in the wrong; yet, so precious to man is the approbation of his kind, that to rest, though but under an imaginary censure applied to but a work of imagination, is no easy thing" (*Pierre, Israel Potter* 1038). Though *Pierre* and *The Confidence-Man* have both been read as parting shots, there is no point in Melville's career where we can say that he gave up on the audience once and for all. His magazine stories tell us something about his ambivalent but persistent commitment to literary professionalism.

When he turned to magazine fiction, Melville was not rejecting the reading public but choosing to work in a popular genre whose practitioners were well paid. The stories he wrote are often about the role of the writer in nineteenth-century America. Even the slightest of the stories, such as "The Fiddler," are interesting to the student of the literary career in America, while others, such as "Bartleby, the Scrivener," are among Melville's greatest works. The magazine years recapitulate Melville's earlier career as a fiction writer and anticipate his later career as a poet, for during these years he produced a substantial but uneven body of work, much of it focused on the issue of writing for the public versus writing for himself.

Every one of Melville's famous attacks on the reading public was followed by some attempt to reconcile his work with the public's expectations. Even *The Confidence-Man* was followed by three seasons of lecturing, an activity even more public and professionalized than fiction writing. Melville is traditionally seen as a romantic genius struggling to maintain his integrity in a corrupt literary marketplace. In fact, he achieved his best work when he tempered his romantic self-conceptions with attempts to reach the existing audience and to articulate the public and professional responsibilities of the writer. Despite the urgency with which Melville assumed the romantic posture in the years after *Mardi*, he continued to produce works in popular forms such as the magazine story and to publish them with commercial firms such as Harper's and Putnam's that served large numbers of readers. In the supposedly silent years after *The Confidence-Man*, Melville published several volumes of verse, including *Battle-Pieces and Aspects of the War* with Harper and Brothers and *Clarel* with Putnam's. Melville's career would have been far less interesting, and probably less productive, if he had simply retreated into the romantic posture of the neglected genius that he adopted in *Mardi* (to declare himself a serious artist) and returned to in *Pierre* (to explain his professional difficulties). Melville's admirers since Hawthorne have noted that he could not rest content with any single intellectual position. That courageous restlessness also applies to his idea of himself as a writer and artist.

At the time Melville wrote *Mardi*, he was a writer with two recently successful works, an eager public, and powerful friends in the publishing world. As soon as he began to think of himself as an artist, he began to think of his readers as an uncomprehending and hostile mass, even before he had any proof that his work would fail with the public.

There are hints in Melville's letters that he was uncomfortable with the romantic attitude toward literary work. In a letter to Richard Bentley, his British publisher, Melville adopted the posture of the great author who will be discovered by posterity: "Your report concerning 'Mardi' was pretty much as I expected; but you know perhaps that there are goodly harvests which ripen late, especially when the grain is remarkably strong. At any rate, . . . let us by all means lay this flattering unction to our souls, since it is so grateful a prospect to you as a publisher, & to me as an author" (*Letters* 87). But he catches himself being flippant and resumes the professional tone of his earlier communications with John Murray, Bentley, and others: "I need not assure you how deeply I regret that, for any period, you should find this venture of 'Mardi' an unprofitable thing for you" (*Letters* 87). Later in the year Melville again tempered his romantic posturing in a letter to his father-in-law, Lemuel Shaw. Everyone knows his statement, "it is my earnest desire to write those sort of books which are said to 'fail,'" but no one quotes the self-deflating qualification that follows: "Pardon this egotism" (*Letters* 92). Here romantic independence at once gives way to Melville's sense of his professional dependence on the public who pays him. Writing to Shaw, who had loaned him money, must have made Melville acutely aware of the conflict between his romantic pose and his actual circumstances. In a capitalist and democratic culture Melville could not forget his dependence on dollars and readers.

In "Hawthorne and His Mosses" the conflict between romantic artist and democratic public is explicit. "Hawthorne and His Mosses" is a complete catalog of romantic denunciations of the nineteenth-century literary institution and its terms.[1] Melville condescends to "the mere critic" and questions the worth of "mere mob renown" (*Pierre, Israel Potter* 1159, 1160). He divides readers into two classes, those "at all capable of fully fathoming" great literature and the majority who cannot. In one sentence he speaks both as democratic writer and as romantic artist, first asking the reader to "read any canto in 'The Faery Queen', and then read 'A Select Party', and decide which pleases you the most," then restricting his invitation to those "qualified to judge" (1169). Melville repeats the romantic arguments that true literature will never be accessible to the public because it appears and recedes according to mysterious laws of its own. Like Shelley in the preface to *Prometheus Unbound* and Hawthorne in "The Custom House," Melville defines the artist as a tantalizing dead man whose spirit is hinted at but never captured in his work: "In Shakespeare's tomb lies infinitely more than Shakespeare ever wrote" (1160).

The problem that Melville confronted but could not resolve in "Hawthorne and His Mosses" was not how to achieve literary fame or even popularity, but how to define literature in a market system that accommodated both serious work and entertaining diversions, truthtellers and storytellers, geniuses and sentimentalists. The American writer was confronted not so much by narrow audience expectations as by a situation in which expectations were not clearly defined and success was as unpredictable as failure. Melville, it must be remembered, had already achieved popular success as a novelist, but was learning to belittle that success, just as Longfellow would do.

Longfellow appealed to Michelangelo, while Melville invoked Shakespeare in his attempt to resolve the conflict between literary professionalism and romantic genius: "Nor must we forget, that, in his own lifetime, Shakespeare was not Shakespeare, but only Master William Shakespeare of the shrewd, thriving, business firm of Condell, Shakespeare & Co., proprietors of the Globe Theater in London" (*Pierre, Israel Potter* 1162). The passage reveals Melville's anxiety over his own creative identity: even Shakespeare "was not Shakespeare" in his own time—that is, he was not the literary immortal of uncontested genius that Melville longed to be. In fact, in his own time, Shakespeare was not a literary artist at all, but a businessman whom Melville defines according to nineteenth-century American terms of success: shrewd, thriving, a partner in a successful concern. Melville was just as troubled as Emerson by the thought of Shakespeare "using his genius for the public amusement." In "Hawthorne and His Mosses" Melville tried to define himself as a writer accepted by the democratic market society but independent of the market's judgments.

In his letters of this period, Melville consistently separated published work from truly creative work. In the November 1851 letter to Hawthorne in which he first mentioned *Pierre* ("I have heard of Krakens"), he coyly directed Hawthorne toward the correct romantic response to *Moby-Dick*: "You did not care a penny for the book. But, now and then as you read, you understood the pervading thought that impelled the book—and that you praised. Was it not so? You were archangel enough to despise the imperfect body, and embrace the soul" (*Letters* 142). A year earlier Melville described himself to Evert Duyckinck as bursting with ideas for books but uncertain about whether his ideas could survive as published products: "But I dont know but a book in a man's brain is better off than a book bound in calf—at any rate it is safer from criticism." Melville wondered if producing an actual book finally "may not be worth the trouble" (*Letters* 117).

The combination of creative exhilaration and professional uncertainty is especially evident in the letters of early 1851. In February of that year Melville was confident enough in his new romantic self-conception (and, as Hershel Parker points out, irritated enough with his friend Evert Duyckinck's failure to understand it) to divorce himself aggressively from the literary world represented by Duyckinck. In response to Duyckinck's request for a sea story and a portrait for one of his magazines, Melville wrote,

> I can not write the thing you want. I am in the humor to lend a hand to a friend, if I can;—but I am not in the humor to write the kind of thing you need—and I am not in the humor to write for Holden's Magazine. If I were to go on to give you all my reasons—you would pronounce me a bore, so I will not do that. You must be content to beleive [*sic*] that I *have* reasons, or else I would not refuse so small a thing.—As for the Daguerreotype . . . that's

what I can not send you, because I have none. And if I had, I would not send it for such a purpose, even to you. . . . The fact is, almost everybody is having his "mug" engraved nowadays; so that this test of distinction is getting to be reversed; and therefore, to see one's "mug" in a magazine, is presumptive evidence that he's a nobody. (*Letters* 120–21)

The letter is a direct and no doubt unexpected attack on Duyckinck's conception of literary work. Duyckinck had little or no reason to believe that Melville thought of himself as anything but a professional author—*Moby-Dick* was not yet published—and he can be forgiven for offering Melville work. But in this letter Melville started to kick himself loose from the existing literary world.[2] He offered his condescending assessment of Hawthorne ("He doesn't patronise the butcher"), and qualified his praise of Hawthorne's "quality of genius, immensely loftier, & more profound, too, than any other American has shown hitherto" by noting that Hawthorne's genius appeared "in the printed form." Given Melville's state of mind at the time, he could only be implicating Hawthorne in the current literary institution that conspired against true geniuses, who keep their masterpieces "in the brain," not bound in calf to be sold to the vulgar public.[3]

Melville's professional frustrations are dramatized in the later books of *Pierre*, but the whole plot of the novel reproduces Melville's high romantic conception of literary work. Pierre must hide his truth from the world just as *Pierre* hides its truth from the audience. But Pierre hides the truth most pointedly from his mother. Pierre's relationship to Mrs. Glendinning is exactly *Pierre*'s relationship to the reading public. The cloying banter between Pierre and his mother in the novel's opening pages masks Pierre's distrust of his mother and his eventual contempt for her, just as the novel's excruciating style was Melville's attempt to mask his hostility toward his audience and his distaste for the task of writing a novel for women.[4]

Mrs. Glendinning is Melville's caricature of the nineteenth-century reading public: female, leisured, prudish, hypocritical, and unable to face dark truths. After Pierre discovers Isabel, he half-conceals and half-reveals the fact to his mother—precisely the literary strategy that

Melville outlined in "Hawthorne and His Mosses." The strategy, of course, alienates his mother and at the same time fails to enlighten her, an ironically accurate foreshadowing of the public's response to *Pierre*. Pierre behaves cryptically toward his mother because he assumes that she will reject the truth just as Melville had assumed since *Mardi* that his audience would reject his more daring experiments. Pierre's self-righteous posture is the stance of the romantic artist: "He who shall be totally honest, though nobler than Ethan Allen; that man shall stand in danger of the meanest mortal's scorn" (130).

The most remarkable thing about *Pierre* was that it did not bring Melville's career to an end. It damaged his reputation, but it was not his farewell to his career as a professional author, as critics once supposed. Melville realized that the romantic posture that informed *Pierre* was a creative as well as a professional dead end, and he soon began to search for a more productive stance toward his audience. In his letter to Bentley of 16 April 1852, written after *Pierre* was finished, Melville implied that he had doubts about the new book and wanted to maintain his career as a professional writer on the very terms he mocked in *Pierre*. He misrepresented the book spectacularly as being "very much more calculated for popularity than anything you have yet published of mine" (*Letters* 150), but he also tried to dissociate himself from the novel by suggesting that it be published under an assumed name. If Melville was persuaded that the portrait of the artist he presented in *Pierre* was a true one, he could simply have stopped writing for the market. Instead, he published the book in the hope that it might interest the reading public after all and perhaps even be a financial success (*Letters* 149–50). After *Pierre* failed, Melville had to admit that it was impossible to write from the adversarial stance he adopted in *Pierre*, and began to search for an alternative.

Melville soon discovered a genre that was both popular and suited to his talents, the magazine story. At this point in his career, when he must have been trying to determine what direction, if any, he could take, *Putnam's* published a long and for the most part favorable discussion of Melville's career from *Typee* to *Pierre*. The February 1853 article by Fitz-James O'Brien, "Our Young Authors—Melville," was a friendly and often astute piece of criticism in which O'Brien used a reading of *Pierre* to analyze the impasse Melville had reached. O'Brien quoted Keats's preface to *Endymion*: "The imagination of a boy is healthy, and the mature imagination of a man is healthy, but there is a space of life between, in which the soul is in ferment, the character undecided, the way of life uncertain, the ambition thick-sighted" (Branch 328). This is an apt description of the crisis that Melville had just experienced and chronicled in *Pierre*. O'Brien sensed that Melville was writing himself into a position that made future work impossible, and warned, "Of his last book [*Pierre*] we would fain not speak, did we not feel that he is just now at that stage of author-life when a little wholesome advice may save him a hundred future follies" (Branch 328).

O'Brien's advice is presented in the nineteenth-century critical voice that modern readers find smug and irritating. It seems unforgivably presumptuous to us for a critic to offer prescriptions to a great writer. But nineteenth-century critics such as O'Brien assumed that the writer's work was to establish some sort of connection between his point of view and the reader's—the same assumption underlying large sections of *Moby-Dick*. He attacked *Pierre* because it at first established no clear relationship with its readers, and then attacked them: "When we first read *Pierre*, we felt a strong inclination to believe the whole thing to be a well-got-up hoax . . . [like] *The Abbess*, in which the stilted style of writing is exposed very funnily" (Branch 328). O'Brien concludes the essay with the often-quoted and often-derided advice to Melville to read less Thomas Browne and more Addison. But this advice is not the product of well-intentioned ignorance or smug superiority; the nineteenth-century reviewer believed that criticism was a dialogue between the author and a critic who speaks for readers.

Nineteenth-century critics such as O'Brien who seem condescending were in fact taking Melville's career very seriously. They assumed that he would read their reviews to find out how actual readers were receiving his work. By October 1852 Melville had received the flattering circular inviting him to contribute to the new *Putnam's*. Hershel Parker has pointed out that O'Brien's review may have encouraged Melville to accept the invitation.[5] During the course of the winter Melville decided that he would write for magazines, and for three years he was a regular contributor to *Harper's*, his publishers' magazine, and to *Putnam's*.

These magazines were among the most interesting and successful of antebellum literary experiments. *Harper's*, in which one of Melville's earliest stories, "Cock-A-Doodle-Do!" appeared, was dedicated by its founder to "the plain people . . . not philosophers and poets" (qtd. in Charvat, *Profession* 279–80). The magazines combined a popular stance with high quality by publishing the best British and American authors, including writers such as Melville whose reputation was uncertain but whose work their editors respected. In addition, as Merton Sealts has written:

> The audience of *Harper's* and *Putnam's* may not have been as effeminate or obtuse as modern interpreters like to assume without necessarily knowing the magazines themselves. . . . *Putnam's* in particular . . . was very receptive to Melville's work, under both George Palmer Putnam and his successors Dix and Edwards, and the magazine itself was not only "charming," as Henry James remembered it in afteryears, but relatively sophisticated: no less a judge than Thackeray, speaking in 1855, called it "much the best Mag. in the world." (Sealts 248)

Melville was paid at the highest rate of five dollars a page, and his stories were often singled out by reviewers as the best offerings in their respective issues.[6] Walter Bezanson has concluded that "in retrospect, it was Melville's good fortune that at a time when he was subject to rather virulent criticism, and was experiencing uncertainties about his career and health, two magazines [*Harper's* and *Putnam's*] of such quality were available to him. They provided a regular market and reasonable pay."[7]

For the most part the magazine stories are now read as Melville's admission of defeat in his war with the reading public or as his continuation of that war using indirection, irony, and conventional narrators whose values are undercut by the stories they tell. Ann Douglas sums up the second view this way: "Melville's newly lowered estimation of his audience was evident in the doll-house proportions of the work he offered them; he deceived his readers, he veiled his insults, partly to demonstrate to them how little worth the effort of attack they were" (315). That such a view of a writer's project seems plausible testifies to the continuing strength of romantic conceptions of the artist as a solitary adversary. Henry James, himself the author of highly ambiguous stories such as "The Turn of the Screw," designed to "trap the wary reader," remembered only his "very young pleasure" in "the prose, as mild and easy as an Indian summer in the woods," of Melville, Curtis, and Donald Grant Mitchell (qtd. in Sealts 234). Like most nineteenth-century readers, James missed the ironies, the veiled insults, the authorial hostility that modern students find in the magazine pieces. The authorial stance in these works is not always conciliatory but it is often self-critical and patterned after popular models. In much of his short fiction, Melville largely abandoned the outright contempt for the taste and intelligence of his readers that he displayed in *Pierre*.

In one of his first stories, "The Fiddler," Melville examined the hostility toward the audience that informed *Pierre*.[8] The story's title echoes the passage in "The Custom House" in which Hawthorne imagines his Puritan ancestors saying of his work as "a writer of story-books": "Why, the degenerate fellow might as well have been a fiddler!" (*Novels* 127). But Melville's story does not attack the American public's supposed contempt for writers; it attempts to define work that both pleases the public and satisfies the writer.

The central character, Helmstone, is a Pierre seen from the outside, a poet with epic pretensions, full of himself and enraged by the mindless public that fails to appreciate his work. He consoles himself for his failure by refusing to admit the right of readers and critics to judge him. Helmstone has recourse to all the romantic rationalizations for failure that Melville himself appealed to in *Mardi* and *Pierre*. In "The Fiddler" Melville suggests that the author must accept some blame if he fails to reach the public. Helmstone muses:

> Then I repeated in my mind that sublime passage in my poem, in which Cleothemes the Argive vindicates the justice of the war. Ay, ay, thought I to myself, did I now leap into the [circus] ring there, and repeat that identical passage, nay, enact the whole tragic poem before them, would they applaud the poet as they applaud the

clown? No! They would hoot me, and call me doting or mad. Then what does this prove? Your infatuation or their insensibility? Perhaps both; but indubitably the first. But why wail? Do you seek admiration from the admirers of a buffoon? Call to mind the saying of the Athenian, who, when the people vociferously applauded in the forum, asked his friend in a whisper, what foolish thing had he said? (*Pierre, Israel Potter* 1197)

The poet's problem is not that his work is too good for the masses but that it is wholly inappropriate to the audience he is addressing. The work is archaic, pretentious, vaguely absurd; it demonstrates a willful ignorance of the existing audience and its needs and expectations. Naturally the circus patrons will hoot him; his work is irrelevant to them and supercilious besides. Though Helmstone briefly glimpses his own foolishness, he turns at once on the foolishness of the audience.

At the circus Helmstone is introduced to Hautboy, a middle-aged man and the fiddler of the title, a man who plays common tunes for the common people. "But common as were the tunes," observes Helmstone, "I was transfixed by something miraculously superior in the style" (1201). Hautboy, it turns out, is a former English child prodigy who played before all the courts of Europe. When Hautboy moved from Europe to America, he became an anonymous artist playing for a democratic audience rather than a famous prodigy playing for aristocrats. He has sacrificed the egotistical urge for fame that underlies Helmstone's romantic self-definitions. Helmstone's friend, emblematically named Standard, challenges him to consider Hautboy's example and abandon his self-defeating concept of literary genius: "You think [Hautboy] no pattern for men in general? affording no lesson of value to neglected merit, genius ignored, or impotent presumption rebuked?—all of which three amount to much the same thing" (1200). When "The Fiddler" ends with Helmstone taking fiddling lessons from Hautboy, Melville has replaced the conception of himself in *Pierre* as a neglected genius with a portrait of himself as an "anonymous" magazine writer.[9] Hautboy's fiddling is the equivalent of Melville's best short stories: a familiar popular entertainment rendered with consummate art.

After completing "The Fiddler" Melville began writing "Bartleby, the Scrivener." The narrator of "Bartleby" has much in common with the genial and self-deprecating narrators of magazine fiction described by Ann Douglas in *The Feminization of American Culture*. He says of himself, "I am a man who, from his youth upwards, has been filled with a profound conviction that the easiest way of life is the best" (*Pierre, Israel Potter* 635), a statement that brings to mind the personas behind regular magazine features like "The Easy Chair" in *Harper's*. Melville mocks his narrator at first and identifies with the uncommunicative Bartleby, who prefers not to write. But the dramatic focus of the story is on the lawyer's effort to understand Bartleby, not on what Bartleby means, for Bartleby's opacity is deliberately impenetrable. The lawyer's effort to understand Bartleby is presented with sympathy; he is not a complacent and myopic man but a far more patient interpreter of Bartleby than most readers would be. The lawyer-narrator represents Melville's attempt to engage genteel magazine readers and at the same time move them beyond the self-approving and sentimental offerings of much current magazine fiction. The story's popularity proves that he was successful in at least the first part of this attempt.

Despite his conversational familiarity with the reader, the lawyer is not a smug sentimentalist. He recognizes his complacency during the course of the story: "Yes. Here I can cheaply purchase a delicious self-approval" (647). He also recognizes his failure to act out his better impulses toward Bartleby: "But this [*sic*] it often is, that the constant friction of illiberal minds wears out at last the best resolves of the more generous" (662). And though he could be accused of indulging his sense of guilt while failing to challenge the reigning social structure, he neither sentimentalizes Bartleby nor claims to have bridged the gulf between them. His most moving and powerful insight into Bartleby's condition, and his own, leaves them both isolated: "I might give alms to his body; but his body did not pain him; it was his soul that suffered, and his soul I could not reach" (653). This is no cheap evasion—the lawyer does offer alms when he can find nothing else to offer, and invites Bartleby home with him without self-congratulation or hope. The lawyer's final lament for Bartleby and humanity suggests that he and humanity are implicated in Bartleby's pain, even though circumstances have made him a comfortable onlooker, like the readers of "Bartleby." Melville begins the story mocking his narrator and identifying with the silent Bartleby, but by the end of the story the lawyer's voice and Melville's have merged.

The last line of the story, "Ah Bartleby! Ah humanity!" transfigures the sentimental vocabulary of antebellum magazine fiction. The lawyer's final utterance is sentimental in tone and rhetorical form, but it also resembles Bartleby's commonplace but incomprehensible remarks. Earlier in the story the lawyer began to speak like Bartleby when he unconsciously used his word *prefer*. In the last line of the story, Melville has the lawyer combine the gentle melancholy he once indulged (and which sentimental readers expected) with the deeper gloom that Bartleby has taught him. The lawyer's response to the human condition becomes as profound as Melville's. Faced with the mystery of Bartleby, both the lawyer and Melville tell a story; and, it is crucial to note, both tell a *magazine* story, directed to the audience for such stories that existed in 1853. Melville may have felt ambivalent about the audience or reluctant to address it on its own terms, but he did not yet choose the cryptic silence of Bartleby. However much he resented the current relations between writers and readers, he acknowledged their validity long enough to produce "Bartleby, the Scrivener."

Like *Moby-Dick*, "Bartleby" represented a temporary solution to Melville's difficulties with nineteenth-century readers. According to Merton Sealts, Melville next embarked on a long narrative about tortoise hunting which he could not complete (see Sealts's "Chronology"). It may be that Melville was trying to return to his old practice of composing from direct personal experience and did not find the subject matter compelling. In any case, he distilled "The Encantadas" from the tortoise hunting manuscript and sold the sketches to *Putnam's*. Melville was evidently trying to resume work in longer forms, but could produce a longer narrative only in fragments. During the fall and winter of 1853–54, Melville returned to the short form and produced an interesting series of experiments with paired tales, "Poor Man's Pudding and Rich Man's Crumbs," "The Two Temples," and "The Paradise of Bachelors and The Tartarus of Maids." In these works Melville returned to the explicit social commentary of *Redburn* and *White-*

Jacket and demonstrated steadily increasing power and subtlety, from the rather pedestrian ironic contrasts of "Poor Man's Pudding" to the deeply felt meditation on the sufferings of factory women in "The Tartarus of Maids." Melville seems to have been trying to find out if he could still write "the other way" and use his fiction to address public issues.

With *Israel Potter*, first published in installments in *Putnam's* (1854–55), Melville set out to continue writing in popular forms—this time, serial fiction—but his attitude toward the audience in this project is difficult to discern. He is not as hostile as he was in *Mardi* or *Pierre*, but neither is he as conciliatory toward his readers as his chosen genre implies. Melville was thinking of "serv[ing] up the Revolutionary narrative of the beggar" at least as early as 1849 (*Israel Potter* 174). Though Melville expressed contempt for *Redburn* and *White-Jacket* as "two jobs" (*Letters* 91), he was nevertheless contemplating a third, and the idea of *Israel Potter* was compelling enough for Melville to sustain it during the next four and a half years of his career. But some creative fatigue is evident in Melville's heavy reliance on a single source for his project, namely, the anonymous *Life and Remarkable Adventures of Israel Potter* (1824).

The opening chapters of Melville's novel are essentially a skillful transcription of the earlier work. Melville always relied on secondary sources for his long works, but not to the extent of taking his major incidents, plot, and characters from a single book. From the early chapters one could conclude that *Israel Potter* was no more than a job conducted by a talented but weary professional writer in need of cash. However, in chapters 5 and 6, Melville began to grow bored with copying another man's narrative. As Walter Bezanson points out, he expanded on the incidents in the *Life* as he became more and more engaged with the novel (*Israel Potter* 190). He began to draw from other sources besides the *Life* and to write in a variety of popular styles and genres: historical drama, sea adventure, Yankee pedlar tale, tall tale.

But *Israel Potter* is finally an uneven and often muted performance, not because it lacks profound speculation, but because it lacks sustained narrative energy and detail. As a British reviewer, possibly G. H. Lewes, remarked, "Mr. Melville follows his hero's fortunes, from the time of his being taken prisoner by the English, with great minuteness in the beginning and middle of the book, and then suddenly generalises towards the end for the sake of getting to the death of 'Israel Potter,' without exceeding the compass of one small volume. . . . an author who ceases to be particular and becomes general, in all cases where the drawing of human character is in question, is sure to lose his hold of the reader in the most disastrous manner" (Branch 342). The novel's one extended scene, and the one most praised by contemporary reviewers, is the battle between the *Bonhomme Richard* and the *Serapis*, which concludes the John Paul Jones section of the novel, the only section largely invented by Melville. In the remainder of the novel Melville's narrative energy flags. He even refuses to tell that part of Israel's story that he at first seemed most interested in:

> But these experiences [of Israel in London], both from their intensity and his solitude, were necessarily squalid. Best not enlarge upon them. For just as extreme suffering, without hope, is intolerable to the victim, so, to others, is its depiction, without some corresponding delusive mitigation. The gloomiest and truthfulest dramatist seldom chooses for his theme the calamaties, however extraordinary, of inferior and private persons; least of all, the pauper's. (606)

Melville is mocking his squeamish readers here and reacting to the critics' complaints about metaphysical digressions in his previous works. But he is also withholding the events of his main character's life, which would have interested contemporary readers familiar with stories of innocent suffering, and refusing to write a democratic story about the fate of an "inferior and private person."

An English reviewer for the *Weekly Chronicle* sensed that Melville was holding something back: "The book leaves the impression of having been carefully and purposely rendered common-place. You must feel that the author is capable of something much better, but for a freak is resolved to curb his fancy and adhere to the dustiest routine" (qtd. in *Israel Potter* 221). *Israel Potter* is uneven because Melville finally refused to satisfy his audience's expectations, not because he compromised with his audience or because the audience forced him to curb his powers. He curbed them himself to produce a novel that for the most part satisfied the taste of its potential readers but interrupted itself when it went too far toward becoming a popular novel.

Perhaps the most astute comment on Melville's attitude toward the reader in *Israel Potter* came in the *National Magazine*, which observed that "a tinge of obscure sarcasm pervades the book, most apparent in its dedication to the Bunker Hill Monument!" (qtd. in *Israel Potter* 217). The dedication was added to the published book after the novel was serialized; it reveals that Melville had returned once again to the romantic posture of *Mardi* and *Pierre*, mocking the reading public and dismissing popular work as unserious. Both *Pierre* and *Israel Potter* were dedicated to inanimate objects, as if no sympathetic human readers were left for the serious artist to address.

Both dedications also used democratic rhetoric to disguise their hostility toward readers, a strategy reminiscent of "Hawthorne and His Mosses." *Pierre* is dedicated to Greylock because the mountain is part of America's antiaristocratic "royalty," Nature; the joke is that Greylock, like the democratic reading public, is indifferent to Melville's work. *Israel Potter* is dedicated to "His Highness The Bunker Hill Monument" so that Melville can contrast aristocratic support for literature with democratic indifference to it: "Israel Potter seems purposely to have waited to make his popular advent under the present exalted patronage" of the Bunker Hill Monument. The original story of Israel Potter and Melville's *Israel Potter* both make their popular advent to dramatize a failed search for patronage. The purpose of the original *Life and Remarkable Adventures* was to help the real Israel Potter secure a pension from the United States government; Melville's dedication to his *Israel Potter* implies that reaching a popular audience with serious work is as futile as the real Potter's struggle to receive his pension. The character and the novel both represent democratic society's failure to support its obscure heroes, military and artistic. Melville's further dedication of his book to "The present exalted patronage"—that is, to no patronage at all—is his obscurely sarcastic swipe at the democratic public.

"Benito Cereno," Melville's next major work after *Israel Potter*, also expresses Melville's dissatisfaction with his audience in an oblique way.

"Benito Cereno" puts the reader in the position of the good-hearted but dim-witted Captain Delano; the story is told so that the first-time reader—the magazine reader—is no more likely than Delano to understand the meaning of events on board the San Dominick. Delano is Melville's hostile version of the average reader, one incapable of recognizing ambiguous events or of drawing conclusions from awful events once they have been revealed to him. "The past is passed," he tells Don Benito; "why moralize upon it?" (*Pierre, Israel Potter* 754). Unlike the lawyer-narrator of "Bartleby," who did moralize on his past, Delano cannot understand the meaning of his experience and complacently refuses to try.

However, Delano is not just a bad reader; he is a moral failure. But Melville made it next to impossible for the contemporary reader to see him as such. Melville used the third-person narrative (unusual in his short fiction) to withhold his moral convictions from the reader, while writing a story that attacked the moral complacency of his readers. The events of the story are uncovered, layer by layer, but the "little lower layer" where the truth lies remains deliberately hidden. First there is the powerful but false revelation to Delano: "Captain Delano, now with the scales dropped from his eyes, saw the negroes, not in misrule, not in tumult, not as if frantically concerned for Don Benito, but with mask torn away, flourishing hatchets and knives, in ferocious piratical revolt" (734). Melville knew that the slaves were driven to commit atrocities to gain their freedom; he also knew that the contemporary reader would see them as Delano does, as terrifying and evil savages. Melville removed himself from this tragic misperception, content to implicate the unwary reader along with the well-meaning but racist Delano.

Then Melville presents Don Benito's deposition, which removes the author still further from his tale and its implications. The deposition seems to reveal the facts that Delano missed or which he could not have known while on board the San Dominick. Yet this graphic account of the criminal deeds of the blacks suppresses the unspoken crime at the heart of the story: the continued conduct of the slave trade, which was outlawed in most of the United States by 1783, sixteen years before "Benito Cereno" takes place. In "Benito Cereno" Melville refused to speak to the issues he raised or to take responsibility for the moral education of his readers. Instead, he took his stand with Babo, who dies rather than speak his truth to the world.

Like Bartleby, Babo defies interpretation, but he is a much fiercer version of the silent scrivener. In "Benito Cereno," Melville used Babo as an image that horrifies but cannot enlighten the reader: "for many days, the head, that hive of subtlety, fixed on a pole in the Plaza, met, unabashed, the gaze of the whites" (755). At the end of "Benito Cereno" the reader is left, like Delano, unable to moralize on this image, but uninstructed by the remote author in how else to respond to it. The shocking final image of Babo's head on a pole represents Melville's silent remoteness, his refusal to speak to an uncomprehending audience.

Melville uses Babo to make his failure to confront the issue of slavery in "Benito Cereno" seem profound rather than evasive. The story raises the most divisive moral issues of the 1850s but withholds comment on them, as if the true artist's function was to offer impenetrable ironies rather than statements on the problems of the day. The plight of the blacks is attributed to a generalized evil in the universe, and Babo becomes Melville's self-serving image of the romantic artist's social and spiritual alienation. When Delano asks Don Benito, "What has cast such a shadow upon you?" he replies, "The negro" (754). The "negro question" was casting a shadow over antebellum America, but in Melville's treatment "the negro" no longer represents specific injustices but inhuman otherness, a grim, impenetrable, paralyzing image beyond which neither writer nor reader can go. As Melville wryly remarks at this point in the story, "there was no more conversation that day" (755).

In "Benito Cereno" the mutual incomprehension of the characters represents Melville's suspension of dialogue with his readers. But if deep truths are unspeakable and readers are fools who could not face them even if they were spoken, then there is no work for the writer to do. Like *Pierre*, "Benito Cereno" put Melville in a position where he had to reassess his attitude toward the audience or stop writing. "The Bell-Tower," Melville's next story, began as a conciliatory piece, like *White-Jacket* after *Mardi* and "The Fiddler" and "Bartleby" after *Pierre*. Leon Howard remarks that the winter during which Melville

composed "Benito Cereno" was "unusually leisurely" for him, probably because the uncertainty about his vocation revealed in "Benito Cereno" made it difficult for him to write (222). By spring, needing
money to support his new daughter and worried about his health,
Melville needed a new story.

"The Bell-Tower" is another self-conscious parable of the literary artist in which Melville reflected on his own difficulties rather than on
public affairs, but it is also a popular performance in the manner of
Hawthorne. As in "I and My Chimney" and "The Apple-Tree Table,"
the other sketches of this period, Melville was searching for another
kind of voice that would allow him to write in a currently acceptable
though still serious way. "The Bell-Tower" is an anomaly among
Melville's works; it is a peculiarly "literary" piece in the antebellum
sense of the term: a historical costume drama with allegorical figures,
decorous treatment of Gothic themes, and a serious but conventional
moral. A bit of Melvillean humor emerges at the end when the sententious moral is qualified by a footnote wryly remarking on "an anachronism or two that occurs in the story" (*Pierre, Israel Potter* 833). Melville
knew that "The Bell-Tower" was not about the Renaissance; it was
about the plight of the artist in nineteenth-century commercial society.
Bannadonna engraves seals for customs house officers, and his creations are compared to the telegraph and the railway (829, 831). But the
story is so full of vague ironies that Melville probably did not know
what sort of attitude toward the artist's plight he meant to convey.
Melville may have been satirizing his own romantic pretensions, as in
"The Fiddler," or he may have been satirizing conventional strictures
on the romantic artist and parodying current "serious" literature. He
probably set out to write a tale about a romantic artist who self-
destructs, but his many changes of heart about the romantic posture
are reflected in his attitude toward Bannadonna, which shifts uncer-
tainly between sympathy and mockery.

The moral of "The Bell-Tower"—"so pride went before the fall"
(833)—could be a genuine piece of self-criticism or intentionally pedestrian and ironic. The story supports both readings. Melville may be ex-
posing and recanting Bannadonna's attitude toward his audience,
which is crudely deceptive; he is outwardly officious toward his pa-

trons but inwardly contemptuous of them and their standards. The story's epigraph expresses Melville's reservations about romantic selfhood and suggests that Bannadonna mistakes alienation for freedom: "Seeking to conquer a larger liberty, man but extends the empire of necessity" (819). And, for a brief moment, Melville humanizes Bannadonna's audience by presenting the thoughts of one of the patrons, who is not fooled by Bannadonna's "ostentatious deference": "the junior magistrate, a kind hearted man, troubled at what seemed to him a certain sardonical disdain, lurking beneath [Bannadonna's] humble mien . . . dimly surmis[ed] what might be the fate of such a cynic solitaire" (824). Here Melville is clearly worried about his own fate as an artist and expressing doubts about the validity of the romantic posture.

But the junior magistrate, and the concession to the potentially sympathetic audience that he represents, soon disappear from the story. Melville approves of the way Bannadonna's art disturbs his patrons: "the visitors forebore further allusion to [Bannadonna's work], unwilling, perhaps, to let the foundling see how easily it lay within his plebeian art to stir the placid dignity of nobles" (823). Bannadonna's description of his engravings resembles the aesthetic Melville presented in "Hawthorne and His Mosses": "Gravity is in the air of all; but, diversified in all. In some, benevolent; in some, ambiguous; in two or three, to a close scrutiny, all but incipiently malign" (825). Bannadonna is much like Pierre, a romantic Satan, independent and self-creating. Bannadonna is killed by his creation, but the tone of the story's moral is unclear, and Bannadonna's death is faintly ludicrous: his mechanical man "dully smote the intervening brain of Bannadonna" as the artist concentrated on other parts of his work. Because these moments could be intentionally ironic or unintentionally comic, it is uncertain whether Melville is condemning Bannadonna's alienation from his audience, or secretly advocating it.[10]

In his next two stories, "I and My Chimney" and "The Apple-Tree Table," Melville assumed the persona of the genial, humorous, and self-deprecating narrator invented for the magazines by Washington Irving and practiced by N. P. Willis and others, although numerous commentators from Merton Sealts to Ann Douglas have found hints of Melville's disaffection beneath the chatty surface of these sketches.

Melville is obviously reflecting on his professional disappointments in "I and My Chimney": "The truth is, my wife, like all the rest of the world, cares not a fig for my philosophical jabber. In dearth of other philosophical companions, I and my chimney have to smoke and philosophize together" (1325). But as in "Bartleby," Melville is here using the contemporary magazine idiom to express personal truth. The final paragraph of "I and My Chimney" is a moving self-portrait, combining good-humored "magazinish" exaggeration and poignant truth: "It is now some seven years since I have stirred from home. My city friends all wonder why I don't come to see them, as in former times. They think I am getting sour and unsocial. Some say that I have become a sort of mossy old misanthrope, while all the time the fact is, I am simply standing guard over my mossy old chimney; for it is resolved between me and my chimney, that I and my chimney will never surrender" (1327). Here Melville's quiet determination to maintain his integrity could still coexist with his deft use of a popular form.

Melville's next attempt to meet the public on its terms as well as his own was *The Piazza Tales*, in particular the introductory sketch which he wrote for that volume, "The Piazza." The collection was initially entitled *Benito Cereno and Other Stories*, but when Melville wrote "The Piazza" he rearranged the volume, placing "The Piazza" first and "The Bell-Tower" last, beginning and ending the collection with parables about the artist and replacing the obliquely hostile "Benito Cereno" with a more conciliatory introductory sketch as the focal point of the volume. "The Piazza," like Hawthorne's "The Old Manse," is a story/preface that attempts to engage the reader by pretending that the exchange between writer and reader takes place in the author's home. The commercial transaction on which the author depends (the reader's buying his book) is subordinated to the intimate domestic site that author and reader agree (in the space of the preface, at least) to prefer. Though certain economic realities are suppressed by this agreement, the suppression is a knowing one which allows the writer to give his voice precedence over the cash transaction that in fact makes it possible for large numbers of readers to "hear" his voice. Melville describes his piazza as a place that combines "the coziness of in-doors with the freedom of out-doors" (*Pierre, Israel Potter* 621), precisely the combination of domestic intimacy and wide circulation made possible by the sketch form.

In "The Piazza" Melville used a popular form to present an uncompromising meditation on his career and on the relationship between his and the public's sense of literary art. The sketch explains why Melville decided to become the writer he was, one who expressed dark realities that he nevertheless hoped would be understood by readers. The narrator of "The Piazza" represents various phases of Melville's literary reputation. He is the writer of sea stories: "I wore a light hat, of yellow sinnet, with white duck trowsers—both relics of my tropic sea-going" (629). He is the writer of chatty and personal magazine sketches like the opening pages of "The Piazza," which describe Melville's Pittsfield farm. And he is the mysteriously morbid soul to whom the critics objected, who "in this ingrate peevishness of my weary convalescence" sees in his flowers, "if you removed the leaves a little, . . . millions of strange, cankerous worms" (626).

This morbid state of mind causes him to leave for "fairy-land," a beautiful cottage in a mountain valley that he can see from his porch; that is, he sets out to tell the kind of tale that Melville's critics demanded of him. The narrator hopes to escape the dullness and vague discontent of his everyday reality, and the story he sets out to tell is the kind of story one would read for such a purpose: either a traditional fairy-story that promises a bag of gold at the end of the rainbow (625), or a contemporary version of such a story that Melville himself might have written: "She [Marianna] shyly started, like some Tahiti girl, secreted for a sacrifice, first catching sight, through palms, of Captain Cook" (629). Instead, the narrator encounters a situation more forlorn than his own and that cannot be transformed into an imaginative or consoling tale. The enchanted cottage is a place of fly-specked windows, wasps, heat, and rot, and Marianna is not a Fayaway but the morbid isolato of Tennyson's poem.

The story functions as an apologia for Melville's art because Melville presents himself, convincingly, I think, as a writer who would genuinely like to write consoling fictions and satisfy the current critical demand that the writer transform sordid reality: "for your sake, Marianna, well could [I] wish that I were that happy one of that happy house you dream you see; for then you would behold him now, and, as you say, this weariness might leave you" (634). The narrator *is*, of course, the inhabitant of the house below, but he cannot bring himself to confirm Marianna's illusions any more than Melville the author could glibly satisfy his audience's more facile expectations. But the narrator is not self-righteous in his integrity; he recently held the same illusion about Marianna's cottage that she holds about his house, and he does not willingly forsake the illusion—he is forced to forsake it. The narrator, Marianna, and the reader of "The Piazza" all share the same delusive hope that stories will always uplift and console. By establishing this common ground with the reader, Melville is able to refute the charge that his dark and "metaphysical" stories proceeded from merely personal morbidity or perversity:

> "Yours are strange fancies, Marianna."
> "They but reflect the things."
> "Then I should have said, 'These are strange things,' rather than 'Yours are strange fancies.'" (631)

The narrator finds that stories, especially fairy stories, cannot alter the brute material realities represented by Marianna's situation, or her sense of hopelessness in the face of them.

"The Piazza" begins as a light-hearted conversational sketch and becomes a fairy story, but it ends as an encounter with the "things" that serious fiction reflects because they are forced on the author, not because he seeks them. The story's last scene is a self-portrait of Melville as the ambivalent author who confused and sometimes exasperated his critics, his readers, his literary friends, and his family. The daytime author takes no more journeys but sticks to his piazza: "the scenery is magical—the illusion so complete" (634). But during the course of the story the piazza itself has been transformed from a cozy and intimate place (which Melville now unmasks as illusory), to a scene of dark and obsessive meditation: "But every night, when the curtain falls, truth comes in with darkness. No light shows from the mountain. To and fro I walk the piazza deck, haunted by Marianna's face, and many as real a story" (634). These real stories are, of course, *The Piazza Tales* themselves, stories of isolation ("Bartleby," "The Encantadas"), slavery and incomprehensible evil ("Benito Cereno"), irrational fear ("The Light-ning-Rod Man"), and self-destruction ("The Bell-Tower"), written by an insomniac author who would sleep if he could.

The Piazza Tales were critically well received but did not sell, partly be-cause the 1857 panic reduced the market for books, but also because Melville's reputation, though strong enough to ensure that his work would be published and reviewed, was no longer strong enough to en-sure sales. By this time some critics and readers were just as ambivalent about Melville as he was about them. Some still felt that Melville was "justly regarded among the first writers of fiction of the present day" and that "the name of the author is a passport to public favor" (qtd. in Inge 44). But in a letter to Melville's publisher, G. W. Curtis said of the planned collection of stories that became *The Piazza Tales*: "I don't think Melville's book will sell a great deal, but he is a good name upon your list. He has lost his prestige,—& I don't believe the Putnam sto-ries will bring it up. But I suppose you can't lose by it. *I* like the Encan-tadas, and Bartleby, very much" (Leyda 510). Perhaps such hopelessly mixed signals reinforced Melville's periodic sense of futility about his literary career. He began work on *The Confidence-Man*, in which he re-sumed his attack on the nineteenth-century reading public.

Because *The Confidence-Man* was the last work of fiction Melville published, it is often read as his final insult to the reading public. This satisfies a long-standing urge to find the point of tragic closure in Melville's career, but in fact his career did not end in 1857. He lectured for three seasons after returning from the Holy Land, and then began writing poetry, most of which he published. The fact that he bothered to write and publish *The Confidence-Man* at all indicates that at some level he was not quite willing to give up on the reading public. His dis-taste for readers is evident in the book, but the last line of the novel does leave open the possibility of a sequel. Melville had recently been invited to contribute to the new *Atlantic Monthly*, so he had objective evidence that his career as a fiction writer could continue (*Letters* 187).

The Confidence-Man actually received a number of mildly favorable reviews despite its opaque style (Branch 369–86). A critic in the *New York Dispatch* even went so far as to assert that "the book will sell, of course, because Melville wrote it," although he warned that "this exceedingly talented author must beware or he will tire out the patience of his readers" (Branch 370). Many readers had lost patience, and Melville turned to lecturing in the winter of 1857 for the money but also, I strongly suspect, because the lecture was a literary genre that was both popular and serious. Melville's lectures were not major works—he did not bother to publish or preserve them—but as Merton Sealts shows in *Melville as Lecturer*, Melville was not only willing to go before the public but to read and respond to reviews of his performances. He altered his topic from the first season's "Statues in Rome" to the more popular "The South Seas," a concession to his audience's expectations that also allowed him to explore subjects not covered in his previous books. Melville was still famous enough to draw crowds for his tours and to be well received, at least on the East Coast. As late as December 1858 Melville professed himself "ready to lecture in Labrador or on the Isle of Desolation of Patagonia," "if they will pay expences, & give a reasonable fee" (*Letters* 193). Though Titus Coan visited Melville during 1858 and reported him as having an "air of one who had suffered from opposition, both literary and social" (qtd. in Howard 262), Melville was still submitting work (probably poems) to magazines as late as the spring of 1859 (*Letters* 194).

When he first turned to poetry in the late 1850s, Melville was determined to write for his own pleasure and to remove his work as far as possible from the taint of commercialism and from his professional reputation. He wanted to see his poems published in a dignified and "literary" way. Melville's memo to his brother Allan about his poems (May 1860) indicates that he wanted to reach a different audience from the one he had been addressing with his fiction and lectures:

> 5—For God's sake don't have *By the author of "Typee" Piddledee &c* on the title-page.
> 7—Dont have any clap-trap announcements and "sensation" puffs—nor any extracts published previous to publication of book—Have a decent publisher, in short. (*Letters* 199)

Though "decent publishers" may have released Melville from some of the pressures of commercialism, the energy of his greatest work had been generated by the need to address a large, undefined, and democratic public, to bring the audience into being along with the work. Like Hawthorne before him, Melville could not produce "high" literature for a genteel public. This first volume of verse was not printed in Melville's lifetime.

The next book that Melville did complete was *Battle-Pieces and Aspects of the War*, which he published in 1866 and which remained in print into the twentieth century. The last twenty-five years of Melville's life will always remain something of a mystery, but it is safe to say that the tension between his professional habits and his romantic self-conceptions persisted. *Battle-Pieces* was one of Melville's most explicit attempts to assume a public role for the writer. In the supplement to that volume he wrote, "the times are such that patriotism . . . urges a claim overriding all literary scruples" (259), thus embracing the public and professional claims on the writer that in other moods he repudiated. Melville envisioned *Battle-Pieces* as a literary artist's contribution to the postwar debate about reconstruction and race.

In 1876, Melville had *Clarel* published by Putnam's, though he would later claim that it was "eminently adapted for unpopularity" (*Letters* 275). His last works, *John Marr* and *Timoleon*, were published in small private editions, and they seem to indicate that Melville had finally accepted the romantic conception of the artist as the most consoling of self-definitions for his old age. *Timoleon* contains poems referring to Keats, Shelley, and Coleridge as martyrs to literary greatness who refused to take "the downward way" of public success from their "lonely Alp" of inspired vision ("Lamia's Song," *Poems* 266; see also "Shelley's Vision," and "C's Lament," which refers to Coleridge).

Melville was also finding romantic consolations in his reading. In the French writer Maurice de Guerin, he underscored these passages: "There is more power and beauty in the *well-kept secret of one's self and one's thoughts*, than in the display of a whole heaven that one may have inside one . . . The literary career seems to me unreal, both in its essence and in the rewards which one seeks from it, and therefore fatally marred by a secret absurdity" (Leyda 703). Melville commented, "This is the finest verbal statement of a truth which every one who thinks in these days must have felt." From Schopenhauer, Melville took the following Blakean meditations:

> What is true and genuine would more easily gain room in the world if it were not that those who are incapable of producing it are also sworn to prevent it from succeeding.

> If he is a man of genius, he will occasionally feel like some noble prisoner of state, condemned to work in the galleys with common criminals; and he will follow his example and try to isolate himself.

> The more a man belongs to posterity, in other words, to humanity in general, the more of an alien he is to his contemporaries; since his work is not meant for them as such. (Leyda 832)

But as Merton Sealts shows in his account of Melville's last years, Melville did not fully give in to these romantic consolations. In his letters he was alternately cynical and breezy about literary fame, but he corresponded gratefully with a number of English admirers; he sat for photographs and his portrait began appearing in encyclopedias and anthologies; and he was willing to have a new edition of his works published (Sealts 218). Most importantly, he returned from poetry to the novel, though we will never know whether Melville intended to publish *Billy Budd*.[11]

By the late nineteenth century the well-established category of romantic visionary could be invoked to explain artists like Melville. W. Clark Russell wrote of *Moby-Dick* in 1884, " It is like a drawing by William Blake, if you please; or, better yet, it is of the 'Ancient Mariner' pattern, madly fantastic in places, full of extraordinary thoughts, yet gloriously coherent" (Branch 410). Some of Melville's early champions, such as Richard Stoddard, H. S. Salt, and Arthur Stedman, wrote about Melville as a professional writer who for reasons of temperament withdrew from the profession. As Salt put it, "he could not, or would not, cultivate the indispensable art of keeping his name before the public" (Branch 431).[12] But it was the view of Melville as a romantic artist compromised by the literary marketplace that became paradigmatic.

Melville was concerned throughout his career with reaching and holding a popular audience, and somewhat successful at doing so, even during the most troubled phases of his career. As a fiction writer in mid-nineteenth-century America, Melville could only work within well-established commercial institutions supported by a democratic ideology that discouraged any total retreat from the public. In a sense he was forced to function as a professional writer addressing a mass public; if he had not been, we would not only have no *Typee*, but no *Moby-Dick*, no "Bartleby," and perhaps no *Billy Budd*. But in another sense, Melville chose to be a professional writer because he willed himself to be a great writer, and a great writer in nineteenth-century America had to address the people. Criticism has still not been able to discover what conditions allow a writer to create great works or why some works achieve popular success while others of equal quality do not. But it is clear that if Melville had not wanted to write for the people—actual readers, not the People of the romantic abstraction—he could never have sustained the tremendous effort he put forth during the decade between *Typee* and *The Confidence-Man*; nor, I suspect, would he have continued to write and to publish during his so-called years of silence and obscurity.

CHAPTER EIGHT

Romantic Genius and Literary Production in the Nineteenth Century

The English romantics developed the idea of the writer as a genius of unquestionable authority as part of the general process of self-definition going on among middle-class people of their period.[1] For writers, the portrait of themselves as geniuses facing an unappreciative reading public was the equivalent for members of the middle class of the solitary, self-willed individual facing industrial society, the hostile arena in which both writers and other individuals had to realize themselves. The romantics tried to create a realm of freedom by addressing the whole Man, not men in their actual social roles. Ironically, this strategy reproduced the tendency to specialize human functions characteristic of industrial capitalist society. Bankers handled men's economic needs; lawyers, men's legal needs; and poets, men's "human needs," which began to seem more insubstantial, marginal, and dispensable the more mystified and private they became. Romantic literature accommodates bourgeois culture by subordinating criticism of specific aspects of the daily life being created by rapid social and historical change to an imagined escape from that life into a private realm of freedom. The changes brought about by the industrial revolution were vast and complex, catastrophic and often brutal, and so were difficult to understand and resist.

Marx diagnosed these changes and stated their consequences in *The German Ideology*:

The division between the personal and the class individual, the accidental nature of the conditions of life for the individual, appears only with the emergence of the class, which is itself a product of the bourgeoisie. This accidental character is only engendered and developed by competition and the struggle of individuals among themselves. Thus, in imagination, individuals seem freer under the dominance of the bourgeoisie than before, because their conditions of life seem accidental; in reality, of course, they are less free, because they are more subjected to the violence of things. (199)

Marx here points out what I believe is a fundamental paradox of romanticism and of bourgeois society alike. By keeping alive private wishes, fantasies of autonomy, and the belief in an unfettered spiritual existence in spite of actual material circumstances, and by separating men's socioeconomic roles from Man as Wordsworth does in his 1802 preface to the *Lyrical Ballads*, romanticism supports the division, which Marx noticed and critiqued as part of bourgeois ideology, between a daily life devoted to material pursuits and an evening life devoted to the domestic and spiritual comforts made possible by the material pursuits. The private and public worlds are kept separate yet related, just as Wemmick keeps his two lives distinct in *Great Expectations*.

In Victorian times such a division between daily and spiritual life was firmly a part of what Raymond Williams calls the structure of feeling. We can see this in an 1847 letter from Mary Shelley to Thomas Medwin imploring him to suppress his memoir of Shelley: "I vindicated the memory of my Shelley and spoke of him as he was—an angel among his fellow mortals—lifted far above this world—a celestial spirit given and taken away, for we were none of us worthy of him. . . . In modern society there is no injury so great as dragging private names and private life before the world" (qtd. in R. M. Smith 29). Mary Shelley used to be deprecated by Shelleyans for "becoming a Victorian," but moments such as that revealed in her letter make it clear that there was no great difference between romantic and Victorian attitudes toward the individual's relationship to society. Mary Shelley's letter confirms the connection Marx noted between otherworldly dreams of freedom and the injury done to individuals when those dreams come into conflict with "the world." In some ways romanticism is not an attack on capitalist culture, but rather supports capitalist and bourgeois assumptions about the ultimate value of private experience.

The link between romanticism and the experience of individuals in capitalist society is confirmed by the growing popularity of Wordsworth, Coleridge, Shelley, and Keats in Victorian England and the United States. The romantic poets came to be prototypical for the culture, which used romantic poetry in the private and therapeutic way that John Stuart Mill used Wordsworth, to learn "that there was real, permanent happiness in tranquil contemplation" (Mill, *Autobiography* 96). The romantic definition of the poet as a man apart from the culture was adopted fully by the culture. The early deaths and belated acceptance of poets like Keats and Shelley also led to the cultural myth closely tied to romanticism, that the great artist is unappreciated in his own lifetime because he is "too good" for his contemporaries. This myth, which is reflected in Mary Shelley's letter when she speaks of the poet as an angel, reproduces the general feeling that the individual is alone and ineffectual in society.

The drama of English romantic literature lies in the conflict between the urgent social and historical pressures of the industrial revolution that confronted the romantics and the extraordinary strategies they developed to compensate for those pressures. Subsequent readers have valued the withdrawal more than the conflict, a preference that does not completely distort the romantic project, which "frees" the individual by abstracting him from society. In the preface to the *Lyrical Ballads* Wordsworth addressed "man in his own nature" rather than in his social relations (*Prose* 1:140). Later, Wordsworth and Keats elevated Man and denigrated men, while Shelley's *Prometheus Unbound* and Blake's *Jerusalem* demonstrated that social change is futile and illusory unless preceded by changes within the self, changes which alone are possible and real. As the romantic poets were incorporated in Victorian times along with the ideology of the self they articulated, writers in general came to represent a certain type of asocial or even antisocial individuality. The Byronic hero was domesticated and, as J. W. Saunders reports, "in time it came to appear the natural thing that writers should be at least a little odd and idiosyncratic" (162).

The romantic view of the great writer's fundamental separation from society evolved into the bourgeois myth of the self-made man. Samuel Smiles's *Self-Help*, a popular Victorian work, exemplifies this connection with its exhaustive catalog of men whose innovative achievements were ignored by a hostile contemporary establishment and only later accepted; with its celebration of energy and will as the most important personal attributes; and with its conclusion that what one *is* is important—one's "character"—not one's social standing or attainments (36). Smiles's bourgeois individualism is the romantic idea of genius domesticated and (to some extent) democratized. Smiles presents his self-helpers as exemplary, though their efforts are extraordinary. His main point, however, is that their efforts are unaided or even hindered by society. The individual becomes what he is in spite of society, not because of it.

Richard Altick noted the connection between romantic and bourgeois ideology, but it appeared to him as a curiosity:

> By one of those queer twists that help make intellectual history so fascinating, the middle-class utilitarians took over the self-taught hero from the romantic idealists and made him serve their own philosophy. Just when Southey was recounting his stories of cottage bards, the Society for the Diffusion of Useful Knowledge published George Lillie Craik's *The Pursuit of Knowledge Under Difficulties*, a biographical dictionary of English and foreign scholars, artists, philosophers, scientists, engineers, and inventors who had toiled up the road of learning against great handicaps. (242)

But the romantic elevation of the self had its darker counterpart in bourgeois despair, the widespread feeling that individuals can do nothing to change a monolithic social order, composed as it is of a "mass" of people and the attendant uncontrollable, inexplicable forces.

American romantic formulations of the relationship between writer and audience often repeated British romantic formulations, usually with their contradictions intact if not exaggerated by the demand on American writers to (in Melville's words) "carry republican progressiveness into Literature, as well as into Life" ("Hawthorne and His Mosses," *Pierre, Israel Potter* 1161). Wordsworth's pronouncements were frequently echoed. In "A Letter to a Young Contributor," which attracted the attention of Emily Dickinson, Thomas Wentworth Higginson counseled: "Remember how many great writers have created the taste by which they were enjoyed, and do not be in a hurry."[2] In *White-Jacket* Melville repeated Wordsworth's distinction between the Public and the People from the 1815 "Essay, Supplementary to the Preface." In his chapter on "Publishing Poetry in a Man-of-War," Melville has Jack Chase say, "The public and the people! Ay, ay, my lads, let us hate the one and cleave to the other" (549). Poe spent his career vacillating between efforts to court the reading public and denunciations of readers as a mob. In 1839, he wrote to a reader of "Ligeia," "As for the mob, let them talk on. I should be aggrieved if I thought they comprehended me" (*Letters* 118). Emily Dickinson repeated the sentiment when she wrote,

> I'm Nobody! Who are you?
> Are you—Nobody—Too?
> Then there's a pair of us!
> Don't tell! they'd advertise—you know!
>
> How dreary—to be—Somebody!
> How public—like a Frog—
> To tell one's name—the livelong June—
> To an admiring Bog! (no. 288)

This romantic satire of the popular writer's career appealed to many writers, but those who chose to make their works public or who did not have the luxury of keeping them private had to "advertise" and address the actual reading public.

Instead of closing the gap between popular and high culture before it became too wide, the American romantics often participated in creating the gap. Thoreau was extreme but not exceptional when he wrote, "Give me a sentence which no intelligence can understand" (qtd. in Buell 62).[3] Even the genteel Higginson could use romantic formulations of the writer's work. In "Literature as an Art" he wrote, "the writer, when he adopts a high aim, must be a law to himself, bide his time, and take the risk of discovering, at last, that his life has been a failure. . . . recognition may not even begin till after his death" (*Atlantic Essays* 43). In light of such a statement, Emily Dickinson's association with Higginson becomes somewhat less mysterious.

Dickinson's idea of the poet was romantic to the core: the poet is the ultimate creative spirit (no. 569), a "Neglected son of Genius" disdained by contemporaries (nos. 1275, 441), contemptuous of the market arrangements governing literary work (no. 709), and independent of any standards but her own and those of her fellow poets (nos. 233, 505). Higginson has been caricatured as a limited prig whose failure to recognize Dickinson's genius prevented her from publishing. But the truth is that Dickinson used Higginson as a buffer between her work and Helen Hunt Jackson's repeated attempts to get her to publish. Dickinson wrote to Higginson in the 1880s:

> Are you willing to tell me what is right? Mrs. Jackson, of Colorado, was with me a few moments this week, and wished me to [publish]. I told her I was unwilling, and she asked me why? I said I was incapable, and she seemed not to believe me. . . . She was so sweetly noble, I would regret to estrange her, and if you would be willing to give me a note saying you disapproved it, and thought me unfit, she would believe you (qtd. in Higginson, *Carlyle's Laugh* 269).

It is easy to sympathize with Jackson's frustration; she had written to Dickinson, "What portfolios of verses you must have.—It is a cruel wrong to your 'day & generation' that you will not give them light" (qtd. in Sewall 587). But by this time the poet had long ago made up her mind to follow the romantic credo. Dickinson owned Edward John Trelawney's memoir of Byron and Shelley, which used this quotation from Shelley's *Defence of Poetry* as its epigraph: "No living Poet ever arrived at the fulness of his fame. The jury which sits in judgement upon a Poet, belonging as he does to all Time, must be composed of his peers; it must be impanelled by Time from the selectest of the wise of many generations" (qtd. in St. Armand 301). Dickinson's determination to be a posthumous poet was, and continues to be, a large part of her appeal, but it is hard to understand how she could ever conceive of her work as "my letter to the World / That never wrote to Me" (no. 441), when precisely the reverse was true.

It has been argued by Ruth Miller and others that Dickinson's desire to publish was fierce, but even if this was the case, she always adopted the romantic posture at the slightest hint of resistance. She wrote Higginson in June 1862, after he expressed some doubts about her work, "I smile when you suggest that I delay 'to publish'—that being foreign to my thought, as Firmament to Fin" (qtd. in *Carlyle's Laugh* 258). She never actually asked her influential friends Higginson or Samuel Bowles to publish her work, nor did she send it to potentially sympathetic readers such as Emerson or Thoreau, whose work she admired and to whom she had access—Emerson was a guest at her brother's house when his lecture tours took him through Amherst. Perhaps she thought about approaching a newspaper editor like Bowles rather than a member of the intellectual elite because she envisioned a popular audience for her work; the subject matter of many of her poems and the common meter she used make this a remote possibility. But she avoided all the available means of bringing her work to the popular audience. Dickinson clearly decided at some point to take the romantic ideal of the artist literally and to hold her work aloof from the corrupting influence of commerce and the faceless mass audience.

It is possible that when she first contacted Higginson in 1862 she was not seeking to publish at all, but responding to the final passages in "A Letter to a Young Contributor," where Higginson opposed the eternal world of poetry to the "disease and manifold disaster" of the social and political world. The politicians are eventually forgotten, argued Higginson, while the poet lives on:

> Who cannot bear a few disappointments, if the vista be so wide that the mute inglorious Miltons of this sphere may in some other sing their Paradise as Found? War or peace, fame or forgetfulness, can bring no real injury to one who has formed the fixed purpose to live nobly day by day. I fancy that in some other realm of existence we may look back with a kindly interest on this scene of our earlier life, and say to one another, "Do you remember yonder planet, where once we went to school"? (*Atlantic Essays* 92)

Higginson, who had already risked his life for the cause of abolition, was about to risk it again in the Civil War at the head of a black regiment. The detached vision of human life he offered here provided him consolation and a temporary respite from the chaos he was about to enter. Dickinson, on the other hand, literalized this detached vision in her life and work, despite Helen Hunt Jackson's argument that "When you are dead, you will be sorry you were so stingy" (qtd. in Sewall 580).

As in the case of Blake, we owe what we know of Dickinson to her early admirers and editors, Higginson and Mabel Todd Loomis, who brought Dickinson's work before the public. Ironically, these editors have been attacked by later readers for mishandling the poems, though Dickinson herself made no effort to prepare her work for publication and probably wanted it destroyed. Dickinson's romantic stance may have freed her to create an unusual and powerful body of work, but, if she had had her way, that work might have been lost permanently. Were it not for Lavinia Dickinson's fortunate reluctance to burn her sister's poems, Jackson's accusation would have been tragically apt. Dickinson's admirers often forget that her work could not and did not become "literature" at all until her scruples were ignored and her work published.

Many of the important midcentury American writers spent as much of their careers retreating from the public as addressing it directly. Many felt, along with Dickinson, that the only way to "tell all the Truth" was to "tell it slant" (no. 1129). But the careers of these writers who took on a public profession only to retreat from the public may have been more representative than they or their audience suspected. In "The Function of the Poet," Lowell made this profound observation:

> Every man is conscious that he leads two lives, the one trivial and ordinary, the other sacred and recluse; the one which he carries to the dinner-table and to his daily work, . . . the other that which is made up of the few inspiring moments of his higher aspiration and attainment, and in which his youth survives for him, his dreams, his unquenchable longings for something nobler than success. It is this life which the poets nourish for him, and sustain

with their immortalizing nectar. . . . His faith in something nobler than gold and iron and cotton comes back to him. . . . The
poets are nature's perpetual pleaders, and protest with us against
what is worldly. (16)

Lowell appeals to Wordsworth's sense of the poet as "the rock of defence for human nature; an upholder and preserver, carrying everywhere with him relationship and love" (1802; *Prose* 1:141). The poet is
the man who restores fragmented selves to themselves. But Lowell's
formulation brings to the surface the sense of despair that is only latent
in Wordsworth: "the generations of mankind are mere apparitions
who come out of the dark for a purposeless moment, and reenter the
dark again after they have performed the nothing they came for" (5).

The sense of desperation in American romantic work is common. In
"A Select Party" Hawthorne deflated the romantic consolations available to the struggling writer: "the cold, icy memory which one generation may retain of another, is but a poor recompense to barter life for"
(*Tales and Sketches* 954). He argued in "The Old Manse" that works that
are "written by men who . . . set themselves apart from their age . . . are
likely to possess little significance when new, and none at all, when old"
(1137). Yet Hawthorne found it difficult to write for his contemporaries
and ultimately gave up the effort. Even Emerson, who made his living
addressing the public directly, nostalgically invoked the age of Shakespeare, when the poet was in "secure possession . . . of the public
mind"; when there was no such thing as literary property, copyright,
or other commercial intrusions on creative work; and when there were
"few readers, many spectators and hearers" (*Representative Men* 191).
The misfortune of the American romantic period was that its great
writers, whose professional experiences were so similar to the aspirations and frustrations of their potential audience, believed that there
were a hundred thousand readers in nineteenth-century America, but
no audience for their work.

Like the British romantics, American writers either wanted or felt
compelled to address the people, the idealized democratic audience,
but found it difficult to address the public—actual groups of readers
whose preferences had to be taken into account. The writer could try

to satisfy, alter, or ignore those preferences, but in antebellum America the reading public, the publishers who served them, and the reviewers who reflected and guided their taste set the terms within or against which writers defined themselves. Many of the major American writers chafed against these terms, but writers like William Cullen Bryant, Walt Whitman, Orestes Brownson, and William Ellery Channing recognized that a large and literate audience might encourage rather than depress literature.

In his 1825 lectures on poetry, Bryant rebutted the already familiar charge that the times were unpoetical and narrowly practical. He argued that the circulation of all kinds of printed matter—"literature," in its eighteenth-century sense—benefited poetry more than past arrangements that restricted it to a single class of readers: "there is strong reason to suppose that [scientific and political writings] have done something to extend [poetry's] influence, for they have certainly multiplied the number of readers, and everybody who reads at all sometimes reads poetry, and generally professes to admire what the best judges pronounce excellent, and, perhaps, in time come to enjoy it" (31). Bryant's claim for poetry was modest compared to high romantic claims, but he supported his contention that poetry was not moribund by citing the romantic poets themselves: "Does the poetry of [England] at the present day—the poetry of Wordsworth, Scott, Coleridge, Byron, Southey, Shelley, and others—smack of the chilling tendencies of the physical sciences? Or, rather, is it not bold, varied, impassioned, irregular, and impatient of precise laws, beyond that of any former age? Indeed, has it not the freshness, the vigor, and perhaps also the disorder, of a new literature?" (31–32). Bryant sensed the paradox of the romantic view of literature: literature was imagined as dying or, at best, as under attack from all quarters, yet great literature was being produced.

Bryant astutely saw that the existence of a number of writers competing to serve the new and larger reading publics in part explained this explosion of talent: the writer reads the works of his contemporaries,

> and whatever excellence he beholds in them, inspires him with a strong desire to rival it—stronger, perhaps, than that excited by the writings of his predecessors; for such is our reverence for the

dead that we are willing to concede to them that superiority which we are anxious to snatch from the living. Even if he should refuse to read the writings of his brethren, he cannot escape the action of their minds on his own. . . . In short, his mind is in a great degree formed by the labors of others. (9)

Here Bryant foresaw the situation that would face American writers throughout the antebellum period and beyond: writers would be motivated by professional competition as much as by a sense of working within a literary tradition.

Whitman also embraced the democratic audience from the start, but even his career was not without its ambivalences. Whitman internalized the struggle between the American writer and his audience and questioned whether poetry was either necessary or possible in a country that was itself a poem. Whitman is the ultimate democratic bard when he repudiates poetry in favor of the common experience of the people: "No one will get at my verses who insists upon viewing them as a literary performance, or attempt at such a performance, or as aiming mainly toward art or aestheticism" (671). The romantic separation of the creative soul from the material work appears in Whitman not as an attack on the insensitivity of the audience but as an attempt to create a poem that is more than a poem. For Whitman a published book was a dead thing. As he wrote in the 1855 version of "Song of Myself," "You shall no longer take things at second or third hand . . . nor look through the eyes of the dead . . . nor feed on the spectres in books" (28). He conceived of *Leaves of Grass* with its green cover and punning title as a living thing. But he refused to pretend that literature was above trade or separate from its material form: he set his own book in type and was willing to risk offending Emerson (more probably, he was unaware of his genteel scruples) by using Emerson's famous letter of tribute to advertise the second edition of his book.

Whitman chose to define the poet in his 1855 preface as one who says to the people, "Come to us on equal terms, Only then can you understand us, We are no better than you, What we enclose you enclose, What we enjoy you may enjoy" (14). But he was not willing to concede the right to judge poetry altogether to the contemporary public. Whitman qualified his belief that "the direct trial of him who would be the greatest poet is today" by claiming, "Still the final test of the poems or any character or work remains. The prescient poet projects himself centuries ahead and judges performer or performance after the changes of time. Does it live through them? Does it still hold on untired?" (24). The romantic appeal to posterity withholds the power of judgment from contemporary readers and places it solely in the hands of the poet himself, who, in Lowell's words, understands "eternal boundaries, such as are laid down on no chart" (9). In an odd way, Whitman was combining romantic and professional attitudes when he usurped the function of contemporary critics and reviewed his work himself.

In spite of his ambivalence, Whitman was more willing than any other American romantic writer to submit to the judgment of the public. As Thomas Bender has written, "the paradox of a people's poet who could not be understood by the people bothered Whitman, more than it bothered others who have presumed to represent democratic art. But he never lost faith in the mass; he never turned against them because his hopes were unfulfilled" (154). But at some points in his career Whitman was tempted to consider himself a neglected genius; as Justin Kaplan has written, in the 1860s Whitman "favored and even welcomed the role of prophet mocked and dishonored in his own country" (305). And late in his life Whitman enacted the ultimate romantic paradox: along with Keats and Shelley, he became famous as a neglected poet (Kaplan 23).

Like most romantic authors, Whitman built an audience into his work, but Whitman tried harder than most to merge his ideal audience and the actual audience; he subsumed all types of potential and actual readers into the self that narrates *Leaves of Grass*. Whitman was the only major writer of the period to realize that the same impulses sent the many to popular literature and the few to the classics. In his open letter to Emerson in the 1856 *Leaves of Grass*, he wrote, "Up to the present . . . the people, like a lot of large boys, have no determined tastes, are quite unaware of the grandeur of themselves, and of their destiny, and of their immense strides—accept with voracity whatever is presented them in novels, histories, newspapers, poems, schools, lectures, everything." (1332). Unlike Emerson and Melville, Whitman sensed that the great artist had to draw his inspiration from this vital popular audience, and that great art emerges from a context in which popular art is being produced and received, not in opposition to or withdrawal from such a context: "Poets here, literats here, are to rest on organic different bases from other countries; not a class set apart, circling only in the circle of themselves, modest and pretty, desperately scratching for rhymes, pallid with white paper, shut off, aware of the old pictures and traditions of the race, but unaware of the actual race around them" (1333). But other great and near-great writers of the period were distrustful of the conditions in which their work was produced. When Whitman wrote that "the American bards shall be marked for generosity and affection and for encouraging competitors" (15), he was pointing to the new conditions in which American writers worked and at the same time voicing the unpersuasive hope that others could see the progressive possibilities of these conditions.

Whitman celebrated the number of readers, libraries, newspapers, sentimental novels, and romances in his open letter to Emerson, and claimed, "I am not troubled at the movement of them, but greatly pleased. . . . What a progress popular reading and writing has made in fifty years! What a progress fifty years hence! The time is at hand when inherent literature will be a main part of These States, as general and real as steam-power, iron, corn, beef, fish" (1329). Whitman's enthusiastic equation of literature and commodity emphasized the new market arrangements that presented opportunities to midcentury writers. By the 1840s most authors received royalties from publishers who assumed risk in exchange for profit; authors no longer paid to have their books printed and sold on commission. Between 1820 and 1860 the number of titles available to the public increased twenty times, and by 1850 American authors were selling twice as many books as British authors in the American market (Nye, *Society and Culture* 76).

In his open letter to Emerson in the second edition of *Leaves of Grass*, Whitman wrote,

> All current nourishments to literature serve. Of authors and editors I do not know how many there are in The States, but there are thousands, each one building his or her step to the stairs by which

giants shall mount. Of the twenty-four modern mammoth two-double, three-double, and four-double cylinder presses now in the world, printing by steam, twenty-one of them are in These States. The twelve thousand large and small shops for dispensing books and newspapers—the same number of public libraries, any one of which has all the reading wanted to equip a man or woman for American reading—the three thousand different newspapers . . . the story papers, various, full of strong-flavored romances, widely circulated—the one-cent and two-cent journals . . . the sentimental novels, numberless copies of them . . . all are prophetic; all waft rapidly on. (1329)

Whitman recognized that technological advances in printing and distributing books, increased literacy, and an abundant popular literature were progressive, and that they helped writers as well as readers by creating an audience for their work. The American Renaissance occurred along with the "strong-flavored romances" and "sentimental novels" of the period, and could not have occurred without them, because neither great writing nor hack work can be produced without a vital audience to bring them forth.

Conclusion:
Romantic Letters
to the World

I have argued that romantic ideas about the writer and his or her audience, such as imagination and genius, are less philosophical constructs
than practical responses to the conditions of nineteenth-century publishing and reviewing practice. And these ideas, while they were used
to explain the writer's failure to reach his or her audience, were ironically accepted by the culture as accurate characterizations of Poetry,
Great Writing, and the Tradition of the English Poet, characterizations
that persisted through the determination of modernist artists to be
alienated from their audience. This determination coincided with and
supported the canonization of the more alienated romantic writers
such as Blake and Melville, and the contemporary practices of Stein,
Joyce, Pound, Eliot, and Beckett.

The coincidence of romantic and modernist ideas about audience
should no longer be surprising to readers who have followed me this
far, but it is an interesting, convoluted, and ironic coincidence that
modernist critics should have found in nineteenth-century authors
what modernist writers were articulating and practicing in their own
work. Other romantic ideas about the isolated self and the self's alienation from society and history are now commonplaces that the frequent
late-twentieth-century appeals to community only serve to highlight.
When Gertrude Stein said that she wrote for "myself and strangers,"
she seemed to be a modernist describing the ultimate form of alienation from one's audience, exactly the opposite of Wordsworth's and
later Hawthorne's conception of writing for an intimate listener or a
small circle of friends. But the English and American romantic conven-

tion of writing to an intimate listener is a response to the fact that the romantics were among the first writers forced to address an audience composed primarily of strangers.

It is a further irony that Stein's work owes its appreciation and acceptance to the interest (and money) of her rather large circle of friends, almost at the same time that Melville and Blake were being canonized by a small but influential circle of interpreters and admirers. Stein's self-conception, romantic to the core, is thus false and true. She was faced with the same mass audience that the American romantics had struggled to reach. In response, she went as far toward obscurity and unintelligibility as prose can go without being randomly generated. And yet the fame she achieved in her lifetime as Writer and Genius is owing in part to the publication of readable works such as *The Autobiography of Alice B. Toklas* (in which she, like Blake, asserted her own claim to being a genius) and in part to the championship of an influential circle of friends and admirers in the art and literary journalistic worlds of the early twentieth century.

I am not trying to deny that reaching a mass audience is a problem for any writer, or that nineteenth-century readers as individuals and as a group were sometimes less intelligent, creative, and careful than the writers who tried to reach them. Many people do go to books for diversion and do not particularly want vatic art or literature that will change the course of their lives or their societies. But the romantic response to this situation, like the later, more extreme modernist response, was sometimes willful, perverse, and unintentionally ironic. For example, when late in his career Melville chose to write a poem in a very popular genre, the tour through the Holy Land, he produced *Clarel*, a work that is almost unreadable and was published in a small, private edition.

Because writers could not receive unanimous favorable assent from the diverse publics of the nineteenth century, many writers at length concluded that serious work could never appeal to a large audience. The writer seemed to have only two choices: to appeal to the lowest common denominator or to the abstract and timeless standards of Literature. Romantic writers often idealized past and supposedly more personal arrangements, overlooked the progressive elements of current arrangements that gave readers access to more books and more kinds of books, and dismissed contemporary readers as inattentive and ignorant.

The innovative nineteenth-century publishers surveyed in chapter 1 saw progress and opportunity while writers such as Wordsworth and Coleridge tended to see only a mass of readers enchanted by inferior work. British romantics anticipated the phenomenon of the mass reading public that would perturb but also energize later generations of American writers. Writers in the United States took over, sometimes verbatim and sometimes with modification, British romantic formulations of the writer's work to suit their needs. Publishers and readers in the United States also took over British romantic formulations about the reading public and its role in shaping the writer's work. Hawthorne thought of his publisher James Fields as mediating between himself and the rough and materialistic public of the nineteenth century, while Emerson and Melville both tried to accommodate their democratic ideals (which led them to want to adapt to marketplace conditions) to the Wordsworthian sense that popular writing was, quite simply, inferior writing. Melville and Hawthorne quoted passages from Wordsworth and Shelley to explain and exorcise the tension they felt between their democratic ideals and their creative endeavors. Even Longfellow, who was as successful as Byron or Hemans in his appeal to contemporaries, adopted romantic conceptions of poetry as being above, or at least outside, the marketplace.

Wordsworth established the paradigm of the writer caught between democratic sympathies on the one hand and devotion to traditional and somewhat abstract standards for Great Poetry on the other. Blake also enacted this pattern, with the interesting complication that religious vocation as well as professional frustration caused him to divide his readers into sheep and goats. Shelley, more radical politically, was yet more "aesthetic" than Wordsworth in his conception of poetry and its standards, which he (like Emerson later) regarded as timeless and without reference to contemporary historical events with which he was otherwise so preoccupied.

In the United States, democratic ideology forced American writers to come to grips with popular taste and marketplace success while the romantic ideology inherited from the British writers made them question popular success as a measure of literary value. Melville, usually seen as a tortured high romantic dissatisfied with the rabble, was really an embattled but serious professional who both courted popular success and rejected it at different points in his career, and sometimes in the course of a single work. His letters show him, oddly enough, denouncing the reading public *before* he had failed with them in *Mardi*. Then his short stories, usually read as ironic and defeatist, show him trying to recapture his audience while at the same time telling them the truths that he felt obliged to tell.

The idea of genius, which appears in writers as different as Coleridge, Blake, Bryant, Brownson, Whitman, and Dickinson, was used to cope with the new system of literary production and pervaded the popular as well as the high romantic literary imagination. The split between "hack work" or popular writing and "literary" literature produced by geniuses that has characterized the twentieth-century discussion of literary art from the modernists on was first noticed and conceptualized by romantic writers and their less well-known colleagues, friends, and competitors.

Romantic ideas about imagination and genius are related to ideas about the personal and professional (or private and public) self, where the personal self is the arena of fulfillment and the professional self is the arena of (few) rewards and (many) frustrations. But the fact that such writers as Poe and Hawthorne achieved some professional success in their lifetimes in no way lessened the bitterness and frustration they felt when attempting to communicate with a new mass society, where old methods of reaching readers were breaking down and new ones were being rapidly invented, improvised, and tested by writers as diverse, and diversely successful, as Blake and Hemans, Whitman and Cummins, Melville and Stowe. This bitterness and frustration was, finally, a part of the lived experience of nineteenth-century life in a boom-or-bust capitalist industrial economy that the romantics inadvertently captured and reified for both the high and popular culture of the twentieth century.

For example, when Blake used the concept of original genius, it was often in an appeal to posterity in response to his professional frustra-

tions, to denounce trade or the market, and to denounce mass commercial society as it was taking shape:

> Advertizements in Newspapers are no proof of Popular approba-
> tion. but often the Contrary . . . for these thirty two Years I am
> Mad or Else you are so both of us cannot be in our right senses
> Posterity will judge by our Works Wooletts & Stranges works are
> like those of Titian & Correggio the Lifes Labour of Ignorant
> Journeymen Suited to the Purposes of Commerce no doubt for
> Commerce Cannot endure Individual Merit its insatiable Maw
> must be fed by What all can do Equally well at least it is so in En-
> gland as I have found to my Cost these Forty Years. ("Public
> Address" 573)

Blake's attack on mass production and consumerism in the arts is a
powerful one, but it is inextricably linked to romantic denunciations of
popular taste and attacks on other practitioners (an unfair attack in this
case, since Woolett and Strange are still considered to be two of the period's best engravers). Blake's target is the impersonal arena that de-
vours "individual merit." His personal difficulties in the new situation
led him to attack market arrangements as a conspiracy against individual genius, particularly his genius.

The idea of genius, which E. J. Hobsbawm calls "one of the most
characteristic inventions of the romantic era," both allowed the artist
to make claims on the reading public and provided consolation if those
claims were unsuccessful (*Age of Revolution* 260). These two functions
were often blurred, so that "genius" could be paired with "unappreciated" while the concept "popular" could be used as a value judgment
implying "inferior" or "uninspired." Thus Wordsworth defends his
poetry and attacks that of others when he writes, "Away, then, with the
senseless iteration of the word, *popular*, applied to new works in poetry,
as if there were no test of excellence in this first of the fine arts but that
all men should run after its productions, as if urged by an appetite, or
constrained by a spell!" (*Prose* 3:83). The idea of genius was frequently
used to justify the writer's confusion about and separation from the
contemporary audience. Hazlitt went so far as to claim that Blake's relatively accessible *Songs of Innocence and of Experience* were "only too

deep for the vulgar" (Bentley 54). But the most striking use of the idea of genius is Blake's statement, "Ages are All Equal. But Genius is Always Above The Age" ("Annotations to Reynold's *Discourses*" 649). The assertion itself is characteristically romantic, but its context is ironic and revealing. Blake made this assertion in the margin of a book. In effect, this bit of marginalia embodies the self-contradictory nature of the English romantic idea of genius. Blake asserted his individual superiority but did so in private because the public conspired against individual merit. Though he claimed a universal significance for art, he addressed the claim to no one in particular. Though he asserted that genius was timeless, his statement would have been lost if his admirers had not preserved a book that he did not even write. There are few more concentrated examples of the tension and ambivalence that characterized romantic addresses to the world and the forms of address the romantics chose.

It is just this tension and ambivalence that cultural histories such as this one are now hard at work attempting to understand. The concern with audience is just as pressing now as it was in the romantic period in Britain and America. As Colin MacCabe of the British Film Institute recently wrote in an issue of the *Times Literary Supplement* devoted to cultural studies,

> The full effect of a cultural studies in active relation to a wide range of audiences is difficult to calculate. One can, however, indicate two essential emphases. The first is that students concerned with pursuing topics in cultural theory and analysis will be constantly confronted and engaged with the artists, architects, film-makers, musicians and writers who are currently engaged in creating new cultural forms. . . . Such an engagement will throw up as a constant theme the relations between commerce and culture. It is impossible for the traditional university not to constitute these two areas as antithetical both in disciplinary and ethical terms. But for those engaged in the practice of culture, there are no such easy oppositions. It is close to impossible to conceive of any art being produced without a potential audience. But to talk of audiences is immediately to talk of money, and it is in the very complicated

relations between artist and audience, between product and market that a renewed cultural studies will find much of its edge. (13)

It should be noted that the traditional university until very recently followed Blake and other romantics in driving a wedge between art and the "maw" of commerce. In some cases the romantic writers' assessment of public taste, and of this relationship between art and commerce, was accurate and revealing, in other cases, disappointing and confusing. But romantic attitudes toward audience, those that were justified and those that were perverse, affected romantic and later work in profound and visible ways.

Notes

1. Leenhardt conducted a sociological survey of five hundred Hungarian and French readers; see his "Toward a Sociology of Reading."

2. See especially Altick's *The English Common Reader*, and Charvat's *Literary Publishing in America, 1790–1850* and *The Profession of Authorship in America.*

   Almost every study of romanticism published in the 1980s and 1990s includes a critical genealogy of forebears, attempting to place the new study into the current, ongoing debate. I see no need to repeat those genealogies here, but I do want to acknowledge their importance and value, and to refer the reader to some I have found most helpful in tracing this movement from literary criticism as practiced from the early part of the twentieth century until now to literary history and scholarship as practiced for the last two decades, with some scholarly antecedents such as Altick and Charvat.

   I would begin with Butler's *Romantics, Rebels, and Reactionaries* and McGann's *The Romantic Ideology.* Levinson's *Wordsworth's Great Period Poems* and Siskin's *The Historicity of Romantic Discourse* also include interesting overviews of modern literary criticism and scholarship. Ferguson gives the official overview of the British territory in "Romantic Studies." See also "American Literary Studies to the Civil War," by Techi, and "New Historicisms," by Montrose.

   Some valuable studies not mentioned in *Redrawing the Boundaries*, edited by Greenblatt and Gunn, are Wilson's *Figures of Speech*, Dauber's *The Idea of Authorship in America*, Fink's *Prophet in the Marketplace*, Brodhead's *Cultures of Letters*, and Andrew Bennett's *Keats, Narrative, and Audience.* For other overviews of the American critical territory, consult the introductions and bibliographies to the anthologies cited in note 3 below.

3. Among recent young scholars of British romanticism, I would list Levin-

son, Klancher, Siskin, Andrew Bennett, and Behrendt as examples of the approach I have been discussing.

In American studies, consult the contributors to five important anthologies: Michaels and Pease, *The American Renaissance Reconsidered*; Bercovitch and Jehlen, *Ideology and Classic American Literature*; Bercovitch, *Reconstructing American Literary History*; Davidson, *Reading in America*; and Machor, *Readers in History*.

4. I am thinking, of course, of the familiar litany of famous romanticists listed, and attacked or modified, in every 1980s study of romanticism: Lovejoy, Peckham, Frye, Abrams, Hirsch, Bloom, Hartman, and many others, depending on the litany.

INTRODUCTION

1. Both, as McGann and others have pointed out, are deeply romantic characterizations of the writer's project.

2. See Hawthorne's preface to *The Marble Faun*.

3. See the discussion of "Literature" in Williams, *Keywords*. Also see the discussion of the interaction between Peacock and Shelley in chap. 4 below.

4. See Brodhead, *The School of Hawthorne*, and chaps. 5 and 8 below.

5. See Jack, *The Poet and His Audience* 104: "Shelley's letters make it clear that his sense of failure was sharpened by the inevitable contrast with Byron."

6. For a contrasting new historicist view of Thoreau, see Fink, *Prophet in the Marketplace*. But see also discussions of Thoreau's turn to a more private mode of composition, his journal, in Sharon Cameron, *Writing Nature* and Howarth, *The Book of Concord*.

7. But see revised anthologies such as McGann's *The New Oxford Book of Romantic Period Verse*, and such canon-challenging studies as Tompkins's *Sensational Designs*.

8. A canon is a useful pedagogical tool that must be, as it has been, examined, critiqued, brought to consciousness, historicized, evaluated, added to and subtracted from. All this has been going on with a vengeance, not simply for the last twenty years but ever since the beginning of literary pedagogy.

But a canon serves one valuable function that is sometimes ignored—it keeps people reading authors and works on whom and on which they might otherwise give up. If they were not canonical works, I doubt that I as a young reader would have made it through to understanding and enjoyment of *King Lear* or *Paradise Lost*. And who can say what the ultimate fate of *Jerusalem* or *Prometheus Unbound* would have been if admirers had not supported those works and eventually saw them canonized?

An *Uncle Tom's Cabin* can make it on its own, and was written with the full intention that it should. But so were large parts of *Moby-Dick*, yet it was not until the high-modernist-led Melville revival of the 1920s that that work was canonized. Today's attacks on and defenses of "the canon" seem to me to ignore how historically fluid and inclusive the various canons of past and present have usually been.

9. Readers interested in the theory and history of alienation and the self should consult the many sources of all political persuasions that exist. As good a place as any to start is Sennett's *The Fall of Public Man*, a study of the rise of the private self in eighteenth- and nineteenth-century European society. A more conservative view of a shorter but pivotal period is Johnson's *The Birth of the Modern*.

Those interested primarily in literature can consult, for the eastern side of the Atlantic, Izenberg's *Impossible Individuality* and the extensive work of Terry Eagleton and Raymond Williams before him. For the western side, consult Shulman, *Social Criticism and Nineteenth-Century American Fictions*, and Gilmore, *American Romanticism and the Marketplace*, as well as recent New Historicist criticism such as Dimock, *Empire for Liberty*; Brown, *Domestic Individualism*; and Pfister, *The Production of Personal Life*.

10. It is interesting to note how accurately romantic literature expresses bourgeois experience. As Siskin expresses it, "Far from being the culmination of English Romanticism, the 1830s marked the moment at which the constructs and strategies of Romantic texts became 'normal' within and for the very culture that produced them" ("Wordsworth's Prescriptions" 305). I would say that this is true for the United States as well as for England.

11. I hope it is clear that I am not using the term *middle-class* as a term of abuse or as a way to debunk romantic work. Writers need readers, and though the romantic (and now popular) cliché is that great writers are not appreciated in their own time, the romantic writers had to write for and to someone. They could not sustain projects addressed to themselves, as my chapters on Shelley, Blake, Hawthorne, and Melville should make clear. In England, the romantic writers shared the radical audience's concern with government oppression, economic dislocation, and social injustice. They shared with

the middle-class audience and with the early mass audience a conception of society as a hostile and impersonal arena. And they both created and discovered a clerisy, or the "Gentle Reader," to serve as an idealized audience for their work, "gentility" being one of the most important middle-class values in Victorian times.

12. At the end of his life, Hawthorne actually had a tower built for himself to use as a writing studio. Brodhead links this act to Hawthorne's creative decline (*School* 80).

13. Sennett discusses how widely held this self-image was in *The Fall of Public Man*, 131 ff.

I. THE ANGLO-AMERICAN LITERARY PROFESSION

"Abrams's tone and vocabulary [in *Natural Supernaturalism*] have become more noticeably exalted and religious than in *The Mirror and the Lamp*: he has kept in step with the marked drift of American critical writing in the past decade and a half toward theology, not necessarily all that displaced" (Butler, "Against Tradition" 43).

2. WORDSWORTH AND THE DIFFICULTY
OF "SPEAKING TO MEN"

1. "Both [Wordsworth and Coleridge] must be seen within the climate of Jacobinism, isolated, the subject of unceasing external vigilance and yet at the same time of inward recoil and confusion—the moment at which the *Lyrical Ballads* were written, the early draft of 'The Ruined Cottage,' and possibly some passages which were to find their way into 'The Prelude'" (Thompson, "Disenchantment or Default?" 155). Thompson makes a convincing case that "the poets, when they went to Germany, were hopping the draft" (168). He quotes James Losh's letter to Robert Southey: "We all agreed that were there any place to go to emigration would be a prudent thing for literary men and the friends of freedom" (169). Thompson concludes that in 1798, "Drummed out of the neighborhood, [Wordsworth and Coleridge] made the decision [to emigrate to Germany] within a week. It was also a withdrawal from the vortex of an unbearable political conflict" (169).

2. "In many ways, Wordsworth, the Cambridge-educated radical, deeply disillusioned with the course he had seen the French Revolution taking, guiltily

aware of the manifest inequalities within his society, wishing at once to transcend its complacently paternalistic attitudes and to affirm a 'common humanity' with those from whom he was separated by privilege, may be seen as a prototype of a certain kind of modern left-wing intellectual. *Lyrical Ballads 1798*, with its awkwardnesses and uncertainties of tone, its sometimes contradictory stances, more directly than any other of his published works reveals the difficulties he faced in finding a position from which to write at all" (Glen 340).

3. Webb points out that the distinction between the Public and the People was used by many counterrevolutionary publications of this period: "In the [*White Dwarf*] of 28 February, 1818, [editor Gibbons Merle] makes a clear distinction between the *populace* and the *people*. The former were apparently written off as hopelessly lost and not worth saving; the task lay with the latter whom he defines as traders, shopkeepers, clerks, and mechanics, who would suffer intensely by the devastation proposed by the agitators" (55).

4. "Henry Taylor, accounting for the dawn of Wordsworth's popularity, put it down to Wilson's articles in *Blackwood's*, and he says: 'This opening was widened, I think, by two articles of mine in the *Quarterly Review*, one of which, I was told by the publisher at the time, had doubled the sale of his works'" (qtd. in Collins 224).

5. See the letter by Charles Lamb wittily narrating Wordsworth's response to Lamb's response to the poetry (Wordsworth, *Letters* 1:316).

3. RELIGIOUS VOCATION AND BLAKE'S OBSCURITY

1. References to Blake's long poems will give the plate and line numbers, followed by the page number in the newly revised Erdman edition of 1982. Other references to prose, letters, annotations, notebook entries, and short poems will give the page number in Erdman.

2. For example, Blake issued some of his works with the pages in different orders so that readers would not be regimented. No surviving copy of *The Book of Urizen* exactly matches any other, a diversity characteristic of all his surviving engraved works.

3. Glen 349, n.7 cites Elizabeth W. Gilboy, *Wages in Eighteenth-Century England* (Cambridge MA: Harvard UP, 1934), 58–59, 260–61.

4. See for example his letter to George Cumberland (Dec. 1808, 769).

5. "Those who cannot see what is implied may remain unable to tolerate what is expressed; and those who can read aright need no index of ours" (Swinburne 225).

6. Blake assembled his 1809 exhibition to counter threats from Robert Cromek to his reputation and therefore to his livelihood. Cromek, an engraver and entrepreneur, was to this period of Blake's life what Hayley was to the Felpham years: the focus of all that Blake resented about his current situation.

   However, his bitterness against Cromek was more justified, for Cromek was unscrupulous in his dealings with Blake. In 1805, after commissioning Blake to create and engrave a set of designs for Blair's *Grave*, he hired another engraver, Luigi Schiavonetti, to produce Blake's designs. Reviewers of the project concluded that Blake could conceive designs but not execute them, the charge he rebuts repeatedly in the 1809–10 documents. Then in 1806, Cromek saw Blake at work on a sketch of the Canterbury pilgrims. He took the idea to Thomas Stothard for an oil painting that Cromek later had engraved. This plagiary rankled Blake for years, and he never spoke to Stothard again, though Stothard was an unwitting accomplice. A good account of Blake's dealings with Cromek is given by Read, "The Context of Blake's 'Public Address.'" For the Canterbury Pilgrims plagiary see Davis, *William Blake*, 120 ff.

7. With the phrase "in a dark corner" Blake objects to the way paintings were hung in commercial galleries and academic exhibitions. He felt paintings were being hung in the dark to obscure their blurred outlines and misplaced emphasis on coloring. He repeatedly denounces Rembrandt, Titian, and Rubens as hacks who imposed this corrupt practice on the public.

8. Blake's hope for a real audience recurs as late as 1818 in another exaggeration of his reception: "The few [illuminated books] I have Printed & Sold are sufficient to have gained me great reputation as an Artist which was the chief thing Intended. But I have never been able to produce a Sufficient number for a general Sale by means of a regular Publisher" (771). These statements are evidence of the deeply felt need for contemporary response that Blake elsewhere denies.

9. Modern critics follow Smith and Swinburne by labeling any form of actual political or social activism as "vulgar." Frye, for example, writes, "'The poet and the dreamer are distinct,' says Keats's Moneta, and Rousseau in Shelley's poem is typically the bastard poet whose work spilled over into action

instead of remaining creative" (148). Note that "creativity" is valued because it is not "action," though how Frye then distinguishes it from mere dreaming is not clear.

10. Great twentieth-century critics such as S. Foster Damon and Northrop Frye have pieced together Blake's myth, but there is an obvious discrepancy between the clarity and force of their explications and the deliberate obscurity of Blake's works. To read Blake's later works now is almost inevitably to read Frye's *Fearful Symmetry* or Harold Bloom's commentary in the Erdman edition. No literary work comes to us unmediated, but Blake's work is unusual, perhaps unique, in the canon of English poetry, for to extract *any* meaning at all from his prophecies, one must approach them by way of commentary. The irony is that Blake's works, which were conceived as documents of human liberation, have by their very nature been consigned to those willing to spend years reasoning out their system. Blake has for the most part been fortunate in his critics, but they do form a priesthood largely untroubled by Blake's obscurity and willing to accept him on his own terms as a source of religious revelation. For example, in his article "William Blake and His Reader in *Jerusalem*," Roger Easson sees Blake's obscurity as a strategy to encourage readers:

> The bard must at once ensure that *Jerusalem* survives as a viable literary work, which will encourage the reader to labor at the furnaces of Los, and ensure that those readers who do not enter in forgiveness and faith will endure throughout a frustrating, though alluring, labyrinth. . . . This aesthetic creates within *Jerusalem* a cunning and magnificently ordered rhetorical screen to separate the sheep from the goats, the saved from the damned, the forgiving, faithful readers from the accusing rational ones. Consequently, Blake's rhetorical apocalypse is more perfectly structured than rational men have acknowledged. (326)

For Easson, *Jerusalem* is a holy book which the devout reader masters and the critical reader rejects at the cost of damnation.

4. SHELLEY AND ROMANTIC SELF-DIVISION

1. "To the Editor of the 'Examiner'," from "Note on *Queen Mab*," in the *Complete Poetical Works*. This text reproduces Mary Shelley's 1839 edition of the

poems, which helped to establish the Victorian views of Shelley that I discuss below. It is substantially the same text as in Hutchinson's edition.

2. My account of Shelley's career is indebted to Holmes and Cameron.

3. Shelley could be moderate, as evidenced by *A Proposal for Putting Reform to the Vote*.

4. The elegy is notable for its despairing, even defeatist conclusion. It has often been compared to *Lycidas* as one of the great pastoral elegies, but where Milton returns his reader to the world, "fresh woods, and pastures new," Shelley unexpectedly yearns to leave it:

> Why linger, why turn back, why shrink, my Heart?
> Thy hopes are gone before; from all things here
> They have departed; thou shouldst now depart!
> (lines 469–71)

Like *The Ruined Cottage*, *Adonais* offers the reader a consolation that is indistinguishable from that of conventional Christianity: the world is a vale of tears, and the only release from "cold mortality" is to enter "the abode where the Eternal are" (lines 486, 495). The conclusion exposes Shelley's disappointed hopes for reaching an audience and using his poetry to effect social change.

5. Recent critical treatments often simply reproduce Shelley's ambivalence and his attempts to overcome it imaginatively. Two examples from modern books on Shelley's politics will illustrate this tendency. In *The Unacknowledged Legislator* Dawson acknowledges the contradiction between Shelley's political hopes and the actual European political situation, but asserts, "Shelley's problems here are the result not so much of any lack of practicality on his part as of the almost insuperable difficulties that face any politics so radical as to deserve the epithet 'millenarian'" (216). The difficulties of millenarian politics are, of course, "almost insuperable" because such politics are not practical. Dawson obscures the difference between practical and millenarian by adopting a Shelleyan sense of what "practical" means, a sense derived from the *Defence*'s pseudoutilitarian argument for poetry's social efficacy. And in *Radical Shelley* Scrivener argues that "poetic ideas, as soon as they are born, are indestructible, even if it takes centuries for them to influence social practices" (253). Like Shelley, Scrivener does not and, I think, cannot explain the discrepancy between poetry's power and its attenuated effect on the world.

5. CONCEPTIONS OF THE WRITER
IN HAWTHORNE AND POE

1. Brodhead writes that "Hawthorne accepted the role of high cultural author in its full official form, Saturday Club lunches, literary pilgrims, and all—and accepted it, apparently, without it having occured to him that he could refuse it or modify its terms. . . . As Hawthorne acceded to the role of canonical author he himself began to find his work a bore. His dominant passions in the years of his greatest fame were apathy, lassitude, and ennui" (*School* 79).

2. As Buell writes, "It is probably no accident that Romanticism started to become a major influence in New England at the time when literary professionalism also started to become a viable option" (69).

3. Shelley separates conception from execution in *A Defence of Poetry*. See the discussion of this theme in chap. 4 above.

4. In *Alastor*, Shelley lamented

> The brave, the gentle, and the beautiful,
> The child of grace and genius. Heartless things
> Are done and said i' the world, and many worms
> And beasts and men live on. (lines 689–92)

5. As Gilmore puts it, if the author "wrote for a 'few,' they were professional men of letters like himself, reviewers and critics for the leading journals of the antebellum era. His real interest was in persuading the 'many' to buy his books" (82).

6. Blake wrote to his patron Hayley in 1804, "I must say that in London every calumny and falsehood utter'd against another of the same trade is thought fair play. Engravers, Painters, Statuaries, Printers, Poets, we are not in a field of battle, but in a City of Assassinations" (751).

7. In "A Select Party" Hawthorne also elevated work that exists only in the artist's imagination over work turned out for the market. In the house where the select party gathers there is a library, "the volumes of which were inestimable, because they consisted not of actual performances, but of the works which the authors only planned, without ever finding the happy season to achieve them. . . . The shelves were crowded; for it would not be too much too affirm that every author has imagined, and shaped out in his thought, more and far better works than those which actually proceeded

from his pen" (*Tales* 955). Like Shelley and Poe, Hawthorne responded to professional crisis here by elevating the thwarted creative impulse over the actual work produced for the market by competitors.

6. EMERSON AS CULTURAL SPOKESMAN

1. Cf. Robinson's analysis of the Emersonian style: "If he used the divine pronouncement effectively, it was in part because he balanced it with the homely metaphor and the vernacular phrase" (178).

2. In an early journal meditation, Emerson echoed Shelley's feeling that no literary work can capture or equal the power of the private consciousness. Looking through the works of Schiller, Emerson found them all wanting and concluded, "so with all his productions, they were the fermentations by which his mind was working itself clear, they were the experiments by which he got his skill & the fruit, the bright pure gold of all was—Schiller himself" (*Journals* 5:55).

3. Cf. *Nature*: "To the body and mind which have been cramped by noxious work or company, nature is medicinal and restores their tone. The tradesman, the attorney comes out of the din and craft of the street and sees the sky and the woods, and is a man again. In their eternal calm, he finds himself" (*Collected Works* 1:13).

4. See my discussion of *The Ruined Cottage*, above, chap. 2.

5. As Emerson would write in *English Traits*, "the best political economy is care and culture of men; for in these [economic] crises all are ruined except such as are proper individuals, capable of thought and of new choice and the application of their talent to new labor" (*Complete Works* 5:162). The class-based insularity of this statement is obvious, especially in light of Charvat's findings in *Profession* that the New England investment class was basically unscathed by the panic, "while other sections of the country were prostrated" (58). Furthermore, in New England, it was only the operatives who lost their jobs.

6. See the discussion of this stanza above, in chap. 4.

7. Cf. the Victorian attacks on reformers as monomaniacs whose inadequate private lives forced them to channel their energies into public causes. The definitive portrait is Mrs. Jellyby in Dickens's *Bleak House*, the missionary who is an incompetent mother. Emerson put forward the identical attack in "Self-Reliance": "If an angry bigot assumes this bountiful cause of Aboli-

tion, and comes to me with his last news from Barbadoes, why should I not say to him, 'Go love thy infant; love thy woodchopper; be good-natured and modest; have that grace; and never varnish your hard, uncharitable ambition with this incredible tenderness for black folk a thousand miles off. Thy love afar is spite at home'" (*Collected Works* 2:30). This argument was authoritative because it replaced efforts to alter specific social circumstances with the private self-culture that the society had already embraced. Emerson's criticism of reformers often diverted attention from the cause at hand to the vulgarity or zeal of those that professed it, diffusing commitment under the guise of sympathy. This familiar strategy persists, for example, in recent conservative criticism of feminism.

7. MELVILLE AS A PROFESSIONAL WRITER

1. Melville had already complained in *Mardi* of critics who "worship some mediocrity of an ancient and mock at the living prophet with the live coal on his lips," and of the fate of the genius destined for immortality but "yesterday cut in the marketplace by a spangled fool!" (1260, 1262).

2. Melville himself makes this sarcastic pun on the title of Duyckinck's journal, the *Literary World*, in another of his assertions of romantic independence: "& for me, I shall write such things as the Great Publisher of Mankind ordained ages before he published 'The World'—this planet, I mean—not the Literary Globe" (*Letters* 96).

3. Ironically, Hawthorne also used this romantic conceit to describe literary work in "A Select Party," a sketch to which Melville referred in his "Mosses" review. Hawthorne describes "a splendid library, the volumes of which were inestimable, because they consisted not of actual performances, but of the works which the authors only planned" (*Tales* 955).

4. Many critics have defended *Pierre*'s style as parodic but, as Baym points out, there is no evidence that Melville had read the sentimental or domestic romances that he supposedly makes fun of in *Pierre*. Even if *Pierre* were a parody, it would have to be considered a clumsy one; a good parody has to reproduce with skill *some* of the features of the genre that it mocks (Baym, "Melville's Quarrel" 919).

5. Historical note to *Pierre; or, The Ambiguities* 394.

6. In its issue for 31 May 1856, the *American Publisher's Circular and Literary Ga-*

zette praised *The Piazza Tales* for "evincing, as they assuredly do, the excellent characteristics of their popular author. . . . they were, in no small degree, instrumental in raising that journal [*Putnam's*] to its present proud position—the best of all American Monthlies." The *New York Dispatch* of 8 June 1856, wrote, "When the 'Encantadas' appeared in 'Putnam's,' the chapters were universally considered among the most interesting papers of that popular Magazine" (qtd. in Inge 37, 44).

7. Historical note to *Israel Potter*, 173.

8. My discussion of Melville's magazine stories uses the chronology established by Sealts.

9. Melville's identity, like that of other well-known authors writing for the magazines, was in fact an open secret.

10. Appropriately enough, the reception of the story was ambiguous as well. George William Curtis at first rejected it for *Putnam's*, but changed his mind the next day, conceding that "to many the style will seem painfully artificial and pompously self-conscious," and offering this curious praise: "But it seems to me well suited to the theme" (qtd. in Leyda 502; see also 738, 819). The story nevertheless struck some sort of chord for its first readers; it was the only one of Melville's stories to be anthologized in the nineteenth century.

11. I suggest that with *Billy Budd* Melville was making one last effort to enter the literary marketplace. This cannot be proven, but he had published all his previous completed fictions, and he must have known that he still had readers. As Leon Howard has shown, "some fifty-six new editions and reissues of his various books had appeared in America and England during his lifetime, and four of his prose works were still in print [at his death]. . . . He lacked renown but not readers" (338). In *Billy Budd* Melville makes it clear that he does not approve of the secular and progressive audience that he must address, but he *does* address them. The work has been read for so long as a coda to Melville's career that it is difficult to see it for what it indisputably is: a late-nineteenth-century work, perhaps more profitably read in the context of post–Gilded Age America than as a late American Renaissance work.

12. Arthur Stedman wrote in "'Marquesan' Melville," "It is generally admitted that had Melville been willing to join freely in the literary movements of New York, his name would have remained before the public and a larger sale

of his works would have been insured. But more and more, as he grew older, he avoided every action on his part and on the part of his family that might look in this direction" (qtd. in Sealts, *Early Lives* 109).

8. ROMANTIC GENIUS AND LITERARY PRODUCTION

During the late eighteenth century the term *genius* was shifting in meaning from "a characteristic disposition or quality" to its current meaning, "extraordinary ability." The changed meaning of *genius* and corrolary terms such as *original* and *creative* parallels the shift during the period in other key romantic terms, such as *imagination*, from descriptions of general characteristics to descriptions of particular individual traits. These shifts were symptomatic of new ways of thinking about the individual's relationship to society that put increasingly higher value on private life and individual experience, while using terms with negative connotations such as *mass* to describe social experience (see "Genius" in Williams, *Keywords*).

2. This was first published in the *Atlantic Monthly* (Oct. 1862); rpt. in *Atlantic Essays* 85. Higginson alludes here to Wordsworth's statement in the 1815 "Essay, Supplementary to the Preface" that "every author, as far as he is great and at the same time *original*, has had the task of *creating* the taste by which he is to be enjoyed."

3. Whitman remarked on Thoreau's "disdain for men, . . . [his] inability to appreciate the average life—even the exceptional life: it seemed to me a want of imagination. He couldn't put his life into any other life—realize why one man was so and another man was not so: was impatient with other people on the street and so forth." Whitman decided that Thoreau possessed "a very aggravated case of superciliousness" (qtd. in Schlesinger 390).

Works Cited

Allott, Miriam. "Attitudes to Shelley: The Vagaries of a Critical Reputation." *Essays on Shelley*. Ed. Allott. Liverpool: Liverpool UP, 1982.

Altick, Richard D. *The English Common Reader: A Social History of the Mass Reading Public 1800–1900*. Chicago: U of Chicago P, 1963.

Antzcak, Frederick J. *Thought and Character: The Rhetoric of Democratic Education*. Ames: Iowa State UP, 1985.

Bank, Stanley, ed. *American Romanticism: A Shape for Fiction*. New York: Putnam, 1969.

Barcus, James E., ed. *Shelley: The Critical Heritage*. London: Routledge, 1975.

Barnes, James J. *Authors, Publishers and Politicians: The Quest for an Anglo-American Copyright Agreement, 1815–1854*. Columbus: Ohio State UP, 1974.

Baym, Nina. "Melville's Quarrel with Fiction." *PMLA* 94 (Oct. 1979):15.

———. *Novels, Readers, and Reviewers: Responses to Fiction in Antebellum America*. Ithaca NY: Cornell UP, 1984.

Behrendt, Stephen. *Shelley and His Audiences*. Lincoln: U of Nebraska P, 1989.

Bell, Michael Davitt. *The Development of American Romance: The Sacrifice of Relation*. Chicago: U of Chicago P, 1980.

Bender, Thomas. *New York Intellect: A History of Intellectual Life in New York City, from 1750 to the Beginnings of Our Own Time*. New York: Knopf, 1987.

Bennett, Andrew. *Keats, Narrative, and Audience: The Posthumous Life of Writing*. New York: Cambridge UP, 1994.

Bennett, Scott. "John Murray's Family Library and the Cheapening of Books in Early Nineteenth-Century Britain." *Studies in Bibliography* 29. Charlottesville: The Bibliographical Society of the U of Virginia, 1979.

Bentley, G. E., Jr., ed. *Blake: The Critical Heritage*. London: Routledge, 1975.

———, ed. *Blake Records*. Oxford: Clarendon, 1969.

Bercovitch, Sacvan, ed. *Reconstructing American Literary History*. Cambridge, MA: Harvard UP, 1986.

Bercovitch, Sacvan, and Myra Jehlen, eds. *Ideology and Classic American Literature*. Cambridge: Cambridge UP, 1986.

Bindman, David. *William Blake: His Art and Times*. London: Thames and Hudson, 1982.

Blake, William. *The Book of Urizen*. Ed. Kay Parkhurst Easson and Roger R. Easson. Boulder CO: Shambhala, 1978.

———. *The Complete Poetry and Prose of William Blake*. Ed. David V. Erdman. Berkeley: U of California P, 1982.

Branch, Watson G., ed. *Melville: The Critical Heritage*. Boston: Routledge, 1974.

Braudel, Fernand. *The Perspective of the World*. New York: Harper and Row, 1984. Vol. 3 of *Civilization and Capitalism, Fifteenth –Eighteenth Century*. 3 vols. 1981–84.

Brett-Smith, H. F. B., ed. *Peacock's Four Ages of Poetry, Shelley's Defence of Poetry, Browning's Essay on Shelley*. Boston: Houghton Mifflin, 1921.

Brodhead, Richard H. *Cultures of Letters: Scenes of Reading and Writing in Nineteenth-Century America*. Chicago: U of Chicago P, 1993.

———. *The School of Hawthorne*. New York: Oxford UP, 1986.

Brown, Gillian. *Domestic Individualism: Imagining Self in Nineteenth-Century America*. Berkeley: U of California P, 1990.

Brownson, Orestes A. *The Writings on Literature*. Ed. Henry F. Brownson. New York: AMS P, 1966. Vol. 19 of *The Works of Orestes A. Brownson*. 20 vols. 1966.

Bryant, William Cullen. "Relation of Poetry to Time and Place." Vol. 1 of *Prose Writings*. Ed. Parke Godwin. New York: Appleton, 1884. 2 vols.

Bryce, James. *The American Commonwealth*. 2 vols. New York: Macmillan, 1914.

Buell, Lawrence. *New England Literary Culture: From Revolution through Renaissance*. New York: Cambridge UP, 1986.

Bulwer-Lytton, Edward. *England and the English*. 2 vols. New York, 1833.

Butler, Marilyn. "Against Tradition: The Case for a Particularized Historical Method." *Historical Studies and Literary Criticism*. Ed. Jerome J. McGann. Oxford: Clarendon, 1985.

———. *Peacock Displayed: A Satirist in His Context*. London: Routledge, 1979.

———. *Romantics, Rebels, and Reactionaries: English Literature and its Background 1760–1830*. New York: Oxford UP, 1981.

Cameron, Kenneth Neill. *Shelley: The Golden Years*. Cambridge MA: Harvard UP, 1974.

Cameron, Sharon. *Writing Nature: Henry Thoreau's Journal*. New York: Oxford UP, 1985.

Carman, Bliss. 1896 rev. of Emily Dickinson's poetry. Rpt. in *The Recognition of Emily Dickinson: Selected Criticism since 1890*. Ed. Caesar R. Blake and Carlton F. Wells. Ann Arbor: U of Michigan P, 1964.

Channing, William Ellery. *Self-Culture*. New York: Arno P, 1838. Rpt. *New York Times*, 1969.

Chard, Leslie F. *Dissenting Republican: Wordsworth's Early Life and Thought in Their Political Context*. The Hague: Mouton, 1972.

Charvat, William. *Literary Publishing in America, 1790–1850*. Philadelphia: U of Pennsylvania P, 1959.

———. *The Profession of Authorship in America, 1800–1870*. Ed. Matthew J. Bruccoli. Columbus: Ohio State UP, 1968.

Chilcott, Tim. *A Publisher and His Circle: The Life and Work of John Taylor, Keats's Publisher*. London: Routledge, 1972.

Clark, David Lee, ed. *Shelley's Prose, or The Trumpet of a Prophecy*. Albuquerque: U of New Mexico P, 1954.

Coleridge, Samuel Taylor. *Biographia Literaria*. Ed. James Engell and W. Jackson Bate. Princeton NJ: Princeton UP, 1983. Vol. 7 of *The Collected Works of Samuel Taylor Coleridge*. 14 vols. 1969–83.

Collins, A. S. *The Profession of Letters: A Study of the Relation of Author to Patron, Publisher, and Public, 1780–1832*. London: Routledge, 1928.

Cremin, Lawrence A. *American Education: The National Experience, 1783–1876*. New York: Harper and Row, 1980.

Crowley, J. Donald, ed. *Hawthorne: The Critical Heritage*. New York: Barnes and Noble, 1970.

Curran, Stuart, and Joseph Anthony Wittreich Jr., eds. *Blake's Sublime Allegory: Essays on The Four Zoas, Milton, Jerusalem*. Madison: U of Wisconsin P, 1973.

Damrosch, Leopold, Jr. *Symbol and Truth in Blake's Myth*. Princeton NJ: Princeton UP, 1980.

Dauber, Kenneth. *The Idea of Authorship in America: Democratic Poetics from Franklin to Melville*. Madison: U of Wisconsin P, 1990.

Davidson, Cathy, ed. *Reading in America: Literature and Social History*. Baltimore: Johns Hopkins UP, 1989.

Davis, Michael. *William Blake: A New Kind of Man*. Berkeley: U of California P, 1977.

Dawson, P. M. S. *The Unacknowledged Legislator: Shelley and Politics*. Oxford: Clarendon, 1980.

Dickinson, Emily. *The Complete Poems of Emily Dickinson*. Ed. Thomas H. Johnson. Boston: Little, Brown, n.d.

Dimock, Wai-Chee. *Empire for Liberty: Melville and the Poetics of Individualism*. Princeton NJ: Princeton UP, 1989.

Dorfman, Deborah. *Blake in the Nineteenth Century: His Reputation as a Poet from Gilchrist to Yeats*. New Haven CT: Yale UP, 1969.

Douglas, Ann. *The Feminization of American Culture*. New York: Knopf, 1977.

Duerksen, Roland A. *Shelleyan Ideas in Victorian Literature*. The Hague: Mouton, 1966.

Duyckinck, Evert, and George Duyckinck. *Cyclopaedia of American Literature*. New York: Scribner's, 1855.

Eagleton, Terry. *Criticism and Ideology: A Study in Marxist Literary Theory*. London: Verso, 1976.

———. *Literary Theory: An Introduction*. Minneapolis: U of Minnesota P, 1983.

———. *Marxism and Literary Criticism*. Berkeley: U of California P, 1976.

Easson, Roger. "William Blake and His Reader in *Jerusalem*." *Blake's Sublime Allegory: Essays on The Four Zoas, Milton, Jerusalem*. Ed. Stuart Curran and Joseph Anthony Wittreich Jr. Madison: U of Wisconsin P, 1973.

Edmundson, Mark. "Criticism Now: The Example of Wordsworth." *Raritan* 10 (Fall 1990):2.

Emerson, Ralph Waldo. *The Collected Works of Ralph Waldo Emerson*. 3 vols. Ed. Robert Spiller et al. Cambridge MA: Belknap, 1971.

———. *The Complete Works of Ralph Waldo Emerson*. Ed. Edward Waldo Emerson. Boston: Houghton Mifflin, 1903.

———. *The Correspondence of Emerson and Carlyle*. Ed. Joseph Slater. New York: Columbia UP, 1964.

———. *The Early Lectures of Ralph Waldo Emerson*. 3 vols. Ed. Stephen Whicher et al. Cambridge MA: Belknap, 1964–71.

———. *Emerson in His Journals*. Ed. Joel Porte. Cambridge MA: Belknap, 1982.

———. *Essays: Second Series*. Ed. Joseph Slater et al. Cambridge MA: Harvard UP, 1983. Vol. 3 of *The Collected Works of Ralph Waldo Emerson*.

————. *The Journals and Miscellaneous Notebooks of Ralph Waldo Emerson*. 16 vols. Ed. William H. Gilman et al. Cambridge MA: Belknap, 1960–82.

————. *Nature, Addresses, and Lectures*. Ed. R. E. Spiller and A. R. Ferguson. Cambridge MA: Harvard UP, 1971.

————. *Representative Men: Seven Lectures*. Boston: Sampson, 1850.

————. *Selections from Ralph Waldo Emerson*. Ed. Stephen E. Whicher. Boston: Houghton Mifflin, 1957.

Erdman, David V. *Blake: Prophet Against Empire*. Princeton NJ: Princeton UP, 1954.

Ferber, Michael. *The Social Vision of William Blake*. Princeton NJ: Princeton UP, 1985.

Ferguson, Frances. "Romantic Studies." *Redrawing the Boundaries: The Transformation of English and American Literary Studies*. Ed. Stephen Greenblatt and Giles Gunn. New York: MLA, 1992.

Fiedler, Leslie. *What Was Literature? Class, Culture and Mass Society*. New York: Simon and Schuster, 1982.

Fields, James T. *Yesterdays with Authors*. Boston: J. R. Osgood, 1874.

Fink, Steven. *Prophet in the Marketplace: Thoreau's Development as a Professional Writer*. Princeton NJ: Princeton UP, 1992.

Frye, Northrop. *Fables of Identity: Studies in Poetic Mythology*. New York: Harcourt Brace, 1963.

————. *Fearful Symmetry: A Study of William Blake*. Princeton, NJ: Princeton UP, 1969.

Gilchrist, Alexander. *Life of William Blake, "Pictor Ignotus"*. London: Macmillan, 1863.

Gilmore, Michael T. *American Romanticism and the Marketplace*. Chicago: U of Chicago P, 1985.

Glen, Heather. *Vision and Disenchantment: Blake's Songs and Wordsworth's Lyrical Ballads*. New York: Cambridge UP, 1983.

Greenblatt, Stephen, and Giles Gunn, eds. *Redrawing the Boundaries: The Transformation of English and American Literary Studies*. New York: MLA, 1992.

Greenspan, Ezra. *Walt Whitman and the American Reader*. New York: Cambridge UP, 1990.

Gross, John. *The Rise and Fall of the Man of Letters*. New York: Macmillan, 1969.

Guinn, John Pollard. *Shelley's Political Thought*. The Hague: Mouton, 1969.

Haskell, Thomas L. *The Emergence of Professional Social Science: The American Social Science Association and the Nineteenth-Century Crisis of Authority*. Urbana: U of Illinois P, 1977.

Hawthorne, Nathaniel. *Novels*. Ed. Millicent Bell. New York: Library of America, 1983.

———. *Tales and Sketches*. Ed. Roy Harvey Pearce. New York, Library of America, 1982.

Hayden, John O., ed. *Romantic Bards and British Reviewers: A Selected Edition of the Contemporary Reviews of the Works of Wordsworth, Coleridge, Byron, Keats, and Shelley*. Lincoln: U of Nebraska P, 1971.

Higginson, Thomas Wentworth. *Carlyle's Laugh and Other Surprises*. Boston: Houghton Mifflin, 1909.

———. "A Letter to a Young Contributor." *Atlantic Essays*. Boston: J. R. Osgood, 1871.

Hobsbawm, E. J. *The Age of Capital, 1848–1875*. New York: Weidenfeld and Nicolson, 1975.

———. *The Age of Revolution: 1789–1848*. Cleveland: World, 1962.

Holmes, Richard. *Shelley: The Pursuit*. New York: Dutton, 1975.

Hoover, Suzanne R. "William Blake in the Wilderness: A Closer Look at His Reputation, 1827–1863." *William Blake: Essays in Honour of Sir Geoffrey Keynes*. Ed. Morton D. Paley and Michael Curtis Phillips. Oxford: Clarendon, 1973.

Howard, John. "An Audience for *The Marriage of Heaven and Hell*." *Blake Studies* 3 (Fall 1970):1.

Howard, Leon. *Herman Melville: A Biography*. Berkeley: U of California P, 1951.

Howarth, William. *The Book of Concord: Thoreau's Life as a Writer*. New York: Viking, 1982.

Howells, William Dean. *Literary Friends and Acquaintance*. Ed. David F. Hiatt and Edwin H. Cady. Bloomington: Indiana UP, 1968.

Inge, M. Thomas, ed. *Bartleby the Inscrutable: A Collection of Commentary on Herman Melville's Tale "Bartleby the Scrivener"*. Hamden CT: Archon Books, 1979.

Izenberg, Gerald N. *Impossible Individuality: Romanticism, Revolution, and the Origins of Modern Selfhood, 1787–1802*. Princeton NJ: Princeton UP, 1992.

Jack, Ian. *English Literature, 1815–1832*. New York: Oxford UP, 1963.

———. *The Poet and His Audience*. New York: Cambridge UP, 1984.

Works Cited

Jacobus, Mary. *Tradition and Experiment in Wordsworth's Lyrical Ballads (1798)*. Oxford: Clarendon, 1976.

Johnson, Paul. *The Birth of the Modern: World Society 1815–1830*. New York: HarperCollins, 1991.

Jordan, John E. *Why the Lyrical Ballads?: The Background, Writing, and Character of Wordsworth's 1798 Lyrical Ballads*. Berkeley: U of California P, 1976.

Kaplan, Justin. *Walt Whitman, A Life*. New York: Simon and Schuster, 1980.

Klancher, Jon. *The Making of English Reading Audiences, 1790–1832*. New York: Oxford UP, 1987.

Knight, Charles. *The Old Printer and the Modern Press*. London: John Murray, 1854.

Konvitz, Milton R., ed. *The Recognition of Ralph Waldo Emerson*. Ann Arbor: U of Michigan P, 1972.

Lackington, James. *Memoirs of the First Forty-five Years of the Life of James Lackington, Written by Himself*. 7th ed. 1794. New York: Garland, 1974.

Leenhardt, Jacques. "Toward a Sociology of Reading." *The Reader in the Text*. Ed. Susan Suleiman and Inge Crossman. Princeton NJ: Princeton UP, 1980.

Levinson, Marjorie. *Wordsworth's Great Period Poems*. New York: Cambridge UP, 1986.

Leyda, Jay, ed. *The Melville Log: A Documentary Life of Herman Melville, 1819–1891*. 2 vols. New York: Harcourt, Brace, 1951.

Long, David Andrew. "Authorial Politics: Poe and the Conservative Ethos in Antebellum American Culture." Diss. Stanford U, 1989.

Longfellow, Henry Wadsworth. *Hyperion* and *Kavanaugh*. Boston: Houghton Mifflin, 1894. Vol. 2 of *The Prose Works of Henry Wadsworth Longfellow*. 2 vols.

———. *Michael Angelo: A Fragment*. Boston: Houghton Mifflin, 1895. Vol. 4 of *Longfellow's Poetical Works*. 6 vols.

Lowell, James Russell. *Literary Criticism of James Russell Lowell*. Ed. Herbert F. Smith. Lincoln: U of Nebraska P, 1969.

MacCabe, Colin. "Tradition Too Has Its Place in Cultural Studies." *Times Literary Supplement* 26 May 1995: 12–13.

Machor, James L., ed. *Readers in History: Nineteenth-Century American Literature and the Contexts of Response*. Baltimore: Johns Hopkins UP, 1993.

Madison, Charles A. *Book Publishing in America*. New York: McGraw-Hill, 1966.

Marx, Karl. *The German Ideology* and *Grundrisse*. *The Marx-Engels Reader*. 2nd ed. Ed. Robert C. Tucker. New York: Norton, 1978.

McGann, Jerome J. *The Beauty of Inflections: Literary Investigations in Historical Method and Theory*. Oxford: Clarendon, 1985.

———. *The Romantic Ideology: A Critical Investigation*. Chicago: U of Chicago P, 1983.

———, ed. *The New Oxford Book of Romantic Period Verse*. New York: Oxford UP, 1993.

Mead, David. *Yankee Eloquence in the Middle West, 1850–1870*. Lansing: Michigan State College P, 1951.

Mellow, James R. *Nathaniel Hawthorne in His Times*. Boston: Houghton Mifflin, 1980.

Melville, Herman. *Battle-Pieces and Aspects of the War*. 1866. Ed. Sidney Kaplan. Amherst: U of Massachusetts P, 1972.

———. *Israel Potter: His Fifty Years of Exile*. Ed. Harrison Hayford et al. Chicago: Northwestern UP and the Newberry Library, 1982.

———. *The Letters of Herman Melville*. Ed. Merrill R. Davis and William H. Gilman. New Haven CT: Yale UP, 1960.

———. *Pierre, Israel Potter, The Piazza Tales, The Confidence-Man, Uncollected Prose, Billy Budd, Sailor*. Ed. Harrison Hayford. New York: Library of America, 1984.

———. *Pierre, or, The Ambiguities*. Ed. Harrison Hayford et al. Chicago: Northwestern UP and the Newberry Library, 1971.

———. *Poems*. New York: Russell and Russell, 1963. Vol. 16 of *The Works of Herman Melville*. 16 vols. 1963.

———. *Redburn, White-Jacket, Moby-Dick*. Ed. G. Thomas Tanselle. New York: Library of America, 1983.

———. *Typee, Omoo, Mardi*. Ed. G. Thomas Tanselle. New York: Library of America, 1982.

Meyers, Marvin. *The Jacksonian Persuasion: Politics and Belief*. New York: Vintage, 1960.

Michaels, Walter Benn, and Donald Pease, eds. *The American Renaissance Reconsidered*. Baltimore: Johns Hopkins UP, 1985.

Mill, John Stuart. *Autobiography*. New York: Liberal Arts P, 1957.

Miller, Perry. *The Raven and the Whale: The War of Words and Wits in the Era of Poe and Melville*. New York: Harcourt, Brace, 1956.

Miller, Ruth. *The Poetry of Emily Dickinson*. Middletown CT: Wesleyan UP, 1960.

Montrose, Louis. "New Historicisms." *Redrawing the Boundaries: The Transformation of English and American Literary Studies*. Ed. Stephen Greenblatt and Giles Gunn. New York: MLA, 1992.

Moorman, Mary. *William Wordsworth: A Biography*. 2 vols. New York: Oxford UP, 1968.

Mott, Frank Luther. *A History of American Magazines, 1741–1850*. New York: Appleton, 1930.

Mumby, Frank Arthur. *Publishing and Bookselling*. 5th ed. London: Jonathan Cape, 1974.

Nye, Russel Blaine. *Society and Culture in America 1830–1860*. New York: Harper and Row, 1976.

———. *The Unembarrassed Muse: The Popular Arts in America*. New York: Dial P, 1970.

Peacock, Thomas Love. *Peacock's Memoir of Shelley*. Ed. H. F. B. Brett-Smith. London: Henry Frowde, 1909.

———. *Nightmare Abbey and Maid Marian*. Ed. H. F. B. Brett-Smith and C. E. Jones. New York: AMS P, 1967. Vol. 3 of *The Works of Thomas Love Peacock*. 10 vols. 1967.

Pfister, Joel. *The Production of Personal Life: Class, Gender, and the Psychological in Hawthorne's Fiction*. Stanford CA: Stanford UP, 1991.

Poe, Edgar Allan. *The Complete Poems and Stories of Edgar Allan Poe, with Selections from His Critical Writings*. Ed. Arthur Hobson Quinn and Edward H. O'Neill. New York: Knopf, 1967.

———. *The Letters of Edgar Allan Poe*. Ed. John Ward Ostrom. New York: Gordian P, 1948.

Poirier, Richard. *The Renewal of Literature: Emersonian Reflections*. New York: Random House, 1987.

Pollard, Arthur, ed. *Crabbe: The Critical Heritage*. London: Routledge, 1972.

Porter, Carolyn. *Seeing and Being: The Plight of the Participant Observer in Emerson, James, Adams, and Faulkner*. Middletown CT: Wesleyan UP, 1981.

Railton, Stephen. *Authorship and Audience: Literary Performance in the American Renaissance*. Princeton NJ: Princeton UP, 1991.

Read, Dennis. "The Context of Blake's 'Public Address': Cromek and the Chalcographic Society." *Philological Quarterly* 60 (Winter 1981): 69–86.

Robinson, David. *Apostle of Culture: Emerson as Preacher and Lecturer*. Philadelphia: U of Pennsylvania P, 1982.

Roper, Derek. *Reviewing Before the Edinburgh: 1788–1802*. Wilmington: U of Delaware P, 1978.

Ruland, Richard, ed. *The Native Muse: Theories of American Literature*. New York: Dutton, 1972.

Ryskamp, Charles. "Wordsworth's *Lyrical Ballads* in Their Time." *From Sensibility to Romanticism: Essays Presented to Frederick A. Pottle*. Ed. Frederick W. Hilles and Harold Bloom. New York: Oxford UP, 1965.

St. Armand, Barton Levi. *Emily Dickinson and Her Culture: The Soul's Society*. New York: Cambridge UP, 1984.

Saunders, J. W. *The Profession of English Letters*. London: Routledge, 1964.

Schlesinger, Arthur M., Jr. *The Age of Jackson*. Boston: Little, Brown, 1945.

Schorer, Mark. *William Blake: The Politics of Vision*. New York: Henry Holt, 1946.

Scott, Donald M. "The Popular Lecture and the Creation of a Public in Mid-Nineteenth-Century America." *Journal of American History* 66 (Mar. 1980): 791–809.

Scrivener, Michael. *Radical Shelley: The Philosophical Anarchism and Utopian Thought of Percy Bysshe Shelley*. Princeton NJ: Princeton UP, 1982.

Sealts, Merton M., Jr. "Alien to His Contemporaries: Melville's Last Years," "The Chronology of Melville's Short Fiction, 1853–1856," and "The Reception of Melville's Short Fiction." *Pursuing Melville 1940–1980*. Madison: U of Wisconsin P, 1982.

———. *The Early Lives of Melville: Nineteenth-Century Biographical Sketches and Their Authors*. Madison: U of Wisconsin P, 1974.

———. *Melville as Lecturer*. Cambridge MA: Harvard UP, 1957.

Sennett, Richard. *The Fall of Public Man: On the Social Psychology of Capitalism*. New York: Knopf, 1977.

Sewall, Richard B. *The Life of Emily Dickinson*. New York: Farrar, Straus and Giroux, 1980.

Shelley, Percy Bysshe. *Complete Poetical Works*. 1839. Ed. Mary Shelley. New York: Modern Library, n.d.

———. *The Letters of Percy Bysshe Shelley*. 2 vols. Ed. Frederick L. Jones. Oxford: Clarendon, 1964.

————. *Shelley: Poetical Works*. Ed. Thomas Hutchinson. New York: Oxford UP, 1967.

Shulman, Robert. *Social Criticism and Nineteenth-Century American Fictions*. Columbia: U of Missouri P, 1987.

Simpson, Lewis P. *The Man of Letters in New England and the South: Essays on the History of the Literary Vocation in America*. Baton Rouge: Louisiana State UP, 1973.

Siskin, Clifford. *The Historicity of Romantic Discourse*. New York: Oxford UP, 1988.

————. "Wordsworth's Prescriptions: Romanticism and Professional Power." *The Romantics and Us: Essays on Literature and Culture*. Ed. Gene W. Ruoff. New Brunswick NJ: Rutgers UP, 1990.

Smiles, Samuel. *Self-Help: with Illustrations of Character and Conduct*. 1859. London: John Murray, 1958.

Smith, Henry Nash. *Democracy and the Novel: Popular Resistance to Classic American Writers*. New York: Oxford UP, 1978.

Smith, Robert Metcalf, et al. *The Shelley Legend*. New York: Scribner's, 1945.

Stern, Milton R. "American Values and Romantic Fiction." *American Fiction: Historical and Critical Essays*. Boston: Northeastern UP, 1977.

Swinburne, Algernon C. *William Blake: A Critical Essay*. Ed. Hugh J. Luke. Lincoln: U of Nebraska P, 1970.

Techi, Cecilia. "American Literary Studies to the Civil War." *Redrawing the Boundaries: The Transformation of English and American Literary Studies*. Ed. Stephen Greenblatt and Giles Gunn. New York: MLA, 1992.

Thompson, E. P. "Disenchantment or Default? A Lay Sermon." *Power and Consciousness*. Ed. Conor Cruise O'Brien and William Dean Vanech. New York: New York UP, 1969.

————. *The Making of the English Working Class*. New York: Vintage, 1963.

Ticknor, Caroline. *Glimpses of Authors*. Boston: Houghton Mifflin, 1922.

————. *Hawthorne and His Publisher*. Boston: Houghton Mifflin, 1913.

Tocqueville, Alexis de. *Democracy in America*. 2 vols. Ed. Phillips Bradley. Trans. Henry Reeve and Francis Bowen. New York: Vintage, 1945.

Tompkins, Jane. *Sensational Designs: The Cultural Work of American Fiction*. New York: Oxford UP, 1985.

von Hubner, J. A. Graf. "Individualism as a Function of Opportunity." *Individ-*

ualism and Conformity in the American Character. Ed. Richard L. Rapson. New York: Heath, 1967.

Webb, R. K. *The British Working Class Reader, 1790–1848: Literacy and Social Tension*. London: Allen and Unwin, 1955.

Whicher, Stephen E. *Freedom and Fate: An Inner Life of Ralph Waldo Emerson*. Philadelphia: U of Pennsylvania P, 1953.

Whitman, Walt. *Complete Poetry and Selected Prose*. Ed. Justin Kaplan. New York: Library of America, 1982.

Williams, Raymond. *Culture and Society: 1780–1950*. London: Penguin, 1963.

———. *Keywords: A Vocabulary of Culture and Society*. Rev. ed. New York: Oxford UP, 1983.

Wilson, R. Jackson. *Figures of Speech: American Writers and the Literary Marketplace, from Benjamin Franklin to Emily Dickinson*. New York: Knopf, 1987.

———. *In Quest of Community: Social Philosophy in the United States, 1860–1920*. New York: Wiley, 1968.

Wittreich, Joseph Anthony, Jr., ed. *Nineteenth-Century Accounts of William Blake*. Gainesville, FL: Scholar's Facsimiles and Reprints, 1970.

Wordsworth, William. *The Letters of William and Dorothy Wordsworth*. 3 vols. Ed. Ernest de Selincourt. Oxford: Clarendon, 1967.

———. *The Poetical Works of William Wordsworth*. Ed. Ernest de Selincourt. Oxford: Clarendon, 1969.

———. The *Prelude: 1799, 1805, 1850*. Ed. Jonathan Wordsworth, M. H. Abrams, and Stephen Gill. New York: Norton, 1979.

———. *The Prose Works of William Wordsworth*. 3 vols. Ed. W. J. B. Owen and Jane Worthington Smyser. Oxford: Clarendon, 1974.

Zapf, Hubert. "English Romanticism and American Transcendentalism: An Intercultural Comparison." *Romantic Continuities*. Ed. Gunther Blaicher and Michael Gassenmeier. Essen, Germany: Verlag Die Blaue Eule, 1992.

Zboray, Ronald J. *A Fictive People: Antebellum Economic Development and the American Reading Public*. New York: Oxford UP, 1993.

Index

DATE DUE

APR 04 2000		
APR 15 2002		
		Printed in USA